Parenting for a Digital Future

Parenting for a Digital Future

How Hopes and Fears about Technology Shape Children's Lives

SONIA LIVINGSTONE AND ALICIA BLUM-ROSS

OXFORD

UNIVERSITY PRESS

Oxford University Press is a department of the University of Oxford. It furthers
the University's objective of excellence in research, scholarship, and education
by publishing worldwide. Oxford is a registered trade mark of Oxford University
Press in the UK and certain other countries.

Published in the United States of America by Oxford University Press
198 Madison Avenue, New York, NY 10016, United States of America.

Library of Congress Cataloging-in-Publication Data
Names: Livingstone, Sonia M., author. | Blum-Ross, Alicia, 1979– author.
Title: Parenting for a digital future : how hopes and fears about technology
shape children's lives / Sonia Livingstone and Alicia Blum-Ross.
Description: New York, NY : Oxford University Press, [2020] |
Includes bibliographical references and index.
Identifiers: LCCN 2020008762 (print) | LCCN 2020008763 (ebook) |
ISBN 9780190874698 (hardback) | ISBN 9780190874704 (paperback) |
ISBN 9780190874728 (epub)
Subjects: LCSH: Parenting—Social aspects. | Internet and children—Safety measures. |
Digital media—Social aspects. | Technology and children.
Classification: LCC HQ755.8 .L577 2020 (print) |
LCC HQ755.8 (ebook) | DDC 004.67/8083—dc23
LC record available at https://lccn.loc.gov/2020008762
LC ebook record available at https://lccn.loc.gov/2020008763

Contents

Acknowledgments

First and foremost, we thank all the parents who talked to us for this book. It is only because of their generosity in giving us their time, and sharing their lives, that we could depict the struggles and joys of parenting in the digital age. We have tried faithfully to represent their views and concerns. We also met many children in our fieldwork and are deeply grateful for their curiosity as they walked us through their digital creations, and showed patience with our many questions.

Our work was supported by educators from our three digital learning field sites. We promised to keep these anonymous to protect their identities, but we wish to record how hugely important they were in welcoming us, sharing their experiences and discussing our findings.

The research for this book was made possible by a grant from the John D. and Catherine T. MacArthur Foundation for the Connected Learning Research Network in connection with its grant-making initiative on Digital Media and Learning. We appreciated how the MacArthur Foundation stayed in touch with the research, hosted meetings, and made introductions, keen to support our work in ways that helped shape our analysis.

Parenting for a Digital Future was one of several research projects conducted by the Connected Learning Research Network. Our work gained enormously from the lively dialogue and critical debate among the network participants. Our thanks to Dalton Conley, Kris Gutierrez, Vera Michalchik, Bill Penuel, Jean Rhodes, Juliet Schor, and S. Craig Watkins, plus the network advisors and fellows—and especially Mizuko Ito, our stellar network director, and Julian Sefton-Green, our collaborator and partner throughout.

The Parenting for a Digital Future survey was ably fielded by CHILDWISE—thanks to its research director, Simon Leggett. Four of the families were originally interviewed as part of a project funded by the Joint Research Centre of the European Commission, and we thank Stephane Chaudron, director of the "Young Children (0–8) and Digital Technology" project. Eight were repeat interviews, as they had been part of *The Class*, written with Julian Sefton-Green, and also funded by the MacArthur Foundation.

We thank the research assistants who worked with us on the book and our linked blog at www.parenting.digital—Alexandra Chernyavskaya, Kate Gilchrist, César Jiménez-Martínez, Paige Mustain, Svenja Ottovordemgenschentfelde, Jenn Pavlick, Rafal Zaborowski, and Dongmiao Zhang. We benefited greatly from your insights.

Writing can be a solitary affair, but fortunately each of us was a member of a writing group that patiently and insightfully critiqued drafts of several chapters of this book. Nothing can replace the kind but tough intellectual contributions of Bart Cammaerts, Lilie Chouliaraki, Ellen Helsper, Peter Lunt, and Shani Orgad (in London) and Morgan Ames, Matt Rafalow, Antero Garcia, and Amber Levinson (in California). We're grateful too to Urszula Dawkins, who painstakingly edited our text, and to Joe Livingstone for trouble-shooting our arguments and expression throughout.

As this book has taken shape, our ideas have been sharpened in conversations with Meryl Alper, Shaku Banaji, Sarah Banet-Weiser, Veronica Barassi, Brigid Barron, Melissa Brough, Anne Collier, Michael Deuzanni, Kirsten Drotner, Nathan Fisk, Richard Graham, Lelia Green, Devorah Heitner, Alexis Hiniker, Henry Jenkins, Amy Jordon, Anya Kamenetz, Vikki Katz, Beeban Kidron, David Kleeman, Michael Levine, Claire Lilley, Sun Sun Lim, George Maier, Jackie Marsh, Gemma Martinez, Giovanna Mascheroni, Rodrigo Muñoz-González, Jessica Piotrowski, Jenny Radesky, Vicky Rideout, Mike Robb, Vicki Shotbolt, Mariya Stoilova, Lori Takeuchi, Amanda Third, Yalda Uhls, Rebecca Willett, Barbie Zelizer, and many more: sorry if we left anyone out—thanks to all!

This book was written under the auspices of the Department of Media and Communications at LSE, ably supported by staff in the LSE's Research Division. It has informed but is independent of the work we have each done since completing the manuscript.

In many ways our own families are threaded throughout this book—as our own experiences as mothers (of children of very different ages) undoubtedly influenced our interviews and our analysis. Sonia is eternally grateful to her partner, Peter, and (now grown-up) children, Joe and Anna—for their ever-creative insights, robust critique, and warm support—and to her own parents, whose amazing parenting this book has often led her to reflect on. Alicia is deeply thankful for Shez's profound teamwork and support, and to

Abe and Penny for their playfulness and patience even when writing this book sometimes meant extra "screen time" all around. Thanks also to Alicia's own parents and siblings, who pitched in with childcare and thoughtful commentary, and who are a reminder that "parenting" as a preoccupation and source of identity doesn't stop when children grow up.

1

Expectations

As we entered Lara and Pawel Mazur's[1] small flat in a comfortable London suburb, Lara began pouring out their disagreements over six-year-old Tomas's digital media use, exclaiming how they'd been looking forward to discussing this with us. Lara, a college administrator originally from Brazil, was full of ideas to enable Tomas's online opportunities—researching educational apps and guiding his search "to build his confidence and make him independent." Pawel, a chef from Poland, was worried about online risks, especially after Tomas's friends introduced him to a violent video game.

Lara wanted Tomas to learn about the ways of the world, saying, "my position is to talk to him about it when it's happening. . . . I'm very open, maybe too open." She was critical of "other mums" and, implicitly, of Pawel for his caution. Pawel, who had set passwords for everyone on the family laptop, offered a hesitant defense. He conceded:

> We need to educate him how to use the internet so he can . . . make the right choices, but you need to be safe as well at the same time. I don't want to control. I just want to be able to view it in case there's something which I'm not able to control.

Tomas told us shyly that he loved football online and offline, along with video games and playing outdoors with the neighborhood children. His parents' divergent approaches to digital technology were not lost on the six-year-old. Tomas observed that his dad didn't always let him play his beloved FIFA when he's "playing too much," but mum usually "says yes."[2]

How should parents manage digital devices and experiences, and what should they expect of them? Why are these questions so contested within families, among policymakers, and in the media? During the fieldwork for this book, anxious,

---

[1] Family 33.

[2] FIFA stands for Fédération Internationale de Football Association. Tomas was playing a video game based on association football (EA Sports, 2018).

Parenting for a Digital Future. Sonia Livingstone and Alicia Blum-Ross, Oxford University Press (2020). © Oxford University Press.
DOI: 10.1093/oso/9780190874698.001.0001

enthusiastic, defensive, or exhausted parents told us about their "parenting philosophy"[3] and where they turned for inspiration or support. Some parents (by which we mean those in a primary domestic caregiving role for children[4]) were consumed with these questions, while others seemed less bothered—whether because they had greater concerns elsewhere or had managed, somehow, to avoid the swirling anxiety about all things digital. As with Lara and Pawel, mothers and fathers often differed in their concerns, and social class and ethnicity also differentiated families, yet not always in predictable ways. This diversity matters because it complicates and contests public and policymakers' assumptions about the role of digital technologies in family life.

Lara and Pawel's disagreement illustrates a point we will often return to throughout this book. Talk or actions that seem to concern children's digital lives are, at heart, rooted in parents' deeper hopes and fears for family life and their children's futures. Building on research conducted over four years with parents, children, and educators, we explore the lives of families variously enjoying the pleasures and wrestling with the challenges of digital technologies. We argue that, as parents strive to understand the profound changes they are living through, digital dilemmas act as a lightning rod for contemporary contestations over values, identity, and responsibility.

Although parenting practices may seem mundane, parenthood is being powerfully renegotiated in increasingly individualized societies. Specifically, we will reveal throughout this book that it is through their everyday practices that families navigate between present desires and material constraints.[5] In introducing the burgeoning field of "parenting culture studies," Ellie Lee, Jan Macvarish, and Jennie Bristow observe:

> What were once considered banal, relatively unimportant, private routines of everyday life for children and families (mealtimes, sleeping, playing, reading nursery rhymes and stories) have become the subject of intense

---

[3] By "parenting philosophy," Lynn Schofield Clark (2013) refers to the way parents share their life stories, cautionary tales, and tried-and-tested experiences with their children as a way of communicating their values.

[4] Recognizing that not all children and young people live in homes with biological parents, by "parenting" we refer to diverse forms of caregiving including, for example, by older siblings, grandparents, or foster parents. Gillies (2008); Webb (2011).

[5] As John Postill (2010) explains, the concept of practice has been variously defined and debated, a minimal definition being "'arrays of activity' in which the human body is the nexus," thereby drawing attention to the unfolding and unequal negotiation between the strategies of powerful organizations and the tactics of ordinary people located in everyday contexts of time, space and social relations.

debates about the effects of parental activities for the next generation and society as a whole.[6]

Family, health, finances, education, social relations—these were once pre-scribed by traditional authorities but are becoming more a matter of choice, with individuals simultaneously empowered and burdened with new opportunities and risks. At the same time, individual choices have societal consequences, and politicians, educators, and policymakers are making in-tense efforts to manage parenting, even though it persistently escapes them.[7] In short, parenting involves, on the one hand, a form of personal care for a child or children but, on the other, it involves practices that are cultural, social, and economic—and that makes parenting political. Thus we make an analytic distinction between the everyday actions of parents and the contested notion of "parenting"—a term that has only recently become pop-ular in everyday discourse. Over and above a description of what parents do, "parenting" as a verb has become popular as a way of pointing to, even constructing, a set of demanding "tasks" for parents in late modernity. This charges parents with the moral obligation "to parent" well, always asking themselves if they meet the standards of "good parenting."

While our fieldwork is grounded in the day-to-day experiences of fami-lies, our broader concern is how arguments about "parenting" have become a crucial means by which society explores pressing dilemmas over how to live, what constitutes well-being, and what "good life" to hope for. We posi-tion parenting in relation to theories of late modernity and the risk society, as discussed later in this chapter. As Stevi Jackson and Sue Scott observe, "greater parental investment in children occurs within what seems to be a less predictable and less safe world."[8] This investment concerns everyone—since "children are the future"—and society's anxious calculations designed to optimize an uncertain future often turn the spotlight on children and childrearing.

---

[6] Lee, Macvarish, & Bristow (2010, p. 294).

[7] Ulrich Beck and Elisabeth Beck-Gernsheim (2002) observe: "On the one hand, individualization means the disintegration of previously existing social forms—for example, the increasing fragility of such categories as class and social status, gender roles, family, neighbourhood etc. [. . . on the other hand] new demands, controls and constraints are being imposed on individuals" (p. 2). See also Jessop (2002).

[8] Jackson & Scott (1999, p. 89). It can also be argued that late modernity's dis-embedding from tra-dition and re-embedding in new forms of commitment to (relatively fragile or even risky) identities or communities (Beck, Giddens, & Lash, 1994; Giddens, 1999) brings both opportunities and risks for children's socialization and life chances (James, 2013; Livingstone, 2009).

Parents' exercise of their responsibilities therefore becomes everyone's concern. So it is not accidental that the public stands at the ready to judge parents' management of their children's use of digital technologies. Being media scholars, we are intrigued that it is digital transformations that crystallize the dilemmas of modern life. And the combination of digital innovation—bringing uncertainty and complexity, and childrearing—being so crucial in its consequences, seems particularly explosive. Contradictory advice from others adds to the anxieties. A steady flow of mass media headlines exhort parents to learn digital skills or buy the latest gadget to keep up, yet also to closely monitor their children to avoid risks online and to limit time spent on "mindless" activities like gaming and social media. Although technological innovation is far from the only change defining the present age, our research has led us to observe, over and over again, how it provokes fundamental anxieties about agency, values, and (the loss of) tradition.

We invited the parents we spoke with to look backward to their childhood to reflect on how they were parented, and then forward to the conditions in which their children might themselves parent in the future. Many parents told us that digital technology represents the single most noticeable difference between their own childhood and that of their children—so of course it attracts their attention and concern. This is not to say that technological change is, truly, the top or only priority for our times, nor even that all parents really think this. Indeed, throughout this book we critically examine what problems are introduced by giving such attention to the digital and, therefore, what other, perhaps deeper, problems are obscured.

Pawel's hope of keeping control was something we heard repeatedly in our fieldwork, as was Lara's optimism about digital opportunities. Lara told us excitedly, "The big policy that is happening—and all the mums are concerned—they are going to learn this semester how to do coding."[9] Asked, "Are [the mums] worried or are they excited?," Lara replied, now agreeing with her husband:

They seem a little bit puzzled by it and so that's something that is happening now and you can't avoid, you know, government policy and their IT classes,

---

[9] During our research, the UK Universities minister, Sam Gyimah, said: "A world-class pipeline of digital skills is essential to the UK's ability to shape our future" (Department for Education, 2018). Funding for a series of computer programming ("coding") initiatives from the early years onward followed (e.g., Dredge, 2014). Of course, schools have taught computer programming since the 1970s, but today's renewed investment in coding is receiving widespread public attention.

and they will go down that way whether you want it or not. So it's good to have some structure or some tools.

The school's new plan to teach coding made Lara fatalistic:

There are lots of new things coming up and I think the speed, I doubt that the parents will be able to follow, I don't know, so I'm just hoping for the best.

Pawel sought to cope by taking on a new digital burden:

I need to stay on top of it so I know what he's able and capable of doing on the computer before I let him loose. . . . [So] I'm going to have to learn about coding.

It wasn't long before "liberal" Lara was calling for stronger government regulation of the media, given the safety and commercial threats that surrounded Tomas. But doubting that this would be effective, she too felt tasked with risk management. Lara and Pawel poured their few resources—primarily their energy and determination—into educating their son to succeed in what they saw as, and what we will argue to be, a risky and uncertain world. Like many parents we interviewed, they were convinced that, though only six, his personal choices were already portentous, for his future was at stake.

Between a remembered past and an imagined future

Who can anticipate the world 20 years hence? Or know the consequences of today's childrearing for tomorrow's adults? While such questions are as old as humanity, they become particularly pressing at times of rapid social change, especially in an increasingly individualized and competitive society. Of the many changes shaping today's society, the widespread embrace of digital technology is clearly one. As the Organisation for Economic Co-operation and Development (OECD) puts it:

The children entering education in 2018 will be young adults in 2030. Schools can prepare them for jobs that have not yet been created, for technologies that have not yet been invented, to solve problems that have not yet been anticipated.[10]

This gives a new and distinctive edge to age-old questions about parenting. How can parents prepare their children to be adults in 2030 or 2040? Or for jobs that haven't been invented yet? How can they anticipate the digital skills needed to thrive in the future when technological transformations and the future labor market are unpredictable? How can they support their development as citizens at a time of information overload, "fake news," and "hacked" elections? Or, faced with "technological progress and demographic changes," spare them a future of being "trapped in insecure, low-value, low-pay employment—or worse, forced out of work altogether"?[11] In short, how can parents promote children's agency and well-being in a digital world that parents themselves struggle to understand or manage?[12]

The years between a child's infancy and adulthood are symbolically laden with many hopes and fears. Our premise in this book is that parents' actions in the present are shaped not only by immediate needs or desires but also, importantly, by memories of the past and visions of the future. Although it is understandable that parents look back to their own childhoods, parenting is inherently future oriented. Each act of parenting has a double meaning—as an intervention in the present and an effort to bring about a particular future, even if this future cannot be fully named and the path to achieving it is uncertain. The sociology of time argues that, in negotiating their "projected futures,"[13] people find themselves, as Vincanne Adams, Michelle Murphy, and Adele Clarke put it, constantly *"tacking back and forth between futures, pasts and presents, framing templates for producing the future."*[14] For most, the

---

[10] OECD (2018, p. 2). The Institute for the Future for Dell Technologies (2017) agrees: "Emerging technologies will . . . intersect with powerful demographic, economic, and cultural forces to upend the conditions of everyday life and reshape how many live and work in 2030" (p. 1). See also UK Digital Skills Taskforce (2014) and Nesta (2019). For critical perspectives, see P. Brown, Lauder, & Ashton (2012, p. 75); Prince's Trust (2018).

[11] Nesta (2019, p. 1).

[12] There's no doubt such questions are on parents' minds. Cameron, middle-class father of two (Family 48), told us, "I think there will be jobs around now that won't be around in 20 years." He elaborated, "I'd like to see them embrace technology and work in something that's always developing and changing and you're always required. You're always needed." Supposedly, children are even more enthusiastic for a digital career than their parents. Or as *The Independent*'s headline of January 23, 2018, read, "Children of Britain's 'Digital Generation' Aiming for Careers in Technology, Study Shows Ambitions to Become Next YouTube Star or Software Developer at Odds with Parents' Preferences." A survey reported in *HR Review* (January 3, 2019) even suggests that one in five UK children wants to be a social media influencer.

[13] Tavory & Eliasoph (2009, p. 910).

[14] Adams, Murphy, & Clarke (2009, p. 246; emphasis in original).

time span of this imaginative recollection and projection stretches back to people's grandparents and forward to their grandchildren. Thus, a window of around a century bounds the timeframe in which change is experienced and decisions are made. When we asked parents to reflect on their own biographies, we often saw how they engaged intensively in making the imaginative, if hazardous, leap from their known past into their "future talk," in which they tried to divine their child's unknown and unknowable future.[15]

In describing their daily lives, including their own guilty pleasures, marital tensions, judgments of others, and anxieties about their children's futures, parents inevitably reflected wider cultural narratives. These narratives, we found, are often fixated on how technological innovation marks both change from the past and prospects for the future. Parents read the daily headlines about "internet addiction," along with advice about limiting screen time, in parenting magazines or the popular press. They empathize with romantic accounts of "free range" childhoods and are terrified by predictions of people replaced by robots or life-changing decisions made by artificial—not human—intelligence. So when it comes to assessing what's best for their children, parents are—like everyone else—influenced by popular imagery.

Middle-class Lena Houben[16] reluctantly left a job in academia to be around more for her children, but, like some other stay-at-home mothers, she then felt isolated, uncertain of her standing in the world, struggling with a "constant sense of being afloat on a sea of hysteria."[17] She spoke of feeling overwhelmed by the "tsunami" of devices in her home, which provoked her to look back to how her own parents had managed her TV viewing when she herself was a child:

> My parents were very strict and I couldn't watch what everyone else was watching; I couldn't join in the discussions. I started to realize that [my daughter] Miriam was probably going to survive without my being excessively protective, so I needed to kind of let go a little bit and let her experiment. That was fine when she was still 11, but it's snowballing, and we've suddenly ended up with three devices in a very short space of time. All my anxiety has come back.

[15] Alper (2019).
[16] Family 6.
[17] Orgad (2019).

Recalling her own frustration as a child was what had led her to try to be more relaxed in her parenting. But, she ruefully observed, keeping her anxiety at bay had proved impossible, so she imposed strict rules on Miriam's internet use—tracked through use of a Google spreadsheet—to "control" its effects. Yet a purely resistant strategy was too limited: Miriam was also learning to code at school using Scratch, which Lena thought was positive, aware of the official view that coding is vital for a digital future:

> It's the new Latin isn't it? It's like, if you couldn't read or write 600 years ago, you were on the outside, you were a peasant. So in the new world you should know how to use HTML or you should be able to construct your own website, you should know some of the tools; you shouldn't just be a passive user.

Like other parents, Lena told us how she remembered a childhood of making your own entertainment or playing outside in the fresh air, while the future provoked talk of a sci-fi world of high-tech jobs, constant surveillance, and everyone separated by their personal screens. She added:

> In comparison to when I was growing up it feels like a brand-new thing that no previous generation of parents has had to deal with. . . . I am the last generation of people who didn't grow up plugged in.[18]

Interpreting the present so as to "shape new futures" is a highly imaginative activity.[19] Not purely personal—this is socially negotiated, politically contested, and heavily mediated. Robin Mansell draws on Charles Taylor's idea that "social imaginaries are widely shared understandings that have achieved general legitimacy" but argues that society is conflicted in its social imaginaries of the internet, generally prioritizing its economic drivers and market logic yet retaining hopes for "a sharing culture in an information commons."[20] A related case can be made for imagining a better future, where, again, a host of competing expert claims and predictions fight for legitimacy in the public imagination.

Since there is no easy answer to parents' questions about whether or how use of digital technologies will bring about a better future, parents become

---

[18] On the role of media in generational change, see Colombo & Fortunati (2011); Fortunati, Taipale, & de Luca (2017); Vittadini, Siibak, Reifová, & Bilandzic (2013).

[19] Appadurai (2013, p. 289).

[20] Adams et al. (2009); Mansell (2012, p. 34); C. Taylor (2003).

absorbed in hedging their bets against guessed-at outcomes. At mundane moments throughout the day, anxious parents read the runes to figure out which of their child's behaviors may yield future benefits or harms, which newly sparked interests could chart a profitable path to adulthood, which missed opportunities will later be regretted, and which easily overlooked problems signal trouble to come. Parents' memories of their own childhoods are hazy, if not downright nostalgic, and when they compare them with their children's it is precisely the absence then and presence now of multiple digital devices in their homes and pockets that mark the difference, separating adults from their own childhoods and articulating their private struggles for control.

By marking the difference, digital technologies also mark out a key terrain, sometimes a battlefield, for the negotiations of domestic life. Whether they also make a difference is a separate question, one we return to in the concluding chapter.

Embrace, balance, resist

The latest media technologies have always raised people's hopes and fears, necessitating shifts in family practices and public policy. At best seen as time wasting and at worst as spreading licentiousness and violence,[21] when TV first arrived there were also fears that it would have a "devastating effect on family relationships and the efficient functioning of the household" and that it would ruin children's eyes and brains or even cause cancer.[22] At the same time, society's investment in and optimism regarding technology is unremitting, with persistent hopes that it will transform children's educational prospects by creating new opportunities and, by reducing barriers to inclusion, democratize access. Notwithstanding that social scientists have long argued over whether such potential will be realized, and for whom, debates over the latest digital technologies recapitulate similar hyperbole.[23] On the one hand, smartphones have "ruined a generation" and social media have

---

[21] Critcher (2003).

[22] Lynn Spigel (1992) describes the adoption of TV as a space of "family togetherness" and yet popular media also presented this "new machine as a kind of modern Frankenstein that threatened to turn against its creator and disrupt traditional patterns of family life" (p. 9). See also Marvin (1988).

[23] Livingstone (2012); Luckin (2018); E. Williamson, Goodenough, Kent, & Ashcroft (2005).

"ended conversation."[24] On the other, parents are called on to help their children gain the "21st-century skills" highlighted by think tanks, needed by employers, and promoted by governments—or risk being left behind.[25]

Lizzie Coriam,[26] mother of Emily (age six) and Toby (age five), was very anxious about safety and violence online, and so kept a close eye on her children. She captured the dilemma facing many parents in telling us:

> I don't want to be judged as a mother who doesn't take the time to do art and craft, to sit down and read, to go on nature walks, to, you know, so . . . that's why I say, I'm careful about how long they can go on the computer for. Some people do judge parents. . . . I am very conflicted though, because they have a lot of cousins in South Africa who are earning a lot of money in the IT field, so I also feel, should it be something that we actively encourage? I don't know. . . . That's what I'm conflicted about. I mean I don't want them to be behind the rest. I do sometimes think, maybe we should learn more, so that they can learn faster and be ahead of the game.

Understanding how parents respond to these polarized visions is a central motivation of this book. We met many parents trying to chart their own course in accordance with their values and preferences, with lots of or little support, and some facing very particular challenges. For some, digital technologies offer support to counter these visions; for others, the challenges go far beyond what technology can or cannot provide.

Contra Tolstoy's famous statement that "Happy families are all alike; every unhappy family is unhappy in its own way," we found complexity and ambivalence in all our families.[27] So, this book will not support the public discourse of widespread family alienation, with parents and children supposedly "plugged in" to their personal screens to the exclusion of togetherness, discipline, or morality.[28] Indeed, we repudiate this discourse as itself adding to the burden of judgment that parents face every day, just as we have been glad to observe how parents, in diverse ways, try to renegotiate the false

---

[24] Turkle (2011); Twenge (2017).
[25] Institute for the Future for Dell Technologies (2017); Nesta (2017); Qualtrough (2018); Tkachuk (2018); UNESCO (2015). A typical statement from the European Commission's Digital Agency warns: "There is an urgent need to boost digital competences in Europe and to improve the uptake of technologies in education" (European Commission, 2018).
[26] Family 31.
[27] Tolstoy (1886).
[28] R. Putnam (2000); Turkle (2011).

position they are put in when simultaneously exhorted to keep up with digital developments and criticized for too much "screen time."

But we do endorse concerns about inequality, finding that parental investment in educational technologies and resources fails to erase enduring socioeconomic differences, and in some ways exacerbates them.[29] Indeed, we will show that the many promises made for digital opportunities are fragile, so often broken that can be read as compounding the hidden (or not so hidden) injuries of class.[30] At the same time we adopt an intersectional approach, attending throughout to the interrelations among class, gender, ethnicity, disability and other factors in shaping families' resources, imaginaries and outcomes. As will become clear, "privilege and oppression do not follow simple, additive models, but rather are personally interpreted in relation to shifting, contextual variables."[31]

Reflecting on the experiences of parents of babies and of teens, those living in multi-million-pound homes or in social housing, we identify three distinct genres for "digital parenting." By genres we mean clusters of practices made meaningful by particular values, beliefs, and imaginaries (social, digital and future), in ways that are not always conscious or coherent.[32] These genres are:

- *embrace*, in which parents seek out digital technologies for themselves or their children to ease family life or to gain valued professional skills or, for some, "future ready" identities and lifestyles;
- *balance*, in which parents try to hedge their bets by encouraging some digital practices and not others, often ad hoc, weighing opportunities and risks salient in the present or future;
- *resist*, in which parents articulate their efforts as attempting, at least some of the time, to stem the seemingly unstoppable incursion of digital technology into family life.

---

[29] J. E. Katz, Rice, & Aspden (2001); Robinson, Cotten, Schulz, Hale, & Williams (2015); Selwyn (2014); Selwyn & Facer (2007).

[30] Sennett & Cobb (1993).

[31] Alper, Katz, & Clark (2016, p. 110); see also Crenshaw (1991).

[32] We build on research on cultural (and to some degree ideological) genres of participation that "specify particular but recognisable social and semiotic conventions for generating, interpreting, and engaging with embedded practices with and through media" (Livingstone & Lunt, 2013, p. 80; see also Ito et al., 2010).

For some, resisting is a way of responding when it seems that technology presents a problem for their particular child, in response to an incident or behavior. Yet resistance is sometimes less reactive than value driven, reflecting a desire to prioritize other activities or futures or as a way of resisting social pressures and commercialism.

Threaded throughout this book, these genres provide a way of reconciling commonality and diversity among families. They remind us that although their individual circumstances lead parents to respond to the technological and the social in diverse, even opposed, ways, nonetheless common patterns can be discerned and analyzed. For example, embedded in Lara's and Pawel's hopes and concerns are distinctive values toward and practices around digital technologies that are both echoed and contested by others. On the one hand, although they were often exhausted by daily travel and work, Lara and Pawel were trying hard to manage Tomas's daily screen time, limiting it to an hour or so. On the other hand, since the family had no relatives in the country, Pawel had tried to get Tomas to Skype his grandparents. But it hadn't really worked; the grandparents weren't comfortable with the technology and, since he barely knew them and did not speak Polish, Tomas wasn't comfortable with them.[33]

Technology symbolized both their fears and their hopes, but that didn't make it easy to negotiate or manage. Lara was more eager to embrace the new opportunities opened up by technology, while Pawel resisted by seeking continuity with traditional values. Yet their orientations were far from static. Pawel resisted before finding a reluctant balance. Lara embraced but then found herself resisting. Each negotiated with and adjusted around the other in an unfolding dynamic that helped them, over time, accommodate to what they increasingly saw as inevitable. As Lara commented, "everything is permeated by media and computers, in all kinds of work, really, so there is no way to avoid it."

Lena Houben balanced with anxious ambivalence. She worried that too much screen time would affect Miriam's "hand–eye coordination and her fine motor skills. . . . [T]he way she expresses herself might atrophy." This mattered because, despite her concerns, Lena encouraged her daughter to blog her poetry, and this gave rise to some conflict with Miriam's father, Avery Dahl, who had recently returned to work in media production after a period of unemployment that tested the middle-class family's finances. Avery feared

---

[33] Share, Williams, & Kerrins (2017).

that Miriam's "juvenilia" could damage her future "brand," while Lena valued her blog as the beginning of an archive of future benefit. Notwithstanding its uncertain outcomes, Avery was "more front-foot on new technology," telling us, "I want the kids to be as fluent in the grammar of coding as they can while their minds are still plastic," and worrying about a digital future in which "a gulf will open up . . . between those who can and those who can't," perhaps because although the family had now gained financial stability, its previous precariousness wasn't forgotten.

Thus, our genres of "embrace," "balance," and "resist" refer to culturally-shared constellations of practices, values, and imaginaries rather than the neat classification of individuals or families. Often we saw parents at one time embrace, at another resist, when seeking a balance that works for their family. Each genre brings its own anxiety, as parents ask themselves: Did I get it right? Will it pay off? Embracing means positioning oneself ahead of the curve, and so one may feel exposed, acting before the social norms and resources are in place to offer support. Balancing is an active and effortful process, like standing on a rolling log. Not simply a compromise, it invites constant self-questioning and adjustment: Is this right? How can I tell? Resisting may mean worrying about missing out professionally or person-ally, or that one is going out on a limb, taking a risk by *not* doing what eve-ryone else seems to be doing.

Insofar as parenting practices are constantly judged as being in advance of, lagging behind, or settling at what appears to be the emerging norm, these genres embed a normative gaze that can isolate parents from each other, as each watches and evaluates the other before determining his or her own approach. This is especially fraught in relation to digital technologies, where little precedent exists and parents must work things out afresh. Lena described her effort to find other like-minded parents at the playground:

> Asking what other people did and sharing information was so fraught, I just didn't want any part of it. I think that's why I've ended up feeling very isolated; I just felt I had walked into a pit of quicksand and you couldn't take a step without someone criticizing or judging what you were doing with your child. It means that you're very much on your own.[34]

[34] Susan Douglas and Meredith Michaels (2005) argue that motherhood is seemingly celebrated on the surface yet bears a castigating set of standards: "The new momism is a highly romanticized and yet demanding view of motherhood in which the standards for success are impossible to meet" (p. 4).

Whether or not they interpret digital technologies with anxiety, we found that many parents greeted these questions with a deeply felt sense of personal responsibility and judgment of one another. Parents evaluate and judge one another on this basis—one parent is judged as lazy or too permissive with "screen time," another as too rigid and restrictive and the children therefore left out or left behind. Parental autonomy—celebrated in late modern societies in the West—brings diversity that we recognize in our book to counter homogenizing accounts of "parents" or "parenting."[35] But autonomy and diversity carry a cost for the individual, as parents realize that decisions made now may cost their child dearly in the future, and a cost to the collective, for when norms weaken and individuals feel threatened, mutual judgment and even shaming can emerge. It is no wonder that, invited to discuss their children, parents were all too keen to open the door to us and spill out their concerns or conclusions over digital technologies and what they have chosen to embrace, balance, or resist.

Changing times, changing families

The parental attention focused on digital technologies, including whether to embrace, balance, or resist them, leads us to ask how far this is merited and how far it obscures other, perhaps more intractable, problems. Lara and Pawel were keen to share their digital doubts and conflicts, but their interview was also telling for what else it reveals. As globalization theorist Arjun Appadurai put it, we are living through long-term shifts in the flow of money, people, technology, media, and ideas, and their entwined histories are generating unpredictable consequences. The lives of families like Lara and Pawel's are evidence of this, shaped by migration, insecure work, fragile forms of community, and uncertain resources. For Lara and Pawel, parenting intensifies the need to negotiate everything afresh in bridging their different continents, languages, and cultures, and this task is not eased by the precariousness of juggling family life in a demanding and expensive global city, with their own parents far away. As they try to give their son the opportunities they themselves had as children, it seems significant that they see the digital as offering a means by which they can pursue their ambitions for him.

---

[35] We find it problematic that both academic and popular talk of "parenting" tend to treat all parents as the same, obscuring very real differences in resources that parents can call upon (Cooper, 2014; LeVine & LeVine, 2016).

Lena's and Avery's struggles, by contrast, invite a gendered lens, with Lena an educated woman undermined by having to give up her career and public standing, a woman who easily doubted herself. While Lena supported her children's pathway to a digital future, she castigated herself for failing to keep up, saying:

I kind of set off in life with lots of advantages . . . but I know that over the course of my lifetime I've slipped back down to the status of peasant, in terms of modern technologies.

Perhaps Lena focused on the digital because society tells her that, more than her career or marriage, this is something she can and should control.

Other families face other challenges, being preoccupied by family breakdown, illness or poverty, or caring for children with special educational needs or disabilities. Most obviously, all our families lived in London, which, like other global cities, sociologist Saskia Sassen characterizes as being situated at the dense intersection of multiple cross-border dynamics and tensions. This contributes to a sense of creative opportunity yet also instability, intense inequality, and an ambivalent relation to place, especially for its transnational and hypermobile population. Moreover, as Sassen writes:

The concept of the global city brings a strong emphasis on the networked economy because of the nature of the industries that tend to be located there: finance and specialized services, the new multimedia sectors, and telecommunications services.[36]

By comparison with the rest of the United Kingdom, London is distinctive in its proportion of multicultural and multilingual families for the job creation opportunities it offers—especially in the technology sector—and for its recent and substantial improvements in school achievement, contributing to some degree of social mobility.[37] It is also noteworthy for its socioeconomic struggles as families search for creative, interesting, or just practical work

---

[36] Sassen (1991, p. 40). See also Appadurai (2013); Beck-Gernsheim (1998); Leurs & Georgiou (2016).

[37] The UK Office for National Statistics (2016) shows that a markedly higher proportion of the London population are migrants compared to the UK population. Further, "the capital provides more opportunities for its residents—including its poorest ones—to progress than elsewhere" (Sutton Trust, 2017, p. iv), although the most deprived still struggle (Boston Consulting Group, 2017).

opportunities in the city, squeezing into homes they can't quite afford to live in a "better" neighborhood, nearer the "good" school.

More generally, family life is being reconfigured by these and other transformations—in family life, sexuality, work, religious affiliation, education systems, migration patterns, and more.[38] The result is new tensions between tradition and innovation, significantly as a result of the globalized flows of people and ideas, in turn reconfiguring the relations among the generations. Of particular significance, economic changes mean that children now growing up in the West are the first generation in living memory forecast to be less prosperous than their own parents. While for postwar generations the overall rate of intergenerational social mobility has been stable, as John Goldthorpe explains:

> Younger generations of men and women now face less favourable mobility prospects than did their parents—or their grandparents: that is, are less likely to experience upward mobility and more likely to experience downward mobility.[39]

This is because although educational opportunities have expanded in recent decades, job outcomes have become more uncertain. Workplaces are increasingly flexible yet also increasingly demanding, permeable, and insecure.[40] Young people experience extended adolescence compared with postwar generations, with more years spent in education and delayed entry into the workforce or independent living. Combined with a similarly extended period of retirement and advances in health for an increasingly aging population, many parents are "sandwiched" between caring responsibilities.[41]

Since World War II especially, the West has seen "a democratisation of the private sphere," as Anthony Giddens puts it.[42] He argues that intimate relations are ever less defined according to kinship, obligation, or religion and ever more dependent on the intrinsic quality of what he termed the

---

[38] Cunningham (2006); Livingstone (2009, 2018); Parker & Livingston (2018). Hill & Tisdall (1997) note, "the idea of family is to some degree a fluid one, with a mix of concepts at its core—direct biological relatedness, parental caring role, long-term cohabitation, permanent belonging" (p. 66).

[39] Goldthorpe (2016, p. 96). On US parents' anxieties about not reproducing their socioeconomic status for their children, see Cooke (2018).

[40] Graham, Hjorth, & Lehdonvirta (2017); Luckman & Thomas (2018).

[41] Hamilton (2016); Jones, O'Sullivan, & Rouse (2007); Twenge (2017).

[42] Giddens (1992, p. 184).

pure relationship—no longer dictated by traditional inequalities in power but, rather, "reflexively organized, in an open fashion, and on a continuous basis."[43] As a result, expectations of family life have expanded considerably, although the means of achieving them are more uncertain. While Giddens is more interested in the refashioning of gender relations, Elisabeth Beck-Gernsheim observes more generally that:

> The character of everyday family life is gradually changing: people used to be able to rely upon well-functioning rules and models, but now . . . more and more things must be negotiated, planned, personally brought about.[44]

In particular, she argues that as children observe how their parents engage in endless "acrobatics of balancing and coordinating,"[45] they are themselves socialized into an individualized culture. This in turn enables a recognition of children's agency. But while children have gained the right to "determine and regulate the conditions of their association,"[46] parents have gained the responsibility to involve them in key decisions, even becoming accountable to their children in a relationship founded ever less on asserting authority and ever more on building mutual respect. This last is proving difficult for parents in relation to digital technologies.

Parenting in the risk society

Scholars of contemporary family life describe the rising anxiety and "intensi-fied" logics by which parents seek to manage bringing up their children under conditions of risk, uncertainty, and rapid social change.[47] In parallel, there are growing warnings of a crisis in childhood.[48] As several recent academic and popular depictions of family life have explored, some parents respond to

---

[43] Giddens (1991, p. 91); Reese & Lipsitt (1978). Contrary to a romantic vision of family as a buffer against, or isolated from, the outside world, Giddens (1991) argues that the "pure relationship" is "thoroughly permeated by mediated influences coming from large-scale, abstract systems" (p. 7). These systems—policy, welfare, economy, media—may not (indeed, often do not) work in families' interests, nor are they equal in their effects, partly because the resources of the reflexive self are themselves stratified by social class (Threadgold & Nilan, 2009).

[44] Beck-Gernsheim (1998, p. 59).

[45] Beck-Gernsheim (1998, p. 67).

[46] Giddens (1993, p. 185).

[47] Nelson (2010). Sharon Hays (1998) suggests that these dominant and accepted logics of intense parental input are naturalized, not given.

[48] For example, Aynsley-Green (2019); R. D. Putnam (2015).

the societal demands on them by seeking to protect their children by wrapping them in "cotton wool," acting like "tiger moms," "helicoptering" to protect them from harm, or using technology as a "digital tether."[49] Others adopt drastically different strategies, hoping to inoculate their children against danger precisely by exposing them to it, building resilience through philosophies like "free range" parenting.[50] Technology offers new challenges to this careful calibration and new forms of visibility for it—not least by fueling the shaming debates that rage in social media parenting groups though also by promising new ways to "optimize" children's outcomes.[51]

But technology represents just one of many challenges facing today's parents. In an individualized, and increasingly neo-liberal society, with welfare safety nets being rolled back or privatized, people are tasked—whether empowered or burdened—with making decisions under conditions of radical uncertainty and contradictory expert advice. The contemporary constellation of real and perceived threats coalesces, in Ulrich Beck's term, into a "risk society" in which, by contrast with natural threats, "risk may be defined as a systematic way of dealing with hazards and insecurities induced and introduced by modernization itself."[52] In the face of manifold risks, parents are newly "responsibilized" for their actions and the consequences that flow from them, engendering an increasing sense of insecurity and anxiety. As Beck and Beck-Gernsheim observe, this burden, including its unequal costs and outcomes, is not the accidental consequence of socioeconomic changes but, rather, a matter of political ideology (they call this "institutionalized individualism") in a competitive, "sink or swim" culture in which social support is contracting.[53] For Frank Furedi, modern parenting is increasingly "paranoid" in part because "being at risk is treated as if it has become a permanent condition that exists separately from any particular problem."[54] In response, the family itself is changing: Philip Webb describes this as a transformation "from a site of affect to be protected from the vagaries of the outside world [to] a modern, transactional institution."[55] However, as will become clear, we

[49] Chua (2011); Cooper (2014); Honore (2008); Villalobos (2014). On helicoptering, see also Bristow's essay in *Parenting Culture Studies* (E. Lee et al., 2014), Laura Hamilton's *Parenting to a Degree* (Hamilton, 2016), and Hofer et al. (2016).
[50] Tracey Jensen (2016) claims resilience has been co-opted as a neo-liberal strategy in which individual families are expected to "bounce back," deflecting critical attention from problematic social structures (Hoffman, 2010; Kohn, 2016; Nelson, 2010; Rimini, Howard, & Ghersengorin, 2016; Steiner & Bronstein, 2017). See W. Davies (2014) on the rise of neo-liberalism in Western societies.
[51] Faircloth, Hoffman, & Layne (2013, p. 8).
[52] Beck (1992, p. 21); Livingstone & Sefton-Green (2016).
[53] Beck & Beck-Gernsheim (2002).
[54] Furedi (1997, p. 4; 2008).
[55] Webb (2011, p. 97).

recognize the pressures families are under but do not fully agree with Furedi or Webb in their bleak prognosis for family life.

Although parenting anxieties are often dubbed "middle class," we will show that diverse parents are, to a greater or lesser degree, engulfed in today's parenting culture, striving for involvement and vigilance within the family and, ultimately, seeking to shape the present so as to optimize their child's future in a risk society.[56] We critique as classed the idea that only for the middle classes is parenting culture a source of fascination and anxiety. Middle-class parents may be more vocal about their anxieties, but we will argue that, precisely because parents hold themselves (and are held by others) as responsible for fostering children's future life chances, the "individualization" of parenting in the risk society also affects disadvantaged families.[57] At the same time, our fieldwork leads us to question the more extreme claims in the public sphere about parental anxiety, both because we found such diversity among families and because, for many, what we might call their "parenting philosophy" offered them some reassurance.

We can illustrate these arguments by reference to Anna Michaels, who became a single mother when still a teenager.[58] Having grown up in a conservative Christian West Indian family in South London, Anna both reacted against and reproduced the demands that had been placed on her as a child. She described herself with some pride as a "pushy parent" of 13-year-old Derrick and 10-year-old Dionne, saying, "I'm a single young mum and I'm a gay young mum so I'm under a lot of categories of negativity to society." Although often struggling for money, she declared that she wanted her children to "have the best . . . [but] I don't want them to think that the best is owed to them." Anna thus worked to counter what she described as the stereotype of "poor families" or "single parents" as irresponsible. By the way that she refused the position allotted her by society, she illustrated both the uncertain promises and the demands of trying to overcome her difficult circumstances in the risk society by her focus on learning, including with digital technologies.

---

[56] Dermott & Pomati (2015); Faircloth et al. (2013); Furedi (2008); Nelson (2010).

[57] Clark (2013); Lareau, Adia Evans, & Yee (2016). It must be said, we were not helped in building this argument by theories of late modernity and the risk society, parenting culture studies, and the new sociology of childhood. Although all have shaped our thinking, they do not fully address problems of social inequality, especially social class (Beck, 1992; Furedi, 1997; Hoffman, 2010; E. Lee et al., 2014; Livingstone & Haddon, 2017). We develop this point in Chapter 3, where we find we must give more emphasis to the importance of established (if changing) social structures and persistent social inequalities.

[58] Family 22.

Anna fashioned her home as a learning environment, supporting her children's homework by buying all the books, giving them quizzes, acting as the teacher, and creating a strict daily timetable, as well as enabling their particular interests: Dionne danced competitively; Derrick did army cadets and taekwondo. Each choice was made after careful consideration of the pros and cons, to steer the children as much away from danger as toward a productive future. As a working mother, she was concerned that if they didn't attend classes, "they would be on the streets, looking after themselves." She added, "There's a lot of gang violence around here, I'm worried about it for my son. . . . He's doing good. He's on the straight and narrow for now." For Derrick, a Black teenage boy living in an area where others his age had experienced violence, the risks were real, leading Anna also to welcome his interest in computers and gaming, as this kept him safely at home when not otherwise occupied. She told us proudly how she let him take apart her old phone, saying he likes "dissecting stuff. He just wanted to know how it works."

As with many other families, the challenges Anna faced were multiple, and it is within this context that she judged that digital transformations could contribute. Her hopes—as we also saw with many other families—led her to equip the home with a mix of technologies, encourage her son's geeky experimentation, and seek to build a bridge between learning at home and at school. In this respect, although she was not so critical of the school as an institution, Anna's lay theory of learning echoes the theory of "connected learning" developed by the MacArthur Foundation–funded Connected Learning Research Network, of which this project is part.[59] However, Anna's approach was one more of balance than of embracing technology, her enthusiasm tempered because Dionne had had "a horrible time," as Anna put it, when she had been cyberbullied by an elementary school classmate. As Anna reflected ruefully, when telling us how angry she had been, "You can't change how technology is moving. You have to adapt to it, but you also have to have the mentality to adapt to it."

In some sense, Anna had embraced the culture of reflexive modernity in which, alongside the risks of inequality, insecurity, and alienation, comes the potential for self-definition—in her case, this including the chance to counter the negative expectations imposed on her by society. Many contemporary

---

[59] The Connected Learning Research Network hypothesizes that learning is enabled when it is interest led, peer supported, collaborative, and production oriented. Youth-centered and sociocultural in its approach, connected learning research and practice critiques traditional schooling insofar as this tends to be curriculum rather than interest led, and test rather than practice focused, establishing hierarchical relations between teachers and students, treated individually, within the closed world of the school. See Ito et al. (2013, 2020).

social and technological changes are opening up new hopes for social mobility, flexible working, reimagined lifestyles, and self-chosen values, as well as new routes by which these may be achieved. Anna's reflections on her life suggested that she had carved out a more open identity for herself, and that she also attempted to do this for her children based on their individual needs and strengths. Rejecting the strictures of her own upbringing and those of a society that views young, Black, gay single mothers in terms of their deficits rather than strengths, she created her own "parenting philosophy," which reframed these experiences as a resource, not a hindrance.[60] Although she had taken on the burden of self-discipline, she had done so to avoid society's potentially punitive "policing" of either herself or her children.[61] In terms of our three genres of parenting in the digital age, she often embraced technology, describing herself as an "Apple junkie," but she balanced her embrace with some hedging. Reflecting on her efforts to prepare Derrick and Dionne for independence, she said, "Technology is the future, but technology is not reliable. You should be able to read and write, not technology doing everything for you. Do it yourself."

Although Anna appeared sanguine about a digital future, critical scholarship is concerned about the risks—especially to disadvantaged families—of so individualized and effortful a strategy.[62] Thus we as researchers must not only hear her optimism but also set this in a wider context of structural inequality and low social mobility (see Chapter 3). Similarly, although parents readily retell the media's stories about the supposed failings of the younger generation, it is important that we recognize these for their tendency to fuel moral panics about "others." After all, recent decades have seen long-term improvements in children's well-being and, even their educational achievements, notwithstanding with the advent of digital technologies during that period.[63]

In the risk society parents are the first in line for blame and shame, and the first to blame themselves if things go wrong, or if their children "fall behind." Everyday parenting actions are imbued with a sense of consequence, causing parents to adopt what Ana Villalobos calls "security strategies" in which they assume the responsibility for trying to "make things better" for their children[64] despite the fact that many of the great social shifts

---

[60] On how LGBT parents were seen as "deficit" parents until recently, a perception that Anna explicitly resists, see Goldberg (2010); Herek (2010).

[61] Donzelot & Hurley (1997).

[62] W. Atkinson (2007); Skeggs (2015); Woodman (2009).

[63] Livingstone (2018).

[64] Cooper (2014); Lareau (2011); Villalobos (2010, 2014).

that contribute to their children's future insecurity are far beyond their control. Technology has become simultaneously a threat to children's security and a promised route to ensuring it.

In Lena Houben's family, both parents and their 12-year-old daughter Miriam were pursuing a digital future, yet the accompanying risks brought anxiety and discord. Having forbidden her daughter to upload anything to YouTube, Lena Houben was livid when Miriam shared a video of herself in the style of popular vlogger Zoella[65] without her mother's knowledge. Miriam's father agreed with Lena's decision but nonetheless embraced YouTube as "the most astonishing resource. . . . It's something that I never envisaged and the fact that it exists is a kind of wonder that I now just take for granted." Yet although she was fiercely protective of Miriam, especially after "some boys from her school found [the second YouTube video the mother and daughter had made together] and started putting up abusive emails," Lena had herself turned to technology, writing a blog about her experiences as a mother, in particular, her unwanted departure from academia, her life balancing work and mothering, and "how hard it is to be a parent."[66]

To help parents navigate the twin challenges of optimizing opportunities while minimizing risks in the digital age, parenting advice is proliferating in the mainstream and social media, generated by policymakers, educators, health professionals, and an emerging category of "parenting experts."[67] Indeed, parents hardly lack for advice on their "sacred" task of parenting.[68] Arguably the considerable growth in government-sponsored and commercially motivated parenting advice and "interventions" is designed to fill the gap created by the withdrawal of institutional and community supports in the risk society, guiding or, as critics would say, surveilling and supervising parents in what one might consider their private lives.[69] Some of it invokes moral panics, scapegoating digital technologies as the supposed cause of

---

[65] Zoe Sugg (AKA Zoella) is a famous English YouTuber who creates beauty, fashion and lifestyle vlogging content.

[66] Having included some parent bloggers in our project, we were intrigued at this effort to build an online community of peer support (Roberts, 2018).

[67] Furedi (2008); Hulbert (2003, p. 361). Christina Hardyment (2007) outlines the history of parenting advice, explaining how it has always been contradictory and has its own agendas.

[68] Zelizer (1985).

[69] See Daly, Ruxton, & Schuurman (2016); Dermott & Pomati (2015); Nelson (2010); Villalobos (2010); Barassi (2017); Macvarish (2016). These critics argue that such trends are reframing parenting away from the "relational bond characterised by love and care" toward a "job requiring particular skills and expertise, which must be taught by formally qualified professionals" (Gillies, 2008, p. 1080). See also Annette Lareau (2011) on discourses of "scientific motherhood," and Furedi (2008) and Faircloth & Murray (2014) on the rise of parenting experts.

today's childhood ills and scapegoating the people who use them "addic-tively."[70] Some is commercially motivated, selling the latest gadgets and serv-ices purportedly in families' best interests, promoting visions of a digital future that are highly normative and aspirationally middle class.

Although these popular visions of "the problem" are compelling, they do not help parents with their immediate, practical puzzles: When should my child have a smartphone? How much is too much to share on social media? What will using a tablet do to my baby's brain? What is coding and should we sign up for a class? Even more problematic, much advice is disciplinary in tone—full of injunctions that leave parents feeling burdened and judged. Much of it also underestimates parents' growing expertise with technology, treating parents as know-nothings or offering bland or simplistic rules (e.g., limit screen time, install filters, keep devices in a family room) that fail to ad-dress the diverse realities of modern family life, in which parents are under increasing pressure and public services to support families are in decline. And little of it helps parents look beyond the digital: their problems may have quite different causes, but alternative coping strategies—individual or collective—are easily overlooked in the popular focus on the digital.

Overview of this book

The title of this book is something of a provocation. Ideally we would put "parenting" and "digital future" in scare quotes throughout, for it is the con-testation that surrounds them and the lived realities shaped by this contes-tation that we examine. Indeed, although speaking of "parents" is relatively straightforward, "parenting" as a verb (and an active intervention) has only emerged recently, referring not just to the task of bringing up children but to a personal, cultural, and even ideological "project" in its own right.[71] In this book, we aim simultaneously for a close focus on parenting experiences and a wider, critical lens on the society in which parenting is situated. Relatedly, although we heard plenty about the impacts of digital technologies on family

---

[70] Note that the theory of moral panics (Critcher, 2003) emphasizes that anxieties about techno-logical harms center on working-class families disproportionately, so their expression is not just a claim about media effects but, more importantly, a (mis-) judgment about how "other people" lack standards and need to be disciplined.

[71] In introducing their volume on "parenting culture studies," Ellie Lee and colleagues report a dra-matic rise in recent decades in books about "parenting" (as opposed to "parents," where interest has been steadier), a rise visible in both academic and popular publishing (E. Lee et al., 2014).

life, we try to avoid a technologically determinist account of contemporary parenting dilemmas, even as we explore the impact of such accounts when promoted in the public sphere and by policymakers. Our main argument, then, is that digital dilemmas crystallize deep-seated anxieties that stem from the many and varied challenges facing families.[72] These include but go far beyond digital challenges. Since these challenges are unequally distributed, families' responses to digital dilemmas, and the forms of support they need, vary accordingly. As we also show, parents' responses often confound popular expectations, and this in itself matters insofar as popular expectations—typically expressed as criticism of parents—tend not only to undermine parents but also to guide policymakers.

Whatever their struggles—whether rooted in structural or interpersonal difficulties—the decades-long project of bringing up a child challenges parents in ways that may be helped or hindered by the fact that they are living through a period of unprecedented digital innovation. By "the digital" we refer to much more than the influx of digital devices and content in our everyday lives to include society's increasing reliance on complex digital infrastructures composed of proprietary and extensively networked systems, which in turn are stimulating the emergence of innovative but precarious forms of work and living.[73] However transformative history may ultimately judge this to be, for parents it is undoubtedly deeply significant and problematic in the here and now. We interviewed many parents who felt they were, individually, charting new territory in parenting in a digital age. Insofar as the digital has become a site in which today's personal, public, and political struggles are staged, we ask what distinctive character this gives the struggle of modern parenting, both as parents themselves see it and as seen by a society constantly speaking for and about parents.

To research this book, we explored the parenting practices, values, and imaginaries of 73 families in London in 2015 and 2016, supported by a survey of 2,000 parents across the United Kingdom in late 2017. We recruited families with dependent children (younger than age 18) who were highly diverse in socioeconomic status, family composition, ethnicity, and age of children, as explained in the appendix. In an effort to listen to

---

[72] Tilly & Carré (2017).

[73] Lievrouw & Livingstone (2009), Lundby (2009). This reliance has reached the point where Jim Steyer, child advocate and founder of Common Sense Media, argues that the media itself has become children's "other parent" (Steyer, 2002).

parents' own voices and experiences, we conducted some intensely emotional interviews, a process itself telling about the experience of parenting in the digital age. Parents told us how they attempt to optimize their imagined future by establishing family values and practices designed to improve their child's life chances, drawing on diverse and highly unequal resources to do so.[74] Within this effort, "the digital" seems to offer a distinct pathway, with children tasked to carry society's hopes into the future, even though such efforts to control the future in turn generate new risks—both in the present and for the future, compounding adult anxieties about today's children and tomorrow's adults.[75]

We also sought out parents who, in one way or another, had confronted the idea of a "digital future" with distinct purposes or from a distinct perspective, meeting them at school parents' evenings, at children's centers, through parenting organizations, or through their children's after-school programs— including code clubs and media arts or digital "making" programs. We included families with children with special educational needs and disabilities (SEN)—both because they are so often excluded and because many interviewees expressed heightened hopes and concerns fears about what digital media might offer their children or saw digital media as a much-needed workaround for social or economic inclusion in the future. We also included self-proclaimed "geeky" parents, along with parents that blogged about their parenting, some with hundreds of thousands of followers and others with just a handful.

Having contextualized and focused our inquiry in the present chapter, in Chapter 2 we use the frame of a single day to reveal the multiple ways in which parents move between and among our genres of digital parenting within the day. Through negotiating the now-mediated activities of getting up, homework, family time, and bedtime, parents articulated their values not only about digital technologies but also, importantly, about family life. We contrast public policy that, problematically, exhorts parents to police their children's "screen time" with parents' efforts to sustain a more "democratic" mode of family life that respects their children's interests in digital technologies. Eschewing the myth of parents as unremittingly digitally ignorant, we

---

[74] Giddens (1999) calls this "colonising" the future.

[75] Hoover and Clark (2008) discuss how parents see parenting and, particularly, parenting with media as something for which they are specifically "accountable," such that their accounts are always "inflected with their assumptions about proper and desirable parental behavior in relation to the media" (p. 5).

reveal how their own interest in and hopes for digital technologies lead them to seek new modes of parenting, surprisingly often focused on shared digital pleasures.

Chapter 3 contrasts the experiences of families living in very different circumstances. It is not only privileged families but also, indeed, families from across the social spectrum that now invest in the kinds of "concerted cultivation" practices by which parents try to realize the future they imagine for their children. This includes practices that embrace the digital. Recognizing the distinctive intersections of cultural and economic capital that exist in a global city like London leads us to qualify sociologists' standard linear classifications of households. The position of educated but low-income families emerges as particularly interesting insofar as they seek creative or alternative ways of engaging with digital technologies. We then trace how class nonetheless remains important in differentiating parenting practices and, therefore, in shaping the unequal opportunities enabled by digital technology.

In Chapter 4 we turn to families that have most actively "voted with their feet" to embrace the idea of a digital future, by considering self-declared "geeky" children and parents. Although these families are in some ways exceptional, their lives reveal the considerable emotional, financial, and time investment required by the premise—avidly promoted by both the public and private sectors—that the future is digital. But the outcomes remain unknown and are, arguably, riskier than more traditional routes in terms of their long-term outcomes. Families accept these terms, we suggest, insofar as they see the adoption of a "geeky" identity as offering them a plausible pathway to overcome some unique biographical challenges. However, we avoid celebrating them, since their future is unknown: they may but may not benefit from being in the vanguard.

Parents of children with special educational needs and disabilities often experience an intensified struggle to balance the risks of digital technologies while embracing the opportunities. Chapter 5 argues that, rather than being the exception, these families illustrate more intensely the dilemmas of the digital age felt in varying degrees by many families. These dilemmas, we note, arise from parents' efforts to chart individualized pathways under conditions of heightened uncertainty and risk, often alongside reduced structural support. Digital technologies, in short, seem to suggest a clear path toward a socially sanctioned and innovative future, along with some creative workarounds to resolve a lack of domestic resources or capacity. However, the hopes raised by digital technologies for some of the families discussed in this chapter may turn out to be false, and the provision of better state services would surely serve them better.

Recognizing that it is the promise of digital learning for a digital future that leads many families to invest in digital technologies along with digital skills and learning opportunities, Chapter 6 explores parents' practical efforts to realize this promise. These efforts span the main learning sites of children's lives—home, school, and extracurricular activities. Since extracurricular activities combine the resources, flexibility, and expertise to experiment with digital learning, our fieldwork contrasts the values and imaginaries of three extracurricular learning sites, bringing together the voices of educators and parents to understand how each conceives of the learning potential associated with digital technologies. Somewhat unexpectedly, although our chosen learning sites vary considerably in resources, each tends to underplay the importance of parents in scaffolding children's digital interests and, through a series of seemingly minor but significant barriers, acts to disconnect parents from their children's learning.

We conclude in Chapter 7 that parents are caught in a pincer movement in late modernity. They are, on the one hand, more burdened with responsibilities, given the erosion of state support and an increasingly uncertain socio-economic future, and, on the other, charged with respecting the agency of their child, leaving much to negotiate in today's "democratic" families. In seeking to manage the often-fraught dilemmas of their lives, parents find themselves looking back to their childhood and forward to an imagined and often-digital future. Through the generational stories that parents tell, often echoed and amplified by public and media discourses, digital technology comes to crystallize parents' deeper hopes and fears. This leads parents variously to embrace, balance, or resist technology in ways that shape—beneficially and problematically—both their family's present and their children's future.

While managing digital risks and opportunities is often challenging, parents' face an even greater challenge linked to the inherent uncertainties of the future. Not only must they determine—often on their own—whether to embrace, balance, or resist the digital even though little is (or can be) known of the consequences of digital decisions. But also the digital has become the terrain for enacting generational changes of multiple kinds—migration, social mobility, family breakdown, economic insecurity, and more. Through everyday *digital* decisions, parents negotiate authority, values, and identity with their children and, indeed, with their own parents, in person, or in their memory. Given that contemporary lives are characterized by risk and inequality, the outcomes for families vary considerably. Reflecting on these findings, and on what parents told us of their concerns, we end with recommendations for action for the key organizations tasked with improving families' lives and their futures, digital and otherwise.

2

Family Life in the Digital Age

Greeting the day

It's early morning in London. The homes appear lifeless from above, but inside there are signs that the day is beginning. Some parents force themselves to greet the morning, whereas others are being yanked against their will into the early dark and cold by enthusiastic young children. On bedside tables, cuddled in blankets, at the breakfast table, in living rooms, the dark is punctuated by the glow of thousands of small and large screens coming to life.

In a terraced house in an outer London suburb, Nicole Saunders constantly wrestles with the debilitating sleeplessness that comes from juggling a new baby and a three-year-old who habitually wakes in the dead of night.[1] Once toddler Eloise climbs into bed in the morning, Nicole helps her open Netflix (having already set up Eloise's profile) or the CBeebies app to try to claw back a bit more sleep. She told us she felt "guilty" and "lazy" about this, knowing that she was taking liberties with the rules about "screen time," but she also recognized that the extra rest (and coffee) was helping her survive. Nicole, whose dark eye circles punctuated her freckled skin and ginger hair, recounted how she had given up her full-time public relations job to stay at home with her daughters. Even before Eloise was born, Nicole had started blogging about her pregnancy and was now reaching hundreds of thousands of readers each month. On Saturdays, it was husband Jeff's turn to do the early mornings with his daughter, both cuddling up on the couch in their pajamas as he gleefully introduced Eloise to the joys of *Star Wars*. Nicole was glad of the lie-in but a little resentful of Jeff—"he will put the TV on, it just feels like it's taking the easy option"—after she'd spent all week finding worthwhile things for Eloise to do.

In a 1960s flat on an inner-city council estate, Habiba Bekele, who migrated to London from Ethiopia decades ago, rouses herself presunrise each day to begin her morning prayers.[2] Habiba told us that after prayers she starts

[1] Family 37.
[2] Family 25.

Parenting for a Digital Future. Sonia Livingstone and Alicia Blum-Ross, Oxford University Press (2020). © Oxford University Press.
DOI: 10.1093/oso/9780190874698.001.0001

up the family laptop to call her Arabic teacher in Egypt while her husband Stephen readies himself for work as a security guard. While her four children (aged 4 to 10) eat breakfast, the family TV is tuned to the satellite channel GuideUS.tv, a Muslim channel from the United States that features sermons alongside segments sent in by parents of their children reciting the *ayahs* (verses of the Qur'an). Her children, she said, practice their own recitation using an app called *Let's Learn Quran with Zaky & Friends*, downloaded on the family iPad.

Habiba was a childminder,[3] she told us, and once her own children were off to school she would welcome those of other local families, careful to limit "screen time" because she knew that the parents of the children in her care did not approve. She had worries about her children too, describing the surliness that four-year-old Dejen's love for *Horrible Histories* seemed to produce, and upset when nine-year-old Dawit saw pornography at a friend's house. She said she monitored the children carefully, musing, "When you let them have it, they don't want to have a family relationship." When she thought her children demanded too much, Habiba quickly moved to correct, taking devices away for a day or two and arranging a "family day" instead.

In an elite central London neighborhood, Sven Olsson,[4] a busy corporate executive from Sweden, generally sets his iPhone alarm to rouse himself for prework exercise. He told us that after checking work emails in bed he sweats on his treadmill and checks on the stock market, gearing himself up for the day. His 10- and 14-year-old boys Sean and George are slow to wake; sometimes (unbeknownst to their parents) they set their alarms to 2:00 a.m. to break into the safe where their parents keep their iPads and laptops to play games. Sean told us, "Sometimes we go in together, so it's not as easy to figure out who really did it. . . . It's really funny that they don't know who it is."

In her leafy suburb, Sweta Fletcher,[5] mother of two, often struggles to get fussy eater Nikhil to eat his breakfast so that she can get to work across town. She told us she'd compared notes with other mothers after school and recounted how others let their children watch shows at breakfast as incentives to *eat*. Though saying this with implied horror, Sweta was nonetheless quick to proclaim, "That's not a judgment!" Still, when four-year-old Nikhil begged for the family iPad, Sweta carefully set a timer for 10 to 15 minutes. She noted

---

[3] She ran an in-home nursery.
[4] Family 59.
[5] Family 8.

that "the conversation about screen time is a big thing, because I think a lot of parents worry firstly about how long is OK and secondly about the impact."

Metok and Dolma Zangpo,[6] aged five and eight, told us they knew better than to ask to watch TV in the mornings, since it was prohibited on school days. They said they knew that if they failed to "be good" in the mornings they'd sacrifice much-coveted time on their Amazon Fire tablets after school.[7] But never mind: Metok was happy to play with his Lego and Playmobil toys, and Dolma loved reading—and in the race to school there wasn't much time to spare anyway.

As the sun rises across the city, millions of families begin their morning routines, many of which involve negotiations—sometimes conflicts—over technology. By taking you through a day in the life of families in the digital age, we explore how families variously embrace, balance, or resist integrating digital technologies into their lives, influenced by their hopes and fears about a digital future. Along the way, we introduce our research methods and the families we interviewed (see appendix). Substantively, we argue that what is at stake in these negotiations is not only the new and uncertain parenting tasks around technology but also the challenges of the newly non-hierarchical "democratic family," with its heightened expectations regarding agency, fairness, and voice. Both, we argue further, are undermined by the oppressive public discourse of "screen time," for this precludes parents from reaching their own judgments about specific uses of digital technologies, whether positive or negative, and reimposes on parents the traditional authoritarian role from which recent decades of cultural change have sought to liberate them.

Digital technologies in the "democratic family"

The democratic family is a notable outcome of socioeconomic and political developments in recent decades, as discussed in the previous chapter. Increasingly "negotiation is the dominant pattern, as a demand" not a choice, as Beck puts it, and with "traditional authority relationships"[8] subject to interrogation, personally and

---

[6] Family 23.

[7] The Fire tablet is manufactured by Amazon using a custom version of an Android operating system. It functions similarly to the Apple iPad but is generally smaller. Some Fire tablets are labeled "Kids Edition" and come preloaded with child-focused features.

[8] Beck (1997, pp. 152 and 165).

politically. Focusing specifically on the parent–child relationship, family historian Howard Gadlin observes that "the most important characteristic of contemporary child rearing is the continued diminution of parental authority and responsibility," to the point where "democracy in family decision-making and parent-child interaction" is now widely expected.[9] But there are few answers to the new questions of how, and how far, parents should negotiate with their children, according to which norms and to achieve which outcomes. Parenting discourse, as promoted by child experts and the popular media (at least in the industrialized West), "highlights the desirability of child-centered forms of parenting [which] provide children with ample opportunities to exercise choice to develop a sense of individual agency."[10]

In a digital world, there is a particularly fertile synergy between popular conceptions of children and childhood, on the one hand, and of the digital environment, on the other—as playful and expressive, free yet transgressive. This fuels the popular notion of the "digital native" (along with the parent as "digital immigrant"). Thus parents love to recount their child's clever ways with technology, even as they find this undermines their authority. Indeed, in this regard, the digital is historically distinctive, children rarely having been admired in the past for any socially or economically valuable competences. From a child's perspective, therefore, the digital offers intriguing prospects for the exercise of agency and challenge to authority. But this prioritization of children's agency,[11] welcome and merited though it is, poses challenges not just to parents' authority, as is often noted, but also to parents' agency, including their values, philosophies, and aspirations and the traditions they either embrace or create alternatives to.

In this chapter, we make two linked arguments. First, digital technologies have become a prominent focus for conducting family negotiations, because changes in the digital environment differentiate parent and child generations so strongly. Second, the intense need for such negotiations has arisen not only from the advent of digital technologies—salient though this is—but also, and more fundamentally, from the rise of the democratic family over a similar time period. The tactics of previous generations—"Mother knows best," "wait till your father gets home," and, most famously, "because I said so"—are out of favor. Today, parents are expected to negotiate with and listen to their children, respecting the rights and interests of all participants; and they are expected to play new roles—being not only authority figure but also mentor, friend, learning partner, or confidant.[12]

[9] Gadlin (1978, p. 253).
[10] Faircloth, Hoffman, & Layne (2013).
[11] Lansdown (2014); Livingstone & Third (2017).
[12] Jamieson (2007).

Democratic family negotiations, whether with teenagers or small children, can be exhausting and demoralizing. The very salience of digital technologies seems to lead families to seize on them as a means of negotiating their conflicting desires and expectations. More prosaically, many parents resort to providing or withdrawing digital technologies to put an end to such wearing negotiations, in effect reinstating the carrot and stick of yesteryear.

But negotiating desires or discipline on the terrain of the digital brings its own problems, amplifying rather than easing family tensions. After all, digital activities are of uncertain value—the companies promoting them make competing and often exaggerated claims, the scientists disagree with each other, the policymakers don't know which way to turn (support the digital economy or restrict risky innovations?), and parents cannot afford to wait till their children are grown up to see if they made the right decisions. Perhaps in consequence, and notwithstanding that parents have invested in digital technologies both financially and in terms of domestic space, time, and effort in the hope that these will bring real benefits, parents find themselves succumbing to the seemingly simple public expectation that they should limit or "police" their children's "screen time."[13]

The notion of screen time, we suggest, seems to offer parents an officially-sanctioned and seemingly straightforward metric of parenting "success," one which reduces the competing interests of family members, together with the uncertainties of technological benefit or harm, to a straightforward rule of thumb.[14] But in practice, far from providing a reasonable path forward, screen time rules have proved a new rod for parents' backs. For example, Leah Crowe[15] described "pulling [her] hair out" trying to find the right "level of exposure" for her oldest son, Reece (12), who is an enthusiast, like Tomas[16] in Chapter 1, both of "real" football and of the football video game FIFA. Leah's likening of the latter to being "addicted" to a "class A drug" seemed exaggerated, since Reece plays both types of game sociably with friends. But Leah was recently divorced and effectively single-parenting

---

[13] The Parenting for a Digital Future survey showed the extent of UK parents' considerable investment in new technology, now including smart home devices (e.g., Amazon Echo, Google Home), wearables, and virtual reality devices. Yet it also showed how, once they have introduced new digital possibilities for communication and learning into the home, parents become critical of their own and their children's interest in them (Livingstone, Blum-Ross, & Zhang, 2018).

[14] Many parents recounted to us a version of the American Academy of Pediatrics (AAP) previous "two-by-two" guidelines (no screen time for children under age two, no more than two hours a day for older children), though they could rarely attribute them. The AAP rewrote its rules in 2011 and 2016, emphasizing more contextual judgment and less clock watching (American Academy of Pediatrics, 2011; Blum-Ross & Livingstone, 2018; Evans, Jordan, & Horner, 2011; Radesky & Christakis, 2016a, 2016b), but this more nuanced advice has not yet gained such widespread purchase.

[15] Family 40.

[16] Family 33.

Reece and his two younger brothers, so the promise of FIFA after school *was* a convenient way to "make a deal" with Reece to help with the school run. In her case and others, we saw how the focus on screen time simultaneously generates guilt (letting your child access a "problematic stimulant") and provides a solution for trying to negotiate with a child when faced with practical pressures.

As we show in this chapter, parents' struggles over screen time obscure some more fundamental problems that are reshaping the modern family from within, as it responds to the new norms of the democratic family, and from without, as it is buffeted by diverse societal risks and pressures. The fact that family life is often played out on the terrain of the digital both helps parents and undermines them.

As the day unfolds

Having finished breakfast, Sweta Fletcher drops Nikhil off at school and confirms that his teacher has received the email that Sweta has sent including photographs from the weekend's adventures on a local farm. The teacher regularly invites parents to send in family photographs so that she can project them onto the interactive whiteboard in the classroom—a form of "show and tell."[17] Elsewhere, Holly Zangpo receives an automated text from her children's school reminding her to donate to the school fête. The text comes from a no-reply number, so she can't respond, even when she has a question.

The increasing digital mediation of everyday life makes for greater interdependence between school and life at home and, in consequence, extends and complicates parental responsibilities.[18] Is it an opportunity or a burden that Sweta is tasked with documenting the family's weekend leisure activity and ensuring it reaches Nikhil's teacher in a timely way? Or that Holly can be reached by the school anytime but lacks a channel to reply? Some parents organize themselves into groups via digital media—a Facebook group for the parent–teacher association (PTA), WhatsApp groups for year 1 parents—to

---

[17] Glover et al. (2005).

[18] Livingstone (2009). Such mediation is not always welcomed by families, especially when schools make demands on them at home (via emails or use of the school intranet or teacher blogs; Livingstone & Sefton-Green, 2016). This trend, which David Buckingham (2000) dubs the "curricularisation" of leisure, is often resisted by children who seek to retain their autonomy and agency outside of school.

fill in gaps in communication.[19] Increasingly, schools too try to reach into the home to organize parents and children in support of the school. At one point, Bluebell Primary School tried to roll out a digital homework platform, but it was plagued by lost passwords, limited functionality, and parents who did not have tablets or computers at home, so the platform never really caught on.[20] We heard of greater success from Declan and Matthew Bardem,[21] who loved the games offered by their school's homework platform, Purple Mash.

Sometimes even when the technology worked it was irksome in its own way, the constant PTA messages haranguing, the numeracy homework app described, ironically, as "addictive." For some families, such digitally mediated connections seemed too invasive, leaving them to try to maintain some disconnection instead.[22] Jacob Bardem commented, about the school's use of class blogs to encourage the children to post what they did over the holidays, "I'm not that happy about that," and Daisy complained that these were time-consuming without obvious benefit. In short, digital connections offer much convenience, as well as opportunities to enhance learning and parental involvement, but sometimes introduce unwelcome intrusions into family life.[23]

Digital technologies are also bound up with the extension of parents' work into the home. This can allow for greater flexibility and control over their work hours but also requires navigating new pressures and constraints. Sven Olsson's early morning emails on his phone were both resented and appreciated: yes, he checks his work email while still in bed, but at least he can work out and have breakfast with his sons. Sweta Fletcher took time off to be with Nikhil, but social media helped her keep in touch with colleagues and friends, facilitating her return to work later. On the other hand, she also struggled with the balance, ruefully recounting how once at the park as she'd been checking Instagram, Nikhil had asked her not to simply glance up from her

[19] "Family engagement platforms" that aim to make school life more visible (and accountable) to parents are proliferating. These raise privacy concerns, because they make disciplinary action visible to parents (and other teachers) and collect (and monetize) data (B. Williamson, 2010). Yet such platforms may be welcomed by parents and teachers for creating easier pathways for sharing insights between home and school, even if they are sometimes burdensome.

[20] Bluebell Primary School is a pseudonym for the primary school where we conducted research—see appendix for details. Similar challenges have been documented for initiatives such as One Laptop per Child (Ames, 2019).

[21] Family 30.

[22] Livingstone & Sefton-Green (2016) showed that the pressures and expectations of "connected learning" (Ito et al., 2013) may override the desire many young people have for the different spheres of their lives to stay precisely *dis*connected.

[23] Carolan & Wasserman (2014); Hollingworth et al. (2011); Livingstone & Sefton-Green (2016).

phone at him, commanding her: "Mummy, look *long*!" After Nicole Saunders completed the school run with Eloise and finally got baby Cora down for a nap, she would pull out her laptop at the kitchen table to write a tongue-in-cheek blog post about her exhaustion. At the same time as building a following for her blog, she worked part time as a social media manager—a uniquely 21st-century job title—for a growing number of brands. Nicole's opportunistic working around Cora's naps underscores that new ways of connecting work and home bring new flexibility but also a pressure to be "always on," ready to respond, produce, and perform around the clock.

For older children, such parental uses of technology allow them an insight into their parents' working lives. We heard that Olu Datong,[24] originally from Nigeria and now an information technology (IT) support worker at a large London hospital, had set up multiple computer monitors in his small bedroom in the family's South London council flat. When Olu was "on call," nine-year-old Braydon took note, leading his mother, Samantha Winston, to wonder if this had influenced her son's desire to sign up for the new coding club at Bluebell Primary School. Knowing that Olu's IT skills had led him to his present career, she hoped that code club might help Braydon get to "the next level; not just literally typing and searching, but getting to actually make something."

Throughout our research we saw multiple ways that digital technologies played a role in mediating relations between home, school, work, and elsewhere—including among family members themselves. Like many parents, Daya Thakur, born and raised in South London and very involved with her extended Bengali family, who also lived locally,[25] told us she gave her son Kaval (age 14) his first phone when he started secondary school to give him greater independence but still allow him to reach his mother if he needed to, and be reachable by her. Sisters Megan and Rosa Bluestone-Solano, at ages 18 and 23,[26] were old enough to be out at night on their own, but they had linked their phones via a geo-location app so that they could keep tabs on each other. Dad Tim liked that Megan could call him on her walk home from the tube, or that he could take his own phone to bed, telling his daughters, "It doesn't matter what time, call me, don't text me, call me and I'll come and get you." Questions of safety and digital technology were intertwined, with some parents assuming that digital technologies introduced new risks

---

[24] Family 13.
[25] Family 10.
[26] Family 71.

and others, like Anna Michaels[27] (whom we met in Chapter 1), finding it felt safer being able to check in with her children from work using technology, given the presence of gang crime in her neighborhood.

Like many other families, and contrary to what the idea of "digital natives"[28] would lead us to believe, parents like Wembe Kazadi,[29] a Congolese asylum seeker and aspiring filmmaker, don't just use technology because of the enthusiasm of their children. They too often enjoy engaging with digital media for togetherness, convenience, professional development, and learning—even if they then feel guilty for doing so. Wembe had left his country when his wife was pregnant with Mani, and for five years the family had communicated solely via free services like Viber and WhatsApp. Just recently, Bintu (age 10) and Mani (age 5) had come to London, leaving their mother behind as the family saved money to bring her over, and Mani met her father in person for the first time. Wembe was keen to initiate digital activities like looking up information or sharing his own films with his children, seeking to reconfigure the boundaries and possibilities of the home and family in various ways. But technology doesn't always help create the connections one might expect. Wembe told us he worried about how Mani is getting on in her class after dropping her off at Bluebell Primary School with her limited English but said he had not really found a way to make quiet Mani's struggles visible to her teachers.

Parents are gaining or are already in possession of a range of technical, creative, critical, and digital skills, although these are not always equal.[30] As yet, however, this is little recognized or drawn upon by their children's schools, perhaps for fear of introducing domestic inequalities into the culture of the classroom, but perhaps also out of an entrenched reluctance of schools to inquire into home life more generally. After Wembe told us about his own filmmaking and screenings, we asked if the school had thought to draw on his work—a film about a woman who resisted colonial oppression in the Congo—for their celebration of Black History Month (a regular feature in UK schools). But he said the school had no idea of his expertise, implying too that he could not find a way to tell them.

---

[27] Family 22.
[28] S. Bennett, Maton, & Kervin (2008); Helsper & Eynon (2010); Livingstone (2009); Prensky (2001).
[29] Family 12.
[30] Livingstone, Mascheroni, & Staksrud (2018); Wallis & Buckingham (2016).

Even those with nondigital jobs find that the requirements of their day-to-day lives require a basic level of digital literacy. Cecilia Apau[31] and Leila Mohammed[32] worked as a low-paid supermarket cashier and home health assistant, respectively. Cecilia's job required her to operate the computer at the till, and Leila had to log in to the Jobcentre website every evening to demonstrate that she was searching for more work, something daughter Nareen occasionally helped with if needed. However, this did not put them on a level playing field with other parents in our study who worked as IT specialists or digital creatives, or had cultivated expertise of different kinds. So while there is no sense in generalizing parents as "digital immigrants," as we discuss in Chapter 3 the reliance on digital technologies has not reversed long-standing social inequalities, and in some cases it has increased them.

However, while digital technologies prove attractive and empowering, they are also anxiety producing, both the key to freedom and the source of (self-) recrimination. Sweta Fletcher recounted just this dissonance: having taken time out of her career to raise her son, she was deeply ashamed when he asked her to "look long." With the increasing pressure to parent intensively, being able to participate online in a supportive community of mothers provided a lifeline for Sweta and others we interviewed. It also, arguably, helps to make parenting itself more visible, a radical act in a society that keeps parenting in the private realm. Yet by making parents more visible to each other, and to the critical gaze of society, online communities potentially increase the sense of competition and insecurity.[33]

Negotiating values

Getting up, coming home from school, going to bed—these are the times in the day when parents and children are together, so they figure large in narratives of family life. In and around these times, family members head off in different directions and then reassemble often in different configurations across the week. In the busy timetables of family life, we found that many parents sought to *manage* their moments of being together, both with and without digital technology. This was important as a value in itself, as we saw with Jeff Saunders in our opening vignette, introducing his small daughter to a favorite film, and as a means of transmitting values, as we saw with Habiba

[31] Family 34.
[32] Family 35.
[33] L. K. Lopez (2009).

Bekele using technology to create an Islamic cultural context for her children growing up in multicultural London. Indeed, for Habiba, whose family was deeply engaged in religious practice, technology was welcomed for coordinating her own religious practice and that of her children on a schedule joined by millions of others worldwide, and with scattered others in her immediate neighborhood.

Contrary to the fearful assumption that today's digital media act largely to isolate family members from each other,[34] many parents and children in our study mentioned using TV or films to create a valued moment of "joint media engagement,"[35] especially enjoying shows with intergenerational appeal such as *Strictly Come Dancing, The Great British Bake Off,* or *Love Island.* Weekends, especially, could include sharing the pleasures of media together via digital services like Netflix or on-demand streaming. This might be accompanied by "multiscreening"— with family members checking their phones even while all watching the big screen—but the result balanced joint and individual needs in a way that sometimes seemed satisfying. The Parenting for a Digital Future survey confirmed this finding from the qualitative research, showing how digital media are used to bring families together through TV, movies, and video games (this last favored by fathers) and, more rarely and mainly among the middle classes, creating music, photos, or videos together.[36]

When describing her perfect family weekend with her nine- and two-year-olds, Samantha Winston placed the pleasures of different forms of media alongside other activities, not especially differentiating between them. She said:

> We go to the cinema. I think we all like technology, we all like games, and we have, you know, a couple Xboxes. We have a Wii. Braydon's got a DS. I've got a DS. My son's got a PS Vita.[37] We just love games and things like that, so we all sit together. We have about six control pads and we'll sit together, like teenagers, and we'll play games. Or we'll go and watch films. We'll go to the

---

[34] Turkle (2015).

[35] Takeuchi & Stevens (2011); Valkenburg et al. (2013).

[36] Livingstone, Blum-Ross, Pavlick, & Ólafsson (2018). See also Chambers (2019).

[37] A DS is a "dual screen," handheld gaming device manufactured by Nintendo. A PS Vita is a similar handheld gaming device made by PlayStation.

park and cinema and we'll read. I bought my daughter about six books on Friday, and she's been sitting there on the carpet reading.

The investment that parents place in certain kinds of leisure activities as "quality time" spent together can be read, in the context of our interviews, as a way of performing a version of "good parenting," even when what "quality time" looks like varies dramatically from one family to the next. For Samantha Winston, what mattered was variety—the PlayStation as well as the park—as this facilitated multiple ways of being together.[38] For Dave Skelton,[39] who worked in telecommunications and had a degree in media studies, watching TV and films with his 12-year-old daughter, Esme, was a valuable "political act." He curated a selection of films and shows with "strong female characters," including those based on the DC Comics canon (Marvel, he complained, is less consistent on female characters) and "feminist" shows like *Buffy the Vampire Slayer*, along with classics like the films of Howard Hawks.

Although Robert Kostas[40] appreciates that technology offers some of the only ways that his two very different sons spend time together, he was far less sanguine regarding his values around technology. Fifteen-year-old Jake has autism, while 12-year-old Dominic is developing typically. The boys often lock horns, but playing games like *MarioKart* or watching parody videos on YouTube smooths their tumultuous relationship. While he can appreciate Jake's digital interests as helping his relationship with his brother and building skills that might even lead to employment (see Chapter 5), Robert is nonetheless eaten up with worry and deeply in conflict with his wife, Constance (whom he perceived as too permissive), about Jake's use of technology. Robert worried, in particular, about the iPad, which he described both as Jake's "solace" and as something that he was "fixated on" and "addicted to."[41] Robert had seen both sons, but especially Jake, "sitting in their bedrooms, like hermits," and feared they would end up "wasting their lives" with technology.

---

[38] Hochschild (1997, p. 50) critiques the notion of "quality time," noting that by creating this stand-alone classification, there is a transfer of the "cult of efficiency from office to home," thereby preserving the time-poor logic of demanding workplaces and shifting it into the domestic space.

[39] Family 53.

[40] Family 3.

[41] Young people with autism, like Jake, are more likely to spend most of their leisure time with digital media than typically developing peers (Shane & Albert, 2008). One study showed that boys with autism may spend twice as much time per week playing video games (Mazurek & Engelhardt, 2013).

Now that digital technologies are embedded in multiple ways in family life, there is no one single conflict that arises, nor any one single benefit that all parents perceive. For example, Daya Thakur confronted digital dilemmas with a mix of bemusement and confidence. Like Habiba Bekele, she valued the religious socialization of her children and was glad that, of her four children, 14-year-old Kaval was interested in exploring Islam, meeting his uncles and cousins at the mosque, and watching YouTube videos about the prophet Mohammed. Yet she worried that Kaval was mad for his Xbox, a gift Daya's ex-husband bought him so he could play remotely with his cousins and friends from school. She made it clear to Kaval's father that Kaval "can't use it all the time. At the end of the day, if he has homework, that's priority." Although Daya eventually agreed to the gift, there were times when she resented having to police it—for the time he spends on it and for the "foul language" he hears while playing games.

However, like Samantha Winston, Daya enjoyed the togetherness that engaging with digital media could bring, telling us with pleasure how she allowed 10-year-old daughter Kiya to practice the YouTube hair tutorials she watched fervently on Daya's hair. Daya's interview was early in our fieldwork and at the time we did not realize how unusual this aspect of her interview was—she could name the YouTuber that her daughter watched, had watched together with her daughter, and had also engaged in the activity that had so absorbed Kiya. Though she had her worries, especially about Kaval, she'd found ways to value digital media and to embrace it so as to communicate with her children on territory that engaged them. This included finding ways to discuss difficult issues—for Daya, this included sexual grooming online, a concern that she fixated on after seeing a news report—with the result that she felt more confident of her children's resilience to risk, having addressed this head on.[42] Such shared connections are not commonly investigated by researchers looking for "positive learning outcomes" from technology use but are nonetheless deeply valued by parents and children.[43] Daya's and Robert's contrasting levels of involvement in their children's media lives underscores the diversity with which parents understand and act in relation to screen time, often due to their different life circumstances. As we show

---

[42] Daya, like Jess Reid from Family 21, recounted to us how she had purposefully asked Kaval to join her in watching news coverage of a shocking story then capturing the attention of many parents of teens—of a 14-year-old who had been killed after meeting an older teen who had groomed the younger boy while playing a multiplayer game online (see Smith 2015).

[43] Gee, Takeuchi, & Wartella (2017).

next, the "screen time" discourse flattens these differences, treating families as equivalent.

The trouble with screen time

"Have you turned your SelfControl on," Susan Scott[44] called to her 14-year-old son, George, who was doing his homework in the next room, during our interview. Puzzled, we asked her to explain. It seems that the members of George's class at his expensive private school had each been given a MacBook Air to do and submit homework,[45] and the laptop came preloaded with the SelfControl app, which blocks certain websites (like social media or games), for a set period of time, as decided by the school and the parents). Since Susan's husband, Sven Olsson, whom we met at the start of this chapter, traveled frequently for work as a corporate executive, she was largely responsible for supervising their three boys, working only part time to fit everything in. Acting on her mixed feelings about their love of video games, she had set up a lunchtime gathering for parents (in the end, all mothers) so they could discuss the best way to channel their sons' "obsession" with games into something "positive." Susan and her friends jokingly called themselves the "gamer enablers." She had turned to the school's policies around digital media to inform her parenting and tried to manage the boys' screen time carefully, although she hopes at some point they will develop "better impulse control"—recall that Susan and Sven did not know about their sons' nocturnal visits to remove their tablets from the family safe.

In describing her parenting style, Susan unhappily called herself a "policewoman" at home; indeed, she'd installed another app called K9 (after the police sniffer dogs) to further monitor her children's devices and block additional sites.[46] This metaphor of policing children's digital activities was one we heard over and over again. It is problematic in two respects. First, it is in contradiction to the long-term cultural trends that have led to the increasing democratization of the family and have generally been embraced by families. To conceive of "good parenting" as "policing" (and children, by implication, as

---

[44] Family 59.
[45] The school required parents to attend an information session and for parent and child to sign a contract: the laptop is only to be used for schoolwork and not to be taken into a bedroom, so parents can monitor its use.
[46] Fisk (2016).

criminals?) undermines the efforts made by parents over recent generations to reconfigure the gendered and hierarchical family power structures exemplified by the figure of the "Victorian" father.[47] It also turns back the clock on Western society's efforts to recognize that children are not just people in the making but also people with a right to "a life of their own," such that parental (and other adult) values cannot simply be imposed but should be mutually negotiated. Relatedly, insofar as adolescence concerns the transition toward independence, so too does it require parental transitions, as parents find themselves revisiting their expectations and practices as they adapt to the unfolding "personness" of their child and the implications for their own identity as parents.[48] This is very evident in the dilemmas presented by digital technologies, many of which seem to force binary decisions about when and how children can be independent users of digital devices or services—when "should" a child get a mobile phone, for instance, or is 13 really the "right" age to use social media?[49]

Second, there is little evidence to show that policing digital technologies is actually effective for the purposes that parents intend, for it tends to generate domestic conflict and it results in children missing opportunities to learn, gain skills, and become resilient—in both digital and other contexts.[50] Our survey showed that, doubtless alienating for their children, parents were far more concerned about screen *time* than the actual activities their children engaged in online, although both were eclipsed by conflicts around sleep and behavior. It also showed how hard UK parents were working to enable children's online opportunities and address risks, an effort erased from public recognition by the screen time discourse.[51]

Such reflections have led us to rethink the sizeable literature on "parental mediation," for this too largely positions parents as the controlling force in managing their children's media use and reduces "successful" parental mediation simply to measures of the reduction in "screen time." This may work

---

[47] Hugh Cunningham (2006) discusses the gendered division of household labor and argues that parental attitudes and support for egalitarian gender roles increase men's contribution to housework.

[48] Beck & Beck-Gernsheim (2002); Scabini, Marta, & Lanz (2006).

[49] Blum-Ross & Livingstone (2017).

[50] Research shows that restrictive parental mediation can reduce exposure to online risk, but at the cost of parent–child conflict and disobedience, leading to evasive or transgressive uses of technology (Evans et al., 2011; S. J. Lee, 2012; Przybylski & Weinstein, 2017; Weinstein & Przybylski, 2019; Zhang & Livingstone, 2019).

[51] With relatively little difference between mothers and fathers or sons and daughters, the survey showed that parents engaged in a range of enabling (active talking) and restrictive (setting rules, banning certain apps) strategies, with the former used more for older children and the latter for younger ones (Livingstone, Blum-Ross, Pavlick, & Ólafsson, 2018; Livingstone et al., 2017).

in the field of health, where less sugar or more exercise is generally useful advice. But in relation to digital technologies, where neither less nor more is the obvious answer in a thoroughly digitally mediated age, a different approach is needed. As we have written elsewhere:

> Parents need to understand their children's use of digital media in terms of its *contexts* (where, how, when and with what effects children are accessing digital media), *content* (what they are watching and using) and *connections* (how digital media are facilitating or undermining relationships) in order to frame their responses. Our contention is that the long-held focus on digital safety, with its message to parents telling them that their main role is to police and restrict, has been at the expense of supporting parents to help their children learn, connect and create through, about and beyond digital media.[52]

Indeed, it may even be said that the traditional research literature on parental mediation shows little interest in *parenting* as an activity per se. Perhaps because such research draws on universalizing accounts of the psychology of child development rather than on a more historically-sensitive sociology of the family, it has narrowly examined the impact of parenting on children's digital experiences, and not widened its lens to recognize parents in their own right, along with their hopes, fears, and the practicalities of family life more broadly.[53] Only recently, too, has this literature looked beyond a conception of parental mediation as one of imposing parental authority to mitigate media harms to recognize children's views, and their influence on their parents.[54]

---

[52] Blum-Ross & Livingstone (2016a, p. 6). See also Blum-Ross & Livingstone (2017); Livingstone, Haddon, & Görzig (2012); Livingstone, Ólafsson, et al. (2017). Society's exhortation to parents to police screen media parallels its exhortation to schools to "ban" mobile phones. Both are top-down, even punitive, strategies that treat all digital activities as equivalent, and as equally problematic, and both run counter to the more nuanced expressions of parents' and children's voices.

[53] Nathanson (1999, 2002); Nathanson & Yang (2003); Valkenburg et al. (2013). As may be surmised, we disagree with the tradition of "media effects" studies that assumes that media use equals harm (Radesky & Christakis, 2016a, 2016b; for a critique, see Millwood Hargrave & Livingstone, 2009). This is partly because the scientific evidence for negative outcomes is contested, and partly because effects research gains a secondary life insofar as parents tend to repeat the "public scripts" framed by the mass media about "addiction," loss of concentration or sleep deficit, and so on, perpetuating a narrow and negative vision of digital technologies and, indeed, of parents. We are also concerned by the tendency among policymakers, educators, and researchers to reduce mediated experiences to binary outcomes ("good" or "bad") or simplistic measures of "time" or "exposure," often confusing or conflating outcomes related to different aspects of children's physical health (obesity, eyesight, sleep), cognitive development, worldview, or socioemotional well-being.

[54] Barron et al. (2009); Livingstone (2013), Livingstone et al. (2017); Nikken & Jansz (2006).

Parental mediation research has long been drawn on by a sometimes-problematic market in parental controls, as Susan Scott's experience illustrates.[55] It is also referred to in the popular discourse of screen "addiction," as several families discussed in this chapter illustrate. Yet many experts question whether it is appropriate to use a term with a precise psychological and medical definition when the vast majority of children (indeed, people) to whom it is applied do not come close to meeting the criteria for such a diagnosis. Nonetheless, the colloquial use of the word "addiction" among public health and internet safety advocates, and even parents and children as a *self*-diagnosis typifies how public discourses become incorporated into personal lives, framing some practices (such as extended use) as "problems" while leaving others unaddressed (because focusing on extent of use displaces the need for a judgment regarding which contents are beneficial or harmful, and to whom).[56]

While screen time worries were salient among families, many were finding ways to articulate the balance they sought between digital and nondigital activities. Holly Zangpo's strict rules about technology were in place to ensure her children, Metok and Dolma, had opportunities to be creative. Her day was punctuated by multiple, seemingly banal moments of negotiation over what was or was not allowed and what counted as time well spent, as "good" or problematic behavior. She talked of her worries about her children being "addicted" to their devices or a game she hated because it "sucked them in." Although she liked that Dolma could quickly research deforestation for her article in the school paper, she kept the Kindles on a high shelf in the bedroom with the internet off and was quick to make sure the children never "accessed [the internet] without me being in the room." While Holly was wary about technology, she also felt, "you can't close your eyes to it, because it's happening. You just have to learn with it; otherwise it's out of your control." Holly's *resistance* contrasts with another mother Nina Robbins's[57] *embrace* (see Chapter 5), although the substance of what each is saying is not so different. For Nina, critiques of technology were "sort of, as weird as having,

---

[55] The tools on offer vary in whether they put the parent in sole charge or also give the child a role, informing them of the parental controls or promoting parent–child discussion. At worst, they promote parental "spying" on children, with no recognition of children's rights to privacy or agency.

[56] Popular media liken technology's "dopamine kicks" to cocaine (Neri, 2018; Nutt et al., 2015) or compare the tech industry to the tobacco industry (Bowles, 2018; Common Sense Media, 2018; Kamenetz, 2018; Balakrishnan & Griffiths, 2018).

[57] Family 65.

some kind of philosophical argument against teaching a child to ride a bike. It's an inherent part of their world."

Holly's perceptions of technology both reflected and challenged her wider parenting values and style. Holly often played Lego with early riser Metok in the wee hours, although occasionally she let him watch a show instead when she "couldn't quite face it." In general, she was a playful and authoritative parent, inclined to explain the values that motivated her rules, although when it came to screen time, she was more likely to be authoritarian, "locking down" the technology. Witnessing the great lengths that otherwise supportive parents went to "lock down" technology (literally and figuratively), we found ourselves asking whether the screen time discourse has itself become so oppressive as to be problematic, engendering guilt in parents while offering little by way of constructive guidance. Although her parenting "style" was otherwise strongly child centric, Holly showed little interest in understanding how Metok and Dolma could use technology to their benefit or how she might apply her creative, collaborative parenting practices to digital, not just *non*digital, activities.

Treating all digital activities as equivalent irrespective of context, content, or connections is, ultimately, too blunt a strategy to succeed, because the days are gone in which digital media and technologies are an optional extra, a luxury rather than a necessity.[58] They have, instead, become part of the infrastructure of everyday life, rendering time-based, context-free efforts to limit screen time ineffective, with the costs greater than the benefits. Families have come to rely on the ease and intimacy that digital technologies bring to family life. From text message groups to apps for household finance management, grocery lists, family trip planning, social media check-ins with friends, or video chats with far-flung relatives, digital media are increasingly "embedded, embodied and everyday"[59] in ways that have become an unremarkable part of family life, albeit often ambivalently. Our survey found that five in six parents who use the internet at least monthly use it to support their parenting activities, with half using it for educational purposes, 4 in 10 using it to search for local activities and events or to download or stream content for their child, and 3 in 10 using it for social arrangements or health information and advice related to their child.[60] Given this context, and notwithstanding

---

[58] The Data & Society Research Institute (2017) filed an amicus brief arguing that mobile phones today are life necessities, not optional extras.

[59] Hine (2015).

[60] While such activities tend to be practiced more often by mothers, and younger and middle-class parents, they are present in some degree in most homes (Livingstone, Blum-Ross, Pavlick, & Ólafsson, 2018).

the comparative ease of measuring screen time over judging the value of children's digital activities, we argue that demanding that parents just watch the clock misses the point of parenting in the digital age.[61]

Keeping the digital in perspective

All the parents we interviewed had something to say about digital technologies, but some were less absorbed by these questions than others. Understanding the full context of family life mitigates against a "one size fits all" model of screen time advice. Father Miles Taylor[62] was the sole caregiver for his 13-year-old son, Jamie, who had autism and a rare chromosomal disorder. Jamie was exuberant and physically affectionate, especially with his father, and was often the center of attention at the digital media arts class at London Youth Arts (LYA) where we first met him. The two lived in a small studio, which was becoming difficult as by then Jamie was the size of a fully grown man. Miles fantasized about a bigger apartment, where he wanted Jamie to have a

> little study area where he will have his computer set up and a desk. He's not going to be a rocket scientist or brain surgeon, I understand, but I just want him to understand the basic principles of maths and reading so that he can go buy something and receive the correct change.

Miles embraced technology for how it helped Jamie, telling us enthusiastically, "He loves music, so he's all over YouTube. Look, the computer has given him access to all these things that he enjoys."

But their challenges were greater than any technological fix could provide. When Miles became Jamie's sole caregiver, he said, he took on a lot:

> There is the government benefits side of what he's entitled to and then there is getting your head around understanding the psychological, emotional, social factors. And then there is promoting his independence and keeping

[61] Blum-Ross & Livingstone (2016a).
[62] Family 5.

his self-esteem up. And then there is all the medical appointments and understanding all of that as well. And, you know, just then the schooling and domestic day-to-day living. So yes, it is a lot. It's very tiring more than anything; it's very wearing, and at times overwhelming.

Miles's role, as he saw it, was not to tend only to Jamie's physical needs but to help him develop as a person, with independence and self-efficacy, by being a warm and responsive father. In short, the ethos of the democratic family meant that Jamie was much better cared for and that Miles was defining a new model of fatherhood. But without support and resources the two seemed powerfully isolated and Miles almost unbearably stretched.

In the digital media class at LYA where we met Jamie, we also met Alex Reid,[63] a 15-year-old with Down syndrome. When we visited Alex's home and interviewed his mother, Jess, we found quite a different scene. Theirs was a large, expensive Victorian home in North London; Alex and his two siblings each had their own room and their own smartphone. A fitness enthusiast, Alex watches workout videos in bed at bedtime, Jess told us. After he is asleep his parents sneak in to take his phone and charge it overnight in the kitchen—also checking on his social media accounts, after a troublesome bullying incident a few years ago. Alex's bedtime fitness videos are more than a passing hobby; Jess and Alex discussed how his interests in fitness and technology might come together if he were to become a fitness trainer, with Jess saying to Alex, "You probably want to be keeping programs of what people are doing, and people able to send the odd email and making appointments and things."

Access to financial resources and other forms of privilege, including higher digital skills or access to equipment, does not erase the impact of challenging circumstances like transnational dislocations, disability, or illness, but it does sometimes ease them. Recall father Wembe Kazadi, who was living with his children in a bed-sit while his asylum claim was processed and while the family saved money to bring his wife from the Congo. Technology had aided in the process of keeping the family together over a great distance, but there remained the monumental challenge of bringing up his children in a startlingly different context, and one in which his own legal and economic status was so uncertain. Although he had thoughts about technology,

---

[63] Family 21.

he was too busy trying to make a living and support his children to worry too much.[64] This is not to say, however, that it is only the well resourced who find themselves consumed by battles over technology.

Across incomes, we found parents who attempted to evade the strictures of measuring and monitoring screen time by aiming instead for a more flexible approach, balancing risks and opportunities. Ariam Parkes,[65] originally from Eritrea, was married to an Irishman and mother to three daughters. The family was comfortable though not well off, living in a privately owned ex-local-authority house at the edge of a large council estate. Ariam had recently purchased tablets for the two older girls, after much lobbying. The devices had an unexpected benefit for Ariam when it came time to punish nine-year-old Elen for a minor misdemeanor. Ariam said, "I can't take her books away . . . [but with the tablet] I find it quite effective as well because she'll do anything to get it back." After school and into the evenings the girls took choir and swimming, did scouts, and played board games as a family. Yet the older two girls occasionally sat "up for hours watching an annoying guy who makes cake balls or something," videos that made Ariam question "the level of appropriateness" or kids' shows that she characterized simply as "brain dead." Yet Ariam didn't see technology as "my main worry in general; I don't lose sleep over it." Hers was a quiet confidence that left a strong impression on us after the interview. She explained:

> I've got one parenting rule that I've learnt from my mother and that's to trust your child enough to be able to make the right decisions. I've got to bring her up right, and hopefully she'll make the right choices. And she might make a few mistakes along the way, but you know, generally, you just have to let them learn and trust them.

This confidence seemed justified: Elen and her sister Hanna (age eight) told us how they had learned to ignore, or sometimes tell a parent, about what they saw as unavoidable and inappropriate YouTube content.

---

[64] Diane Hoffman (2010) argues, of the currently fashionable concept of resilience, that its focus on "individual strengths that encourage successful adaptation in the face of adversity" (p. 386) is classist, "because resilience concerns itself with largely 'bumps and bruises' concerns in daily life, rather than serious trauma or structural limitations that may be experienced by children from higher risk families" (p. 391).

[65] Family 11.

So, for some parents, blanket screen time advice doesn't work precisely because it ignores these contextual relationships, divorcing time use from the nature and quality of digital activities.[66] Ariam's interview also demonstrated how some parents do find resonance with longer-established parenting practices (encouraging good decision making and independence) even if the presenting signals (the technology) are seemingly little connected to their own childhoods. Ariam recalled advice from her mother as useful, even if her mother had little to say about social media and technology directly.

Negotiations over technology sit alongside other family negotiations— over food and exercise,[67] choice of school or neighborhood, "good" uses of leisure time,[68] money or lack thereof, contact with extended family, and more. These questions preoccupied parents as much as did decisions around digital technology, if not more, although, as we have seen in this chapter, these are interdependent, with meals, care, schooling, bedtime, expenditure, and leisure all having some actual or potential digital dimension. As media scholars, while we are highly aware of how families' daily lives are increasingly "media saturated"[69] and full of digital "stuff,"[70] we wish neither to overstate their importance nor to assume that technology has had a unidirectional impact on parenting and family life. We see our work as part of a tradition of scholarship that shows how families are not simply altered by but, rather, actively find ways to adjust to and attribute meaning to digital (and predigital) technologies in their own ways.[71] We have sought to put digital technologies "in their place," so to speak, recognizing how they are embedded in the messy context of everyday life, "placed" alongside cups of coffee or at bedsides or on high shelves, more or less important depending on the context.[72]

---

[66] Lisa Guernsey (2012) proposes three Cs to consider with screen time: context, content, and the individual child.

[67] Faircloth (2013); Ochs & Shohet (2006).

[68] Ochs & Kremer-Sadlik (2013).

[69] Pink & Leder Mackley (2013).

[70] D. Miller (2009).

[71] Chambers (2013); Clark (2013).

[72] Domestication theory explains how technologies are incorporated into homes in ways often not expected by manufacturers, acquiring both individual and collective symbolic value through active processes of adoption, acculturation, and appropriation and resulting in considerable diversity in the uses of any particular device (Haddon, 2006; Silverstone, 2006; Silverstone & Hirsch, 1992; Berker et al., 2006; D. Miller et al., 2016).

At the end of the day

As London families head toward bedtime, new negotiations invariably begin. Daya Thakur, for example, has four children and lives in a small, two-bedroom council flat. As the only boy, her son, Kaval, has his own room, and he's begged her to have a TV in it—but Daya told us she said no: "The bedroom is a place for quiet. It's time to chill out and sleep. And because I want to be able to keep an eye on what he's doing." But for the girls—the older two shared a room while the youngest shared Daya's room—watching TV with headphones on was precisely the way to carve out a degree of personal space. Habiba Bekele, after her 5.00 a.m. start for prayers, ended each day, she said, by moving around the furniture in her two-room flat, so that the daytime play area for her charges was instead covered in mats for her own sons to sleep on. Sven Olsson and Susan Scott, in their large flat, told us they did no physical rearranging but occasionally played "musical beds" when 10-year-old Sean started coming into their bed at night, frightened by violent video games he'd played with his brothers.

Families negotiate norms around privacy in different ways, with resources and space having an impact, although not always in well-defined ways. Wealthy mother Kylie Smithson[73] had bought her 12-year-old son, Oliver, a wearable activity tracker after some difficult arguments over sleep. She explained, "We can set him a target . . . and say to him you need to start getting to bed earlier, so it's quite useful to have that." She logged into the app on her phone to check his "steps and if he's not doing enough" and to demonstrate to him how much sleep he was getting—or wasn't, since he constantly tried to stay up late. Wearable devices like the Fitbit did not feature prominently in our fieldwork,[74] but we imagine similar negotiations will only take on more meaning in family life as ubiquitous computing and the "internet of things" become more embedded in homes.[75]

Increasingly, parents look for support online to find necessary solutions for troublesome bedtimes. The internet has become the first port of call for most parents when dealing with a host of parenting dilemmas. The Parenting for a Digital Future survey found that for digital and nondigital dilemmas, parents most often search online. This is unequal, however: wealthier parents

[73] Family 52.
[74] Livingstone, Blum-Ross, & Zhang (2018).
[75] Blum-Ross et al. (2018).

are more likely to turn to online sources, while the poorest parents are most likely to have "nowhere" to turn, as are parents of infants to-four-year-olds. Parents are also particularly in need of advice for digital dilemmas, compared with other parenting problems, since few feel they can turn to their own parents for digital advice.[76]

After struggling with her eight-year-old son over bedtime and with her husband about how strict she should be about his tantrums when told to stop playing computer games, Janet Daly[77] turned to Netmums (an online forum) for advice, reading the responses hungrily. Similarly at her wits' end with a sleepless child and unable to turn to her own strict, "old school" Indian parents for advice because she found their methods out of touch (advising her to let her son "cry it out"), mum-blogger Anisha Kumar[78] had started a group on Facebook with over a thousand members interested in "gentle sleep training" who shared tips and research. Anisha's digital confidence far eclipsed Janet's, and so did the form (and intensity) of her digital participation. Thus, she could go beyond reading what existed already on the internet and use her skills to create a new community according to her own values.

In both these cases it was mothers who had taken on the task of "sorting out" the bedtimes, and though we met plenty of fathers who also took responsibility for caring for children, this was not often to the same extent as mothers. In the digital age, mothers seem to gain more than fathers from parent blogs, as is clear from the titles of top UK parenting sites like Netmums and Mumsnet[79] (though we deliberately sought out "dad bloggers" in addition to mothers; see appendix). They also seem to have gained the primary responsibility to manage children's screen time, along with various other digital and nondigital parenting dilemmas, though again there were exceptions.

At the end of the day, like Jake Kostas and many other children with autism, Jamie Taylor struggled with sleep, partly because of his active imagination and difficulty discerning fantasy from reality. His father, Miles, described how "these things can almost become real in his mind, he has quite vivid dreams and is disruptive throughout the night." So technology presents challenges to sleep but also ways of easing into it (as in families who watch shows or listen to stories as part of winding down) and

---

[76] While there are other sources of support in parents' lives—partners, friends and relatives, health professionals, or a child's school—the survey found that these are more often turned to for nondigital rather than digital questions (Livingstone, Blum-Ross, Pavlick, & Ólafsson, 2018).

[77] Family 17.

[78] Family 41.

[79] Jensen (2013); Phillips & Broderick (2014).

certainly gives respite to parents during busy days with kids or to relax themselves after their children have gone to sleep.[80]

Conclusions

This tour through a day in the life of a broad swathe of families reveals the
pressures parents are under and the tactics they deploy as they try to respond to competing desires and demands in circumstances of constrained
resources, to prioritize negotiation with their children over the imposition
of authority, and to prepare for an uncertain future at a time of multifaceted
social change. Whatever their circumstances, parents generally take seriously their responsibility to raise their children, drawing on their available
resources, including an implicit "parental belief system"[81] or even an explicit "parenting philosophy." But parenting is often hard, and the deep current of emotion that runs through our interviews underscores the anxieties
and insecurities that many feel, often experiencing themselves as different or
even deficient.[82]

Across the gamut of parenting practices, this chapter has shown how
digital technologies now play a role—exacerbating or alleviating tensions,
posing dilemmas, reconfiguring risks and opportunities, and connecting
and disconnecting people. But whether the outcome is the transformation
or reproduction of traditional family practices, we have also shown how, in
the democratic family of contemporary Western culture, much depends on
processes of negotiation.

The *Oxford English Dictionary* identifies three meanings for "negotiate,"
all of them pertinent: "(i) Obtain or bring about by discussion; (ii) Find a
way over or through (an obstacle or difficult route); (iii) Transfer to the legal
ownership of another person, who thus becomes entitled to any benefit."[83]
Discussion is crucial. During the conduct of their daily lives, parents engage
in numerous discussions: between parents; sometimes with friends, peers, or

---

[80] Netflix CEO Reed Hastings declared that its biggest competitor is sleep (Raphael, 2017). The
AAP recommends that children aged six and older are set consistent screen time restrictions and
highlights the need to ensure that media use does not interfere with adequate sleep (American
Academy of Pediatrics, 2016a). Research shows that media exposure disrupts sleep patterns and
results in reduced duration and quality of sleep (Radesky & Christakis, 2016b).

[81] Harkness & Super (1996).

[82] Hochschild (1997); Perrier (2012); Reece (2013).

[83] Oxford English Dictionary (2018).

the extended family; and incessantly between parents and children as they negotiate family practices, decisions, and values. Digital technologies play a double role here. They are meaningful resources in and of themselves that demand to be fitted in or adjusted to so that the opportunities are maximized and associated risks are mitigated through negotiation. How they are used also reveals other, perhaps deeper struggles families face, since negotiations over technologies are often also, explicitly or implicitly, negotiations over gender or culture or resources.

The second meaning of "negotiate," we suggest, captures the ways in which parents navigate their way through the day, and through their lives. Digital technologies are often acquired in the hope that they will provide a way over or through life's obstacles and difficulties—entertaining children when alternatives are impractical, supporting learning so that children don't fall behind, or providing a workaround when special circumstances demand. But not only is their effectiveness uncertain; they also bring with them the new problems popularly linked to screen time, among others, to the point where reducing screen time has become a priority in its own right.

As regards the third meaning of "negotiate," concerned with the question of entitlement—or who gets to decide—we suggest that conflicts over digital technologies often stand for deeper questions of parent-versus-child agency. In the short term, parents may retain their authority, though even this remains at risk, but in the longer term their task is to enable their child to choose for themselves. A parent's generational narrative (see Chapter 1)—which looks back to a particular past (the parent's childhood), through to the present (family life), and then to an imagined future (the child's adulthood)—is often told in terms of the process of the parent first gaining, then exercising, and then passing on to the child the power of self-determination. A child's growing into independent ownership and use of digital technologies is a crucial way in which this process can occurs in today's families.

For multiple reasons, therefore, digital technologies have become a key terrain on which child autonomy is to be asserted and parental authority enacted. Although—or perhaps because—the long term outcomes of "digital parenting" are unclear, the democratic family seeks to embrace, balance, or resist change in ways that accommodate the needs and interests of its members, and this in turn is highly absorbing, often emotional, and increasingly mediated. Beyond the families discussed in this chapter, our survey too shows that roughly half of parents said that "I try to limit or resist my family's use of digital media" and roughly half said that "When it comes to

new technologies, I like to be ahead." Rather than this marking out two mutually exclusive strategies, this points to parents who adopt various combin-
ations of resistance (more often limiting or resisting technology), embracing
(and thus trying to get ahead), and balancing.[84]

Even for those who try to balance the role of technology in their family's
life, screen time rules may be welcomed by exhausted or uncertain parents
as a way to resolve the deluge of contradictory parenting advice and obviate
the need for a complex and continual balancing act between resisting and
embracing. Yet while the rules promise an authorized way to cut short seemingly unending family negotiations, the result is often quite the contrary.
It isn't just that allowing or withdrawing digital technologies has become
parents' go-to reward or punishment and, all too often, children's chosen
field of battle. More profoundly, with social norms in flux, previous generations seemingly of little help, future pathways precarious, and experts dis-
agreeing over optimal strategies, parents struggle to find legitimacy for their
view of what's best.

Added pressure comes from the fact that parenting is under heavy scrutiny from the public as well as among and between parents themselves.
Contradictorily, in parenting discourses promoted by policy makers, industry and the media, technology is persistently positioned as both the
problem and the solution. Furthermore, for parents who access "expert"
input, including advice from teachers, there are many moments of dissonance when practices do not match up with the official advice, adding to
parental anxiety and guilt. This dissonance arises because, too often, official
advice conjures a normative vision of how (typically, middle-class) family life
should look,[85] contrasted with popular but problematic assumptions about
the "digital immigrant" and ignorant parents shirking their responsibilities,
and with too little recognition of the realities of how or why digital technologies are being incorporated into family lives.[86]

In reaching these conclusions, we have found it somewhat frustrating
that much of the literature concerned with families and media is narrowly focused on media harms to children and their parents' mediation
strategies and fails to contextualize the changing place of digital media in

---

[84] Livingstone, Blum-Ross, Pavlick, & Ólafsson (2018).
[85] Blum-Ross & Livingstone (2018); Mares et al. (2018).
[86] As domestication theorists have long argued, beliefs about and uses of technology are highly
diverse and dependent on the personal, domestic, and cultural contexts of use (D. Miller, 2011;
Silverstone, 2006).

family life, especially as regards parents' positionality, biography, identity, connections, and values. In short, while far from apologists for the media, since there are plenty of grounds for critique, we do seek to respect both children's and parents' agency in embracing, resisting, or, most often, balancing the place of media and digital technologies in their lives. The discursive construction of the umbrella concept of "screen time" obscures important specificities of what (the content), how, where, when (the context), why, and with whom (the connections) children are watching, playing, and doing things with media, along with people's judgments and values regarding these activities.[87]

Even if advice to parents manages to transcend the contradictory messages—on the one hand in favor of digital educational opportunities but on the other warning against excessive screen time—there will remain a considerable distance between parents' everyday dilemmas and the public rhetoric that promises that the jobs of the future will be "digital jobs" or that digital skills could contribute to a more creative, inclusive, or self-actualizing future if only parents invested appropriately in their children's present lives. While we support the growing call from researchers and some enlightened policymakers for parents to focus less on time spent and more on the content, context, and connections enabled or constrained by technologies, this hardly eases the task of parents, for such judgments of value rather than, more simply, time spent are demanding, and little guidance is available.[88]

Since, as we have argued, reducing parenting in the digital age to a simplistic conception of policing screen time does a disservice to all concerned, what is needed? Can we recognize and promote a wider spectrum of ways that parents can mediate their children's digital activities—as co-learners, resource providers, "brokers," teachers, and beyond?[89] This highlights what is arguably a new and important task for parents: namely, guiding children to benefit from the potential of digital technologies while also building their resilience to manage the pitfalls, to "trust your child," not just saying "don't do this, don't do that," as Ariam Parkes succinctly put it. As some parents see it,

---

[87] Blum-Ross & Livingstone (2018); Guernsey & Levine (2015).

[88] Blum-Ross & Livingstone (2016a). In 2019, the UK's Royal College of Paediatrics and Child Health joined critics of screen time rules, citing a new review article concluding that the evidence for screen-based harms was weak to nonexistent and advising parents to decide for themselves what's good for their child (Stiglic & Viner, 2019; Therrien & Wakefield, 2019). But this came after our fieldwork and, while relieving parents of near-impossible screen time limits, hardly helps them with the value judgments still to be made.

[89] Barron et al. (2009).

digital technologies offer benefits for their children's learning—from gaining basic literacy to exam preparation to religious and cultural engagement.[90] For others, they offer a space for creativity and expression or the promise of future flexibility and dreams fulfilled, sometimes in contrast to parents' own feelings that they have been professionally or personally constrained. We see these hopes in the narratives of parents throughout this book, often from low-income or migrant parents, though also from those with more resources.[91]

All these ambitions are sidelined by screen time guidance for parents, as are, perhaps ironically, parents' ambitions to keep their children safe online—for safety cannot be facilitated nor resilience gained from approaches that ignore the nature of digital contents and activities. In practice, as we have shown, many parents are finding alternatives to the screen time discourse, choosing which activities to champion, which to tolerate, and which to (try to) outright ban. Nonetheless, when it comes to questions about how to manage technology, many seem drawn to the potent discourse of screen time rules and, by implication, to a model of top-down parenting (or "policing"), undermining their deeper efforts to democratize parent–child relations.[92] Further, parents often lack a language, and public approval, for their search for an approach that respects their growing digital expertise and their digital hopes and fears for their child.

In this chapter, we have recognized the diversity and emotionality of parents' accounts of parenting in the digital age and have been led deep into the cultural and temporal conditions of their lives, as they variously look back to their childhoods and forward to their children's futures. As we discussed in Chapter 1, society is devolving more responsibility to parents by rolling back the welfare state and replacing it with market-led policy and neoliberal discourse around individual "empowerment" and "choice," altering the family's external ecology. At the same time, it is reconfiguring the family internally to be more "democratic." As a result, parents feel the burden of choices—lifestyle, education, values, prospects (even though they may not in practice have any more freedom than did their parents, and often their resources are rather less). They must negotiate these choices, such as they are, between themselves and with their children "respectfully,"[93] acknowledging

---

[90] Lim (2018).
[91] Brough, Cho, & Mustain (forthcoming).
[92] Research has shown that screen time rules lead to parent–child conflict, resulting in more authoritarian or "top-down" parenting (Blum-Ross & Livingstone, 2016a).
[93] Beck (1992); Giddens (1991); Lansbury (2014); Reece (2013).

their rights to self-determination now that traditional hierarchies of gender and generation have lost public legitimacy (though, for sure, they often persist in private).

While, undoubtedly, there are substantial ways in which these shifts are "classed," as we explore in the next chapter, we contend that all—or nearly all—parents share in these societal changes. In most families, gone are the days when children "should be seen but not heard," with values determined from on high and behavior a matter of duty, to be replaced by a world in which children are highly visible in their embrace of the new, the expensive, and, for many parents, the uncertain. The democratic family must give considerable time and effort to negotiating the interests of all its members if it is not to become embattled. And "digital parenting" should, surely, be no more blind to the relationships, identities, and ambitions at the heart of family life than parenting in general.

3

Social Inequality

Throughout our interview with Cecilia Apau,[1] the screen of the desktop computer in the corner of the room was flashing. The black screen was alarmingly cut with bars of irregular, pixelated, bright colors—the telltale signs of a virus. Two of her three children played on a supermarket-brand tablet and a smartphone, with another tablet lying broken in the corner. The apartment was high up in the tower block of a large council estate[2] and was sparsely but comfortably furnished. In the small living room, as well as the three screens already mentioned, a flat-screen TV loomed over an old stereo—also broken. When we asked Cecilia, a single mother who worked as a cashier in a low-cost grocery, what happened to the computer, she shrugged, unsure of what had gone wrong or how to fix it. Although Cecilia had sent her first email only in response to the request to participate in our research, she knew the basics of how to navigate the internet, showing youngest son Eric (age four) how to put the search term "Jack and the Beanstalk" into the YouTube search bar to find a video of a book's pages being turned so he could "read" (as she put it) while she made dinner.

In contrast, the home of Susan Scott and Sven Olsson[3] was filled with top-of-the-line technology. Each of their three sons had his own tablet and computer—the older two had had brand-new laptops issued to them by their elite private school. The expansive flat was immaculate, with views overlooking a manicured London park, individual rooms for the three boys, offices for the parents, and even an exercise room for Sven. At the time of our visit, Susan had hired a personal organizer who was busily helping 10-year-old Sean clean out his room for the start of the school year. Sean told us about Susan's "screen time" system, explaining that as the boys got older they got additional time, but that, actually, 16-year-old Niall barely got to use his as he was so busy with his robotics club in the evenings. Sean described how "sometimes when I am playing my screens my mum times me."

[1] Family 34.
[2] Council housing in the United Kingdom is akin to housing projects in the United States—public housing provided for lower-income residents, who can apply to rent them.
[3] Family 59.

Parenting for a Digital Future. Sonia Livingstone and Alicia Blum-Ross, Oxford University Press (2020). © Oxford University Press.
DOI: 10.1093/oso/9780190874698.001.0001

These two families represent some of the contrasts in family life in London, and yet there are also similarities. Both were migrant families, common in London. Cecilia Apau came to London from Ghana, Susan Scott from the United States, and Sven Olsson from Sweden. Although their lives were different in many respects, both homes were filled with digital technologies and inhabited by digital-enthusiast children, including sons (14-year-old George and 10-year-old Sean Scott-Olsson and 8-year-old Eugene Apau) who were learning to code. Yet the differences are important. In terms of technologies—and other consumer goods—the number of digital devices in the Apau and Scott-Olsson households was not dissimilar. But for the Apaus these were the most affordable and therefore had more restricted capacity, albeit adding up to a much more significant percentage of Cecilia's limited income. The Scott-Olsson family thought little of upgrading their devices to the latest models.[4] The boys' interest in coding also looked very different in its pursuit. George and Sean were excited about attending DigiCamp, an expensive summer camp where they would learn to design their own games using a program called GameSalad. Eugene attended a free, weekly after-school program at his primary school, Bluebell, following printed worksheets to learn the free coding program Scratch. Despite his initial enthusiasm he became bored—and anyhow, the club only lasted a term.[5]

How shall we characterize this mix of similarities and, especially, of differences? Of the social science literature on parenting that concerns itself with social class, including that relating to digital technologies, much of it takes a strongly binary approach, contrasting middle-class versus working-class families rather than recognizing sufficiently the overlapping or changing nature of such a classification. For instance, in her influential book *Unequal Childhoods,* Annette Lareau draws on sociologist Pierre Bourdieu's analysis of the reproduction of social inequality (and, thereby, the persistence of low social mobility[6]), focusing her analysis by contrasting the practices

---

[4] Parents and children from higher-socioeconomic-status or more educated homes have access to more and better devices, as shown by the Parenting for a Digital Future survey (Livingstone, Blum-Ross, & Zhang, 2018). Parents with more education report more digital skills, but interestingly, parents' level of education and socioeconomic status are not related to the child's digital skills.

[5] Scratch was developed by the Lifelong Kindergarten group at the MIT Media Lab. Introduced into the UK national computing curriculum in 2013 (Dredge, 2014; MIT Scratch Team, 2018), it is a free tool for teaching coding and programming syntax and concepts. GameSalad (2010) is known for its graphical drag-and-drop programming; it enables users to test their games on Apple devices and publish them in the App Store. GameSalad requires a subscription, whereas Scratch is free, which is telling of the boys' different socioeconomic statuses.

[6] See Social Mobility Commission (2017).

of American "middle class" and "working class" parents.[7] She describes how working-class parents expect their children to be obedient and respectful when required, otherwise leaving them free to do as they wish, while middle-class parents pressure themselves and their children to compete and achieve, often through a rigorous schedule of adult-organized out-of-school enrichment activities (which she terms "concerted cultivation") and often at the cost of free leisure time or family and community loyalty. Relatedly, though different in recognizing the importance of digital technologies in the contemporary family, Lynn Schofield Clark's *The Parent App* builds on Roger Silverstone's concept of the "moral economy" of the household[8] to reveal a strong ethic of "expressive empowerment" among what Clark terms "upper income" families, who encourage media use for learning and self-development and discourage distraction or time wasting (as they perceive it). This she contrasts with an ethic of "respectful connectedness" among "lower income" families, where the emphasis is on media uses that are responsible, compliant, and family focused.

Beyond the work of Lareau and Clark, other ethnographic studies show a similar tendency to contrast middle- and working-class families. For instance, Alison Pugh claims that wealthy US parents practice "symbolic deprivation" by limiting what they spend on or allow for their children, because they believe they have the "right values," while poorer parents practice what she calls "symbolic indulgence" in an effort to preserve their children's dignity among their peers and reward them for not being "in trouble."[9] Yet while the empirical insights on offer have value, including in analyzing the reproduction of social inequalities, some researchers appear to have doubts about the class binaries into which the data are fitted.[10] Clark expresses discomfort with the label "working class," preferring to say "would-be middle class"—perhaps to capture the sense of striving for something better among poorer families that we too found in our study. There are problems too with some of the characterizations of families with few resources. Lareau has

---

[7] Lareau (2011). She explains that she prefers "a categorical analysis" because "family practices cohere by social class" (p. 236). See also Gutiérrez, Izquierdo, & Kremer-Sadlik (2010); Kremer-Sadlik, Izquierdo, & Fatigante (2010); Ochs & Kremer-Sadlik (2013); Wajcman, Bittman, & Brown (2008).

[8] Clark (2013); Silverstone & Hirsch (1992).

[9] Pugh (2009).

[10] Quantitative studies more often use a binary scheme to classify parents by socioeconomic status. However, in the field of children and media, most quantitative research avoids social class analyses (possibly because of the predominance of psychological, rather than sociological, approaches).

since reflected on criticism of her framing of working-class parenting in terms of the belief in "natural growth," given that this description could seem to imply thoughtless neglect.[11]

Other studies have instead focused on the lengths to which working-class parents go to support their children, whether or not using technology, and yet also how they are more vulnerable to the increasing job precariousness and austerity measures we discussed in Chapter 1, making these efforts disproportionately difficult.[12] What these authors underscore is that seemingly commonplace definitions of "good parenting" are often based on middle-class models of "intensive" engagement, which are taken as representative of all parents (and a measure against which parents may be judged deficient).[13] Sociologist Bev Skeggs has highlighted that, given that most researchers and policymakers are from middle-class backgrounds themselves, there is a tendency to describe "what exists for a privileged few and then [suggest] this is a perspective that applies to many others."[14] The tendency to view middle-class practices as the norm also pervades the tech industry, in which a tendency for well-resourced executives and engineers to design for people like themselves (or their own children, or with nostalgia for themselves as children) has predominated.[15] This reinforces middle-class values and practices as the normative default, as we saw reflected in diverse parents' discourses.

In our own fieldwork, while a few of the families we interviewed were living well below the poverty line and a few were earning almost inconceivably high salaries (the two families we begin this chapter with illustrate this disparity well), many were hard to classify neatly as either middle class or working class. Certainly it was challenging to classify them using established UK government or market research classifications.[16] We had tried to do this for two reasons. The first was methodological: to check that we had recruited a sufficiently

[11] In her second edition, Lareau (2011) responds to "concern" from readers that her formulation of "natural growth" underemphasizes how working-class parents support their children. Yet she still argues that these parents "did not seem to view children's leisure time as their responsibility; nor did they see themselves as responsible for assertively intervening in their children's school experiences" (p. 342). As will be clear, we did not find this in our fieldwork. See also Gutiérrez, Zitlali Morales, & Martinez (2009).
[12] Hays (2004); Hochschild (1997); Katz, Moran, & Gonzalez (2018). Some of these books are by academics who identify as being from a working-class background and see writing about their own communities as a corrective to middle-class academic discourses (Mckenzie, 2015; Reay, 2017).
[13] Hays (1998).
[14] Skeggs (2004, p. 48).
[15] See Ochs & Kremer-Sadlik (2015); Ames et al. (2011); Ogata (2013).
[16] The UK Market Research Society typically classifies households using a scale from A (professional) to E (unemployed), although since E includes casual workers, unemployed people, caregivers,

wide range of families, we kept a spreadsheet noting occupation, education, ethnicity, age, family composition, number of children, and so forth. This part was relatively unproblematic, although summarizing family circumstances (see appendix) was not straightforward. Second, and more problematically, we had tried to group families as more or less privileged, labeling them—as is common in social and cultural research on childhood socialization—"middle class" and "working class" to situate our findings within the relevant research literature. But this, we found, we could not do. This was both because we found it near impossible to identify "the dividing line between the middle and working class," as sociologist Mike Savage puts it,[17] and because even the families that could be classified according to standard approaches seemed anomalous in important ways. We met many families whose educational level suggested greater economic security than they had actually achieved, often for reasons of migration or family breakdown, though also because of value-led lifestyle choices. As the families with whom we open this chapter illustrate, both the poor and the rich extremes in our sample fit poorly within familiar cultural imagery associated with working- or middle-class lives.

None of this is accidental. London is distinctive in the UK context in several respects. Socioeconomic status is closely intertwined with patterns of migration and ethnicity. The extremes of rich and poor are greater than in the rest of the country. The proportion of households that cannot be fitted neatly into a binary (or even further subdivided) class structure is considerable. Among these "anomalous" households are a good many families seeking a creative, and sometimes digital, lifestyle that the global city is unusually able to support.[18]

In exploring differences among families in relation to their digital present and imagined future, we have sought to stay open to the crucial inequalities shaping the lives of the families in late modernity.[19] Thus, we agree with Savage that

---

and the retired, it is of dubious validity. The government classifies households using the Office for National Statistics scale, which allows for more categories but still only partially captures the diversity of our families, given complexities of ethnicity, precarity, and other factors.

[17] As Savage (2015a) observes critically, "in the British context, the boundary between middle and working classes came to be a key arena for symbolic mobilization and contestation, and through this process has become reified" (p. 224). See also T. Bennett et al. (2010); Savage (2015b); Skeggs (2004, 2015).

[18] Fishwick (2017); Tech Nation (2018).

[19] Beck & Beck-Gernsheim (2002).

rather than seek to exercise conceptual closure over the concept of class, we should therefore welcome the concept's contested nature and use it as a broad interpretative tool to explore the interplay of economic polarization, the remaking of cultural hierarchies in a mediatized environment, the power of exclusive social networks and the exclusive character of political mobilization.[20]

To this end, we found it helpful to construct intersecting groupings of the families in our fieldwork by drawing on Bourdieu's concepts of economic and cultural capital to grasp the diversification of classed lifestyles in late modernity, especially in the global city. But rather than contrasting middle-class and working-class families, for the reasons presented earlier we focus on the ways of life that challenge or complicate some of the prevailing arguments in the field. This allows us still to recognize how financial resources, whether earned or inherited (theorized by Bourdieu as "economic capital"), and parents' education, cultural knowledge, and practices (theorized as "cultural capital") influence the ways in which digital technologies become integrated into the family and in the social reproduction of inequality. However, we also identify where there are commonalities across class, as well as how some parents are making efforts to construct alternative lifestyles that seek to harness the distinct and still-emerging affordances of the digital age so as to sidestep the strictures of traditional class categories.

Below the poverty line

To get to the door of the Mohammed family's[21] council flat in a midrise block in South London, one has to pass through a series of security gates and down several long halls. Near a major intersection, the building is covered in slowly accumulating grime. Leila Mohammed answered the door wearing a long black *khimar* (a form of hijab that loosely covers the body), covering her hair and flowing over her upper body. She moved nervously; the flat was filled with workmen from the council, who were fixing something in the lounge. With dust everywhere and the flat in upheaval, Leila was visibly annoyed at the presence of the workers but seemed powerless to ask them to clean up.

---

[20] Savage (2015b, p. 225).
[21] Family 35.

The situation had exacerbated daughter Safia's respiratory issues, recently landing her in the hospital after a severe asthma attack.

When we retreated to the kitchen, Leila relaxed a little as she offered tea and told us about her journey to the United Kingdom from Ethiopia and her lively daughters Nareen (age 10) and Safia (age 8), born in London. As she was a single mother earning less than £15,000 a year working as an in-home care assistant, we had thought perhaps that Leila wanted to be interviewed in part for the honorarium on offer. Yet she seemed taken aback at the voucher, then asked whether she could use it to buy a bicycle for her daughters.[22] In addition to Safia's health, Leila had other pressures. She alluded to past troubles with Nareen and Safia's father, without going into detail, and said, "When you're a single mum it's very difficult. I don't have anyone next to me." After waking up early for prayers, a childminder collected the girls and took them to school so that Leila could head to her job as an in-home healthcare assistant for a boy with severe disabilities. She was overstretched, exhausted. Recounting her long days, she was almost in tears:

> I have to wake up at five because I have to make breakfast; I have to leave at seven exactly. We don't have time now. I can't wait for holiday to come. I want to spend it with my kids. I'm tired.

She worried that she must save money to get what "every parent would wish for children, a good education for future life." Leila paid for her daughters to go to Qur'an school on Saturdays and extra math and English tutoring on Sundays, all this taking a considerable chunk of her very limited income. She explained that the money was worth it:

LEILA: I don't have the knowledge and they're teaching me this, you know.
ALICIA: Oh the children are teaching you?
LEILA: Yes even I don't read so much and I didn't know how to write . . . so now they're teaching me writing now.

Leila had high hopes for her daughters in the future, calling Nareen "my engineer" and musing that Safia might want to be a doctor. She said she told them:

---

[22] We offered a post office voucher for £40, which Leila intended to use at a budget shop.

Look I don't have good knowledge; I don't have good money; when you finish your uni, what good job you're getting, you could buy what you want; you have to have good education. That's why I'm working a rubbish job, I said to her, I do not have knowledge.

Leila had, with the help of her former father-in-law, purchased a computer—a solid desktop that looked to have been purchased at least five years before. She was glad not to have to go to the library to use a computer, this being necessary to demonstrate to the job center that she was searching for work. The girls also used the computer for homework—although Leila was vague about exactly what they did, waving her hand and saying, "literacy." Leila and her daughters loved listening to *nasheeds* that they found online—a cappella Muslim songs that contain moral messages.[23] Leila let Nareen use her phone occasionally, but after hearing about a £200 bill a friend received after giving her kids her phone, Leila was wary.

When the family had problems with the computer, Leila turned to Nareen for help. Once, she proudly recalled, Nareen had fixed the computer by taking the front off the hard drive and doing something Leila didn't quite understand but was impressed by.[24] She did not fully celebrate technology, however, worrying—in common with other religious parents we spoke with, especially—that "sometimes there's so many bad things, you know, I don't want them to see this." She did little to explain or discuss with her daughters the content they engaged with, but she monitored their time online carefully. As she explained:

In the news, the scientists said no more than two hours. So after one hour I say stop, go out, do what you want. More than one hour and a half on the computer and on the TV, it's not good sense.[25]

Despite her worries, Leila was "happy with the computer. The bill is too much but you need it, you know, technology is growing." Indeed, it had become useful for her work and her daughters' schoolwork; even her relatives in Ethiopia had computers and tablets for their small businesses.

[23] Kahf (2007).
[24] See Bakardjieva (2005).
[25] Here she refers to the widely known Academy of Pediatrics (AAP) "two-by-two" guidelines (American Academy of Pediatrics, 2011), which stipulate that children should watch a maximum of two hours a day of TV and no TV at all for children under twos. The guidelines were revised in 2016 to be less prescriptive (American Academy of Pediatrics, 2016b).

Leila Mohammed and Cecilia Apau were both multiply marginalized—migrant, Black, single mothers living on low incomes and struggling with childcare.[26] Like 28% of UK children, their children would be defined as living in poverty.[27] According to our survey, parents experience more barriers to internet use if they are Black or have a child with special educational needs. Also, one in five children from low-socioeconomic-status homes never or hardly ever uses the internet.[28] Leila's limited English, gained since she arrived in the United Kingdom, meant that she was shy about speaking in official settings, thus struggling to access services or connections that might have been useful to her or to Safia and Nareen.[29] While they were determined to invest in the benefits of technology for their children, neither Cecilia nor Leila had a detailed level of knowledge about specific digital opportunities, the benefits of one program versus another, or how digital interests might lead to other skills or employment.

So while both mothers were positive about technology, they were not well placed to encourage their children toward more advanced independent or creative pursuits that would give them digital skills to support them when it comes time to seek opportunities for further study or employment.[30] While possible, it seemed unlikely that Eugene Apau would pursue his interest in coding, given that he had already started to move on from it. Additionally, as a young Black man from a low-income family, he would face considerable barriers were he to pursue this as a career.[31] Even when lower-income or minority youth develop forms of cultural capital that are recognized by their peers, these do not transfer into other forms of advantage conferred by mainly White teachers and employers,[32] and considerable

---

[26] Most of the low-income, noncreative parents we interviewed were non-White migrant families, largely due to our having recruited parents in inner London suburbs, while the "traditional" White, working-class families familiar to readers of the seminal *Learning to Labour* (Willis, 1977) are more likely to have moved to the outer suburbs (see Rienzo & Vargas-Silva, 2017, on the percentage of migrant families in London).

[27] This is based on having a household income of less than 60% of the median income for household size. See Child Poverty Action Group (2018).

[28] Livingstone, Blum-Ross, & Zhang (2018).

[29] See Sennet & Cobb (1993).

[30] Brough et al. (forthcoming); Tripp (2011).

[31] As sociologist Matt Rafalow (forthcoming) argues of young people's digital interests, middle-class (often White) children are more likely to be encouraged by parents and teachers who see them as a possible "next Steve Jobs." On the other hand, the digital pursuits of lower-income children (often children of color) are often read instead as either time wasting or disruptive "hacking."

[32] Watkins (2012, p. 4) argues that "not all formations of cultural capital are equal. For example, middle-class-oriented forms of cultural capital—a preference for classical music or modern American literature—are assigned greater recognition and institutional value." Further, Black young people are less likely overall to pursue study or careers in STEM-related fields, not because they do

emotional labor is required to sustain the self-belief that enables the bucking of these great odds.[33] Although there is much talk about the availability of digital jobs, the overall prospects for young people of color in these industries remains, for many deep-seated reasons, "abysmal."[34]

The experiences of low-income families are only cursorily referred to in the one-size-fits-all advice about "screen time," as we discussed in Chapter 2.[35] Although they receive more attention in policies designed to promote digital inclusion, it is crucial to keep in mind the persistent but often hidden nature of their problems with poor connectivity, difficulties in updating and troubleshooting, unpaid bills, or insufficient data plans on their mobile devices. So while many families, irrespective of cultural or economic capital, regard digital technologies as likely to facilitate a particularly promising pathway to future success, there are many gradations in their ability to realize their aspirations, and too many instances of missed opportunities and wasted resources.[36] Given these barriers, including their own relative lack of knowledge and expertise to support their children's learning, it is striking that, nonetheless, both Cecilia Apau and Leila Mohammed were investing substantially in their children's futures and embracing technology to do so.[37]

Elite families, elite skills

The Thiebault family's[38] penthouse apartment in a luxury gated development near the Thames resembled an antiques shop, with carefully curated *objets d'art,* marble walls, and expensive-looking taxidermy, in addition to at least 15 top-of-the-line digital devices scattered through the house—including game consoles, tablets, TVs, and laptops. But to father Michel Thiebault, a high-ranking corporate executive in a technology company, and

not attain the relevant expertise but because they perceive, informed by structural barriers, that such careers are not "for them." See also Archer, Dewitt, & Osborne (2015); Koshy et al. (2018).

[33] Kvansy, Joshi, & Trauth (2015); Sefton-Green & Erstad (2016).
[34] Joshi et al. (2017).
[35] Alper, Katz, & Clark (2016); Blum-Ross & Livingstone (2016a).
[36] Clark, Demont-Heinrich, & Webber (2005); Livingstone & Helsper (2012); Rideout & Katz (2016).
[37] Lower-income households are, like the Apau family, often media rich (Livingstone, 2002). Certain ethnic groups, often migrants (e.g., Latinx in the United States), invest especially heavily in digital media (M. H. Lopez, Gonzalez-Barrera, & Patten, 2013). See also Dermott & Pomati (2015); Mayo & Siraj (2015, p. 54).
[38] Family 57.

stay-at-home mother Josephine (both originally from France), the cost was negligible.

For Michel, teaching his sons about technology was as necessary as understanding the mechanics of a bicycle to improve one's cycling:

> If you take just the bicycle, the fact you know how it works helps you understand, can you accelerate, can you start, can you turn, can you do this or can you do that? . . . It is the same with the digital environment; if you don't understand how it works, you are going to struggle in your life.

Josephine shared Michel's enthusiasm, signing the boys up for technology camps including DigiCamp, the intensive—and expensive—summer camp where we first met Marc (age 13) in his Python II class. These parents and children were digitally literate in that they had set up a "smart home" with interconnected devices, parental filters, and monitoring systems—although, as Marc told us, the sons had already found "ways to engineer around" them. Marc's PS4 was hooked up to the family network, so his parents could see what he was playing from another room (to his chagrin), and his father occasionally turned off the Wi-Fi at the router to ensure Marc got some sleep at night. Despite their monitoring, neither parent seemed especially concerned about what their children would encounter online, trusting them for the most part and nodding when Marc said, with seeming awareness of the screen time discourse, that he "balances" his interests in technology "with everything—socializing, playing games with my friends . . . playing outside, sports, chess."

From a young age Marc had attended a series of technology camps, also teaching himself Java to create "mods" (user-made modifications) in *Minecraft*, followed by Codecadamy tutorials on YouTube to continue his Python class and create his own "RPG" (role-playing game). His digital skills were a source of personal pride, and he scoffed at school friends who "just have an iPhone. They just play on it, but they don't even know how it works." However, although Marc and his older brother Pierre (age 18) were digitally skilled, they spent plenty of time doing other activities too—like French club and tennis. Michel and Josephine emphasized the importance of learning to create rather than passively consuming technology and had educated themselves substantially to be able to support and encourage their sons' interests, as well as playing games such as *Destiny* and *Sniper Elite* with them. Although she didn't work in technology herself, Josephine could tell us fluently about the benefits and limitations of coding languages like Java or Python and nodded approvingly when Pierre described coding as "just like learning how to write."

Michel and Josephine were confident of their sons' futures and of their own continued role in brokering their opportunities.[39] Michel anticipated a world of "sensors, artificial intelligence systems" and noted that "if you don't understand a piece of that, you are going to be completely lost." Unlike the "pathetic" others who "don't have a clue about computing," who use computers uncritically (he evocatively described bank tellers as acting "like robots"), and for whom this technology may come to look "magical," Michel went so far in his social comparison as to call his sons' advanced digital skills those which "any gentleman should have." Josephine tempered his language but shared Michel's vision of their sons' competitive advantage, saying:

> I think if you understand the digital economy you will be more independent, and you will have more choice. I don't want them to be passive guys; I would like them to be active in this future.[40]

Bourdieu's argument in *Distinction: A Social Critique of the Judgement of Taste* is that such efforts made by wealthy families, while perhaps understandable from the viewpoint of those individual families, have the effect of forging new ways in which they maintain their relative advantage, at the cost of increased inequalities.[41] The Thiebault boys were learning to talk the talk of the digital age and to claim new resources, digital and otherwise, as they became available. But this was not merely a matter of acquiring credentials. They were also gaining a knowledge of the digital environment and the skills required to thrive in it that would advantage them relative to the poorer families trying to keep up in a less resourced context, pointing to the challenge for policymakers concerned with digital inclusion. Josephine and Michel had access not only to the resources to pay for their children's digital pursuits but also to the specific and specialized sets of knowledge that

---

[39] Barron et al. (2009); Hamid et al. (2016).
[40] Here she also speaks the language of choice that itself reveals her privileged status in a classed society (Biressi & Nunn, 2013).
[41] Bourdieu (1986).

surround them—from differentiating between programming languages to understanding the market toward which these entrepreneurial discourses are aimed.[42]

"Coding" as a policy and educational initiative is particularly ambiguous in this context. It is likely that coding will help some children attain careers in the new digital markets that reward making, creating, and tinkering, while a few will become high-level corporate executives. But as key distinctions emerge between future entrepreneurs, creative makers, and programmers at different levels, for many, coding may lead to the digital equivalent of blue-collar jobs[43]—"learning to labor" as Paul Willis put it decades ago.[44] Thus, despite public optimism and official predictions about the need for digital skills, it is likely that "digital jobs," including those not yet invented,[45] will be as diverse as the classed jobs they replace. And it is by no means guaranteed that technological expertise will lead to relevant future employment at all, given the rapid pace of technological innovation coupled with increasingly insecure employment practices in many parts of the economy.[46]

Living creatively

Not fitting neatly into polarized accounts of class, some families presented us with a confusing array of class symbols. They had high cultural capital, in that they had pursued advanced degrees or described themselves as "arty" in their interests and outlook.[47] Yet despite the ease with which they accessed cultural institutions, many earned low or precarious incomes and lived in cramped, overfilled, or even crumbling homes.[48] For these families, *London*

[42] As Elinor Ochs and Tamar Kremer-Sadlik (2015) explain, entrepreneurialism is the extension of postindustrial, middle-class parenting values.

[43] Thompson (2017).

[44] Willis (1977).

[45] Claims about the need to "skill up" to prepare for jobs that have not yet been invented is pervasive in public discourse, from technology companies to government agencies (Lomas, 2018; Schleicher, 2011).

[46] G. Morgan, Wood, & Nelligan (2013); Savage (2015b); Schor (2004).

[47] Aaron Reeves (2014) shows that educational achievements especially (rather than social class) predict participation in artistic activities and employment, and that the consequence is often a low to average income.

[48] Our interviews often revealed how traditional class categories fail to account for particular pressures and opportunities that such parents experience. In his revision of traditional social class categories, Savage (2015b) would call these "emerging service workers": people "who have extensive cultural capital and considerable social networks but don't have that much economic capital" (p. 172). However, our low-economic/high-cultural-capital families were not clustered in service

itself, and all that it represents, featured strongly in their conception of their parenting. Although they may have felt it a necessity, these parents' lifestyle represents a degree of choice, itself privileged in some ways: to give up the material comforts that other areas of the country would offer, stretching, perhaps overreaching themselves, to enjoy the advantages of London's cultural and artistic diversity.[49]

Craft-maker Mary and primary school teacher Stephen Aronson[50] had three children attending low-cost activities at LYA. Stephen explained:

> We're living in London; it is a place of opportunities, most of which you might have to pay for, but the opportunities are there and if you look hard enough you can find places where you don't have to pay so much and that's what we've done.

Similarly, mother-of-three Daisy Bardem[51] described herself as "very into getting out and doing as much as, you know, I can. . . . There's quite a lot local going on." Attracted to all that was on offer even within her London neighborhood, she learned about free and low-cost activities from friends and notices in local cafes, as well as from an app called Hoop, developed by and for London parents for just this purpose.[52]

Like the Aronsons, the Bardem family lived in a small flat full of art above a parade of shops in South London. As soon as we walked through the door we were greeted by (bumped into, actually) papier-mâché sculptures made by father Jacob—Star Wars figures, a shark, and more—swinging from the low ceiling. Jacob had worked as a photographer; his arresting images lined the walls, but he had retrained as a paramedic after recurring unemployment. Daisy trained in silversmithing and metalwork at art college and worked for a time for a jeweler but found it hard to make a living doing things other than basic repairs. Having found that her peers from college had gone on to

occupations, and a fair few were small-scale entrepreneurs. Nor does Savage's proposal capture the creative or arty nature of these people's lives (McRobbie, 2015; see also T. Bennett et al., 2010).

[49] London's creative and cultural industries represent a significant portion of London's economy (Togni, 2015), and its concentration of cultural industries accounts for a significant part of the UK economy (Centre for Economic and Business Research, 2017). That access to museums and other publicly funded arts exhibits is free yet predominantly enjoyed by middle- and upper-class populations is a concern in UK cultural policy (Martin, 2003).

[50] Family 18.

[51] Family 30. Both Daisy and husband Jacob are White, although Jacob alluded to some southern European heritage and both had art degrees.

[52] Feiler (2017); Hoop (2018).

do uninteresting work like "restoring old railings" and that you almost in-evitably "have to end up making things that you don't really want to do," she became a stay-at-home mother to Matthew (age eight), Declan (age six), and Nico (age three) and threw herself into family life.[53]

The flat had three computers: an old desktop that Jacob kept because it worked with his out-of-date photo scanner, a more recent desktop that the boys used, and a laptop that Daisy mainly used for "general browsing." There was a shared tablet and both parents had smartphones. Although Matthew had begun asking for his own phone, his parents agreed that at age eight it was still too early. Indeed, his school had asked children not to bring in phones, although Daisy had some sympathy for the many big-city children who "might be walking home on their own." In the evenings, the boys some-times watched films, although Jacob said, pointedly, "If it's on they'll watch it. If you give them a reasonable or better alternative, they'll take it." Daisy did not often watch films with the kids since they were usually on when she was cooking, but Jacob liked to join in if it wasn't something like Disney's "*Frozen* for the millionth time." Jacob especially appreciated shows like *I Can Cook* (a children's cooking show produced by the BBC) because "it gets kids inter-ested in doing something."

Daisy and Jacob limited the boys' access to their smartphones and tablets during the week (although the boys told a different story, saying they watched *Doctor Who* on the tablet in the mornings sometimes) but were more lib-eral on the weekend and when needed. So on long car trips to visit Daisy's family in Wales or when the boys waited for each other at swim lessons, the tablet filled the time. Daisy and Jacob had strong opinions about the media their children accessed, taking their responsibility as cultural curators se-riously. Daisy had found a game called *Monument Valley*, with "steam-punk"-style graphics, which, she thought, resembled a "drawing by Escher. It's very beautiful to look at." To assess content, Daisy compared notes with the other mothers, deciding Matthew was too young for a game he'd asked for (which Jacob described as like "*Grand Theft Auto* for kids"). The parents were happy that the boys played *Minecraft* but lacked knowledge of the game themselves—for example, they were not sure if they were playing in "social" (with others) or "creative" (only themselves) mode. Daisy was less happy

[53] See Orgad (2019).

upon noticing that Declan had downloaded the game *Zombie Annihilation*, explaining to his mum, "There'll be people coming around."[54]

As Daisy was the main caregiver, much of the boys' digital competence came through her. Only recently had she explained to Declan how she bought things online; Declan told us how she "got [a ninja costume] on the internet" and that it would soon be delivered in a box. He also knew it was usually his mum who chose the games for the iPad, though once a "soldier fighting game" seemed to magically appear when he was visiting his grandparents. Loving "finishing off the goblins and playing with the bad fairy," Declan was thrilled that Granny and Granddad had allowed him to play (perhaps because, as he says, they "know nothing" about the iPad). Although Daisy worried about how much "screen time" her parents allowed, the grandparents were into crafts too—an activity they shared with the boys.

Overall, the family had found a balance between embracing and resisting digital technologies in their lives. When they embraced it was partly pragmatic—a matter of going along with the children's enthusiasm in playing with friends, at their grandparents' place, on the weekends—but it was also led by their creative interests, evident in Daisy's curation of apps and games and in how the family talked about technology. Their resistance mixed the common parental anxiety about screen time, especially regarding scary or violent games, with the family's particular pleasure and competence in crafting, artisan, and artistic activities. Outdoor activities were also important: the parents told us about camping, climbing trees, and a recent trip to a local nature reserve to learn about apple-scrumping and making cider.

Looking into the future, Jacob imagined:

The iPad and the laptop is the thing of today; it's the notebook of today and that's what they're using. It's only a matter of time before that is integrated into the windowpanes and windscreens of cars. I'm not going to shy away from it, I take it as it comes, but the sadness I'm going to feel is when their grandchildren say to me, "Can you explain to me *books*?"

---

[54] As Pugh (2009) observes, children do "facework" to participate in commercialized peer culture, even if they lack access to the resources that others have.

However, although Jacob and Daisy were working to prepare their children for this imagined digital future, their main efforts were directed toward nondigital ways of being, creating, learning, and interacting. Daisy appreciated that video games taught "patience" in having to try the same moves over and over again or in needing to make "quick decisions," but she couldn't imagine enjoying a game with her sons in the way they all sat down around the detective board game Cluedo. Although Jacob described himself as having been "dragged kicking and screaming into the digital age," he thought computers would be essential for his sons—musing that all of Nico's homework would likely be online by the time he gets to school—but his ambivalence at what might be lost was clear. As so often in our fieldwork, we saw how family practices and meanings in the present were framed by the imaginative activities of both looking back and looking forward.

In emphasizing creative and "human" ways of being, these parents are not ignoring digital skills but ultimately working to create, as Nelson puts it, "adaptable children with multifaceted skills and abilities. . . . They must remain alert for evidence of particular talents even as they discourage settling too early on a narrow route to achievement."[55] Many of these high-cultural-capital but low-economic-capital families had similarities with the high-income parents in terms of their aspirations for self-fulfillment for their children and their ability to investigate the strengths and weaknesses of particular digital opportunities, but this was differently cultivated. We might say that although there was a similar ethic of "expressive empowerment," to use Clark's term,[56] the aim of empowerment among these families was not financial success so much as creativity and self-efficacy. Parents' values are often implicitly understood by children, so their choices are made and rules established according to the parents' particular criteria and assessment of what is aesthetically pleasing, creatively supportive, and *interesting*.[57] This presents children with an alternative vision of what "success" in the digital future might look like.

[55] Nelson (2010, p. 31).
[56] Clark (2013).
[57] As with many parenting discussions, there is an element of performance in these conversations, since parents' philosophies are variously undermined by children's own desires—along with those of peers, grandparents, and siblings—and by the practical constraints of time, skill, and energy.

Making privilege count

We cannot know the long-term outcomes for the children whose families we visited, but it is telling that when Lareau returned to her fieldwork families 10 years later, the original social class differences were still very much in evidence. As she reflects:

> Although all parents wanted their children to succeed, the working-class and poor families experienced more heartbreak. . . . The middle-class parents' interventions, although often insignificant as individual acts, yielded cumulative advantages.[58]

Lareau offers a compelling explanation for these persistent inequalities by pointing to parental practices of "concerted cultivation." Drawing on Bourdieu's analysis of cultural capital, she shows how middle-class parents distinctively take advantage of extracurricular enrichment activities to prepare their children for a competitive future by guiding them in the skills and confidence to *convert* their experiences into value in institutional settings. They thereby transmit their "differential advantage"[59] to their children, generating a sense of entitlement as they learn how to manage or even "game" the "cultural logic" of societal institutions, notably school.[60] Time and again, Lareau observes how middle-class parents

> proactively tried to alter the conditions under which their children functioned. They were often able to anticipate potential problems before they arose and to redirect their children or intervene strategically to prevent the potential problem from altering a child's trajectory.[61]

In consequence, middle-class children become better able to navigate the structures and rules in their schools and, later, universities, because they feel themselves more entitled and because they are able to

---

[58] Lareau (2011, p. 264). See also Lareau et al. (2016); Livingstone & Sefton-Green (2016); MacLeod (2005); Thomson (2011).

[59] Lareau (2011, p. 5).

[60] Carlson & England (2011); Lareau et al. (2016).

[61] Lareau (2011, p. 153).

command the attention of those who act as gatekeepers to valuable resources—teachers, university admissions tutors, and more. Most obviously, this is an issue of cost, but it is also because of the cultural capital required to locate and recognize the potential value of the eclectic—but often hard-to-find—opportunities available, especially in the global city. Thus, it is likely that despite all their efforts, Cecilia's or Leila's children will not get as far ahead as they hope, though the mothers may succeed in their efforts to not let their children fall behind. It is also likely that the wealthy Thiebault boys will do well, as will the children of Susan Scott and Sven Olsson—enthusiastically adapting to the digital age and preparing for a digital future.

Oddly for a book updated in 2011, Lareau says little about digital technology, except for sporadic mentions of (seemingly problematic) practices of unrestricted TV viewing in working-class homes. Yet in the digital age, many hope that poorer families' willingness to engage with digital technologies, along with their children's considerable enthusiasm for them, might counteract or overcome the persistent forces driving the social reproduction of inequality. Published in 2013, Clark's *The Parent App: Understanding Families in the Digital Age* explores the practices associated with the already-thorough embedding of computers and other digital media in American families. Supporting Lareau, Clark argues that inequalities are exacerbated through digital practices, as social and educational systems are largely set up to recognize the value of the "expressive empowerment" that better-off families work toward, rather than lower-income families' pursuit of "respectful connectedness." She therefore concludes:

> Digital and mobile media are reinforcing trends toward a deeply divided society in which certain ideals and images of an ever-consuming and time-poor middle-class life are normalized.[62]

---

[62] Clark (2013). By contrast, parents who do not conform to middle-class values and practices are construed as "troubling" (Ribbens McCarthy, Gillies, & Hooper, 2013). For example, Hinton, Laverty, and Robinson (2013) found that parents in the north of England whose children were exposed to second-hand smoke (often for reasons relating to poverty) were seen as "morally deviant and problematic" by social workers (p. 73). Similarly, Jaysane-Darr (2013) explores the unequal processes of acculturation to middle-class (often White) values in studying "parenting" classes for Sudanese refugee mothers in the United States.

This persists even though, Clark adds, middle-class families may be envious of the warmth of working-class families. Yet, because the middle-class families cannot give up on their competitive, individualistic aspirations, they are unable to emulate the benefits of connectedness experienced by working-class families (think of Daya Thakur[63] and her daughter doing each other's hair in Chapter 2) or even to reflect on the hidden costs of their own high-stress lifestyles.[64] Pierre Thiebault, for example, listed his activities leading up to his end-of-school A-level exams as grueling months of study, extracurricular activities, competitiveness, and worry.

Meanwhile, as Lareau stresses, poorer parents are preoccupied with immediate needs rather than future possibilities, given their more insecure jobs, greater financial worries, or caring responsibilities, among other pressures. Digital technologies, we see here, offer not only an accessible way of working toward an imagined future but also benefits and conveniences for parents and children in the present (e.g., Leila's searching of the Jobcentre site, Cecilia's use of YouTube to help Eric read while she cooks dinner). But although both better-off and poorer parents try to use technologies to confer advantage, they are very differently positioned to do so. So while both wealthy and poor children are learning coding and other forms of technological expertise, the outcomes are very different. Marc Thiebault and Sean Scott-Olsson had more developed digital skills than Eugene Apau, because they were doing more advanced forms of creation (using techniques like Python coding, building their own games), encouraged and supported by parents who had drawn on their own knowledge and networks to find the classes for them to learn these skills.[65] Meanwhile, Eugene was using a more "standard" language because it was what was offered for free at his school (indeed, Scratch is already integrated into the computing curriculum in England), thus offering only moderate advantage.[66] Although his mother was broadly supportive of his interests, she lacked the time, technological resources, and cultural vocabulary to encourage or "scaffold" it into either a deeper engagement with coding itself or other opportunities (as discussed in Chapter 6).[67]

---

[63] Family 10.

[64] Reay (2004) notes related emotional costs experienced by the children of such high-pressure middle-class parents.

[65] Ching et al. (2015); Hamid et al. (2016).

[66] Dredge (2014).

[67] "Scaffolding" "enables a child or novice to solve a problem, carry out a task, or achieve a goal which would be beyond his unassisted efforts. This scaffolding consists essentially of the adult 'controlling' those elements of the task that are initially beyond the learner's capacity, thus permitting him to concentrate upon and complete only those elements that are within his range of competence" (Wood, Bruner, & Ross, 1976, p. 90). See also Vygotsky (1934/1986).

Middle-class parents also draw on their privileged experiences and institutional knowledge above and beyond their knowledge of technology. For example, Susan Scott's knowledge of university life informed her parenting. She explained, "If you're going off to college, you need to have facility and confidence about using computers as your learning tool; that's the way education is now." So even though 10-year-old Sean said that he actually didn't "really like sitting in front of a screen all day and doing programming, I would rather be running around in the park playing soccer," he acceded to his mother's view that coding might be helpful in his future, although privately describing those who engage in such activities as "nerds." In Chapter 2, we discussed parent–child negotiation in the democratic family: here we see how this can be driven not merely by an effort to manage competing desires in the present but, significantly, as a way of subordinating present desires to a vision of the future. Susan Scott rationalized this exercise of her parenting responsibilities in terms of the value she placed on expressive empowerment—for her family and society. As she said of her oldest son, Niall:

> He is super-creative, making stuff all the time. . . . I think my job as a parent
> is just to help them find a way to be able to use their gifts and to hopefully
> make the world a better place in the process of doing that.

This relative privilege also smooths the relation between home and school, as noted earlier. Susan Scott drew on her elite status to seek out multiple sources of support and expert advice for her parenting decisions—from the school, professionals such as psychologists and therapists, and parenting groups that she had either organized or joined.[68] Josephine Thiebault was even on the board of DigiCamp. And while the Bardems certainly lacked the wealth of the Thiebaults or Scott-Olssons, Jacob and Daisy Bardem could call on considerable cultural capital to pressure their children's teachers for support as needed and to a home environment conducive to confident learning and expression.

By contrast, to the extent that parents like Leila and Cecilia were visible to their children's teachers, they risked being seen as "deficient"[69]—certainly we saw little evidence of effective outreach or of other institutional

---

[68] Arguably, her cultural capital compensated for the migrant's relative lack of social capital and connections, a strategy that Cecilia and Leila would find harder to enact (V. S. Katz, Gonzalez, & Clark, 2017).

[69] Alper et al. (2016); Ribbens McCarthy et al. (2013); Te Riele (2006).

structures helping them to connect their or their children's digital (or other) engagements at home into academic or other achievement.[70] Cecilia Apau told us that while she sought advice from friends, she did not receive much help from her church or her children's school; indeed, after some frustration she had found the latter so unresponsive to her queries that she had stopped asking. Leila Mohammed, similarly, lacked a clear line of communication to her children's teachers and received no indication that her significant investment of time and money in finding extra tuition and support for Safia and Nareen was noticed by their school.[71] This suggests that, unless deliberate efforts are made to design learning environments inclusively, they will foster connections that exacerbate rather than ameliorate pre-existing inequalities.[72]

Insofar as children are not equally able to convert knowledge gained at home and in their community into value that is recognized and rewarded by schools, universities, or employers, we conclude that this is less a failure of individual effort and more a consequence of structural inequalities in society.[73] One problem lies in the institutional design of educators' outreach and engagement with parents and their receptiveness to the interests, knowledge, or achievements of poorer and minority children (as well as being, more fundamentally, the result of a society that unequally resources its children). As Norma González, Luis Moll, and Cathy Amanti argue, though too often unacknowledged, poor families "have knowledge, and their life experiences have given them that knowledge."[74] Yet they may not find ways to communicate their practices to schools and are often overlooked in educational interventions.[75] Notably, Leila's investment in tuition and technology at home were invisible to the school, as was the energy she expended to bring her daughters up in her Muslim faith. The benefits she considered this to

---

[70] Rafalow (forthcoming).

[71] Leila relied on a childminder to drop her children off at school, so her interactions with teachers were limited at best. Indeed, inverting the idea that (middle-class) parents broker opportunities for their children, in her work with migrant families, Vikki S. Katz (2014) found that digital media play a central role not only in the enactment of parenting but also in the administration of family life, as children help "broker" their parents' interactions with external systems by answering calls, translating emails, and beyond—as, for example, did Cecilia Apau's 12-year-old daughter for her.

[72] This matters for the theory of connected learning, and for others keen to foster better home-school links. See Ito et al (2018, 2020).

[73] Dermott and Pomati (2015) found that low-income, less well-educated parents engaged in many of the activities considered to be "good parenting," albeit with less intensity (and perhaps less success) than their wealthier, more well-educated counterparts. See also Lareau (2011); Nelson (2010); Reece (2013); Reay (2004).

[74] González, Moll, & Amanti (2005, p. 19).

[75] For example, there are only a few brief mentions of parents in Selwyn (2014) and Spector (2016).

bring are not (thus far) legible to, nor convertible in, the mainstream. Rather than supporting interventions based on "overgeneralized" understandings of low-income families, Kris Gutiérrez and Barbara Rogoff call for educators to ground interventions in a recognition that families bring with them diverse "repertoires of practice" based on their experiences, knowledge, and values.[76] While their call is not new, it applies also to learning with digital technologies, given that these are "sold" to parents precisely as a means of supporting their children's learning at home, but often with no meaningful relation to either domestic or school practices and policies.

Conclusions

The mass adoption of digital technologies brings potentially beneficial opportunities for families, promising new pathways for parents to facilitate their children's prospects in relation to an emerging and still-uncertain digital future. Most of the homes we visited were filled with digital "stuff," testament to public imaginaries and shared parental desires and hopes for digital technologies. Across class and other differences, parents appeared united in the view that technology offers *something* that, through the work of parenting, "can be cultivated to produce positive outcomes,"[77] agreeing that it was their responsibility to harness potential to support their children in a competitive world and for an imagined digital future. This sense of responsibility is, however, the means by which normative pressures dictate how parents should provision the home and cultivate their children's achievement, even at the cost of stressful family negotiations and the "curricularization" of leisure and private life.[78]

By comparison with earlier expectations on parents—for instance, to support children's homework by providing quiet space and time in the domestic routine—the forms of parental support likely to be effective in relation to digital technology are simultaneously demanding and frustratingly unclear, given the lack of established knowledge about their value for the present or, especially, the future. Consider that, of the 20 to 30 apps Cecilia

---

[76] Gutiérrez & Rogoff (2003).

[77] Furedi (2014). Here, Furedi speaks of parenting more generally, but we contend that today the digital provides a focus and a test for the work of parenting itself.

[78] Buckingham (2000). This contributes to the overextended, time-pressured, and often guilt-ridden nature of contemporary family life (Hochschild, 1997; Schor, 1991).

had downloaded because she believed them to be "educational," of only a few could she say whether or what her children were learning as a result.[79] Nor could the middle-class families we interviewed tell us convincingly what value such apps provided, so opaque is the promise of the digital (by contrast, say, to the world of books they seem to displace) and so ambivalent, therefore, are parents about their value. However, poorer families' investments are often disproportionate to those of others, as are the opportunities they miss out on. By contrast, for confident, creative families that lack financial resources—like Daisy and Jacob Bardem—digital technologies suggest a promising innovation worth taking a chance on, so long as they are balanced by nontechnical opportunities, because they see a way to bring their alternative aesthetic and values to bear in this interpretatively flexible field.[80] And for some privileged parents like the Scott-Olssons— who implicitly know what it takes to get ahead in life—technological innovation may introduce worrying uncertainty compared with their own childhoods, but the risks are nonetheless probably low (except, perhaps, in those cases where technology becomes so all-consuming a fascination that other forms of concerted cultivation are displaced, as we explore in the next chapters).

The combination of opportunities, pressures, and uncertainties helps to explain some of the intensity and anxiety associated with parental (and policy) discussions of digital technology. In our fieldwork, we were regaled with hopes and fears from parents of all walks of life, leading us to disagree with Lareau's contention that concerted cultivation—defined as the effortful provision of individual resources to advantage one's child in consequential ways—preoccupies *only* the middle classes while working-class parents rely instead on what she calls the assumption of "natural growth."[81] Habiba Bekele[82] illustrated the commitment expressed to us by a good number of low-income families when she said, "I do encourage

---

[79] Marsh et al. (2015).

[80] Of higher-income parents, only 30% say they are "very" or "somewhat" likely to use digital media (including computers, tablets, and TV) for educational purposes, but this rises to 52% for lower-income parents (V. S. Katz & Levine, 2015; Wartella et al., 2013).

[81] Lareau (2011).

[82] Family 25. She explained: "I want all of them to have their own future. They decide. My daughter, she said she wants to be a doctor; my son, he said he wants to be a teacher; and then my small girl, she says she wants to be a doctor too like her sister. So that's their hope, that's how you want them to make their goal. So better children, better student, better to the future."

them [with technology], because this is their future." Meanwhile, it was educated families like the Bardems that came closest to a parental vision of natural growth in their romantic emphasis on a spontaneous and creative childhood, instead of an instrumental focus on future economic success.[83]

More generally, we see the rise of a common parenting culture—arguably middle class in its ethos of individualized achievement and itself a response to the individualization of risk in reflexive modernity—that encompasses poorer families too. We say "arguably" middle class, for such a parenting culture can clearly be read as against the interests of working-class families, especially as the consequences remain as unequal as ever, so that for poorer families, the hopes are generally delusory. However, from what the families we interviewed told us, their hopes appeared widely shared, seriously held, and commonly acted upon. At the core was the view that responsible parenting, including in relation to digital technologies, could deliver greater choice, agency, and self-actualization, together with new pathways to social mobility. The fears also were widely shared and widely promoted (usually by the mass media)—although it was, perhaps, distinctive of Cecilia, by contrast with many middle-class parents, that she didn't worry about online risks, "because I know my children. If I tell them not to do it, they won't go. They have limits where to go and what not to do."[84]

Such hopes, we suggest, are particularly widely held in relation to digital technologies, both because of the sizeable national investment in digital technologies in schools, workplaces, services, and communities and because hopes of digitally mediated learning and employment appear particularly resonant in a context of labor market instability and prominent

[83] One might argue that there is some valorization of "natural growth" in Ito and colleagues' emphasis on the importance of "hanging around" and "messing around" as vital to interest-led learning with long-term academic benefits. While often lacking Ito et al.'s commitment to social justice-oriented interventions, we found "natural growth" tends to be endorsed more among middle-class parents, thus inverting Lareau's class analysis (Ito et al., 2010; Lareau, 2011).

[84] This may have been, reasonably enough, because Cecilia had bigger worries on her mind. Marianne Cooper (2014) observes, of the wealthier parents she interviewed, that they managed both to amplify their own anxieties and to set a benchmark against which parents with fewer resources were perceived to be deficient if they did not parent (and worry) with similar intensity. However, given the contemporary climate of anxieties about the internet, it is striking to us that, regarding a fair number of parents, including Cecilia, our fieldnotes record "no real worries about exposure to anything online."

technology-led social change. Fears of the digitally mediated risks of falling behind, losing out, or experiencing harm appear equally resonant in a context of reduced welfare provision.

Participating in a common parenting culture hardly eliminates inequalities. This chapter has also shown that, for high-income families, new technology-related forms of concerted cultivation have quickly come to complement long-established ways in which they are able to bring about a successful future for their children. These parents can provide both high-quality devices and relevant expertise (creative, technological, professional) to guide the sustained development of their children's digital activities. As knowledge gap and digital divide research has shown clearly,[85] the more middle-class parents exploit their available financial and cultural resources to maintain their advantage and reduce their risk in uncertain and competitive times, the more they raise the bar for disadvantaged families trying to keep up. But for poorer families, the availability of and discourses around digital technologies mean that this pathway still seems uniquely accessible.

A decade or two ago, would Cecilia or Leila have invested as heavily in books and other educational resources as they do today in digital technology? Perhaps, but perhaps not: we suspect that the attraction of devices and services makes digital investments particularly appealing, mixing educational promise with entertaining realities in a beguiling way, while children's own enthusiasm for digital acquisitions was hardly applicable to the multivolume family encyclopedia. Yet in such families, the gap between the promise and reality of digital technology use at home is particularly challenging, with the financial commitments and practicalities hard to manage—often unexpectedly so—and a paucity of people they can call upon for help, beyond their own children.[86]

But the consequence is not a simple or polarized landscape of more and less privileged families—especially in London, a global city subject to multiple intersecting forces. First, some families who lack institutionally recognized

---

[85] Bourdieu (1986); Helsper (2017); Mascheroni & Olafsson (2015); Pugh (2009); Schor (2004); Van Dijk (2005). Bourdieu's theory of social reproduction has stimulated some discussion of the possibility of technical capital, somewhat akin to that of human capital, to refer to skills that enable both learning and marketable value (T. Bennett et al., 2010).

[86] Cecilia's desire to buy a computer, despite the hardship it brought and her inability to help support its use, is consistent with the finding that poorer parents are equally, if not more, likely to identify educational benefits for computers (Buckingham, 2000; V. S. Katz, 2014; Wartella et al., 2013; Dermott & Pomati, 2015; Mayo & Siraj, 2015).

forms of cultural capital (access to higher education, confidence with official bodies) may nonetheless have access to forms of alternative forms of "capital"[87]—for example, knowledge that is grounded and meaningful within minority ethnic or religious cultures. These they deliberately cultivate in their children—resulting in a range of benefits including community belonging, additional languages, religious knowledge, diasporic family connections, and (sub) cultural or other forms of expertise. Yet these children are likely to struggle to convert the knowledge gained through these experiences into value that is recognized and rewarded by schools, universities, or employers.[88] In this effort, digital technologies can be particularly helpful insofar as they sustain connections among communities that are physically dispersed. Recall how Leila encouraged her daughters to find and enjoy Muslim songs found online—surely otherwise hard to locate within British mainstream culture—or Habiba Bekele's use of Skype to study Arabic with her teacher in Egypt, and her children's use of apps and satellite TV to ensure they become good Muslims in a largely secular country (Chapter 2).[89] Similarly, Jehovah's Witness parents Afua Osei and Kwame Tuffuor[90] encouraged their three children's use of the "JW" app and website for religious learning and play.[91] Other families used services for "niche" interests from language development to craft, harnessing digital media's "long tail" of content to diverse ends.[92] Claudia Ferreira,[93] originally from Portugal, found Portuguese internet radio and TV channels that she could share with her daughter Mariana (age nine), encouraging her to learn her parents' native language so that Mariana could speak with her extended family when they visited. She also used sites like YouTube to pursue other forms of learning, watching tutorials when Mariana wanted to learn to knit, a hobby that mother and daughter soon engaged in together. Yet only some of these activities are legible to the other sites of children's lives that might confer advantage—school, university, the world of work—and most are probably not.

Second, we have highlighted the approach of families who are highly educated, often creative or subcultural, yet living on relatively low or very low

[87] Linking Bourdieu's analysis of capital to ethnic-minority experiences within Western societies, Sandra Trienekens (2002) discusses community-based forms of cultural capital that operate within but not beyond an ethnic-minority community (see also T. Bennett et al., 2010).
[88] Livingstone & Sefton-Green (2016).
[89] Family 25.
[90] Family 24.
[91] JW.org is a Jehovah's Witness website with some animation and morality stories.
[92] C. Anderson (2006).
[93] Family 16.

income. London is home to well-established creative and cultural industries like art, music, and theater as well as emergent industries like game design, this adding a fascinating complication to class-based accounts of parenting. In his characterization of the "new petite bourgeoisie," Bourdieu describes such people as inhabiting "the most indeterminate zone . . . towards the cultural [rather than economic] pole of the middle class," even suggesting they "invented" this position to take advantage of emerging opportunities in the economy, thereby compensating for their otherwise limited resources, and notwithstanding that this promises only a risky future.[94] Thus, the "commonplace diversity" of languages, cuisines, values, and culture evident in London and other global cities allows for intersectional ways of living that fall outside "middle class" and "working class" classifications as traditionally conceived.[95] This not only includes the distinctively creative or bohemian values of the Bardems, Aronsons, and other low-income families with high cultural capital, some of whom are deliberately seeking their own workarounds to the discourse of middle-class anxiety. It also includes a range of alternative forms of capital—arguably better labeled "community based" or "subcultural" capital—grounded in religious, linguistic, or ethnic-minority knowledge.[96] Recognizing the specific opportunities for "creative labor" in London, along with other global cities, Angela McRobbie argues that this strategy involves the pursuit of particularly "passionate work."[97] Certainly it was no coincidence that when recruiting parents in London we found ourselves interviewing self-employed filmmakers, artists, makers, crafters, photographers, web designers, and more. Digital technologies, as

[94] Bourdieu (1986).

[95] See Crenshaw (1991) for a discussion of intersectionality, and Wessendorf (2014) on "super-diverse" cities. It may be observed that we do not refer to the creative families in terms of Richard Florida's (2014) thesis of the creative class. This is partly because of the controversy his work has attracted, and it is not our point to make grand claims about the economic contribution of such families; it is also because in our fieldwork, these families stood out for their relatively low incomes, it being the disjunction between their economic and cultural capital, in Bourdieu's terms, that we believe leads them so heavily and distinctively to invest in their children's future.

[96] Trienekens (2002) and T. Bennett and colleagues (2010) refer to the largely nonconvertible knowledge of an ethnic-minority culture as "community-based forms of cultural capital," and Sarah Thorton (1996) calls "subcultural capital" the niche taste cultures developed, for instance, around rave culture. For both our creative/bohemian and ethnic-minority families, specific cultural practices network people in ways that transcend their geographic separation, resulting in shared values and forms of expertise, notwithstanding that these are little noticed or valued by mainstream society.

[97] McRobbie (2015) is concerned that this results in little collective identification or political representation. As she says, "A now very swollen youthful middle class bypasses mainstream employment with its trade unions and its tranches of welfare and protection in favour of the challenge and excitement of being a creative entrepreneur" (p. 11). In the public discourse, she worries, we hear of successful creative or craft-focused enterprises but not the precarity they entail.

we explored in relation to the Bardem family, are seized upon for affording an innovative workaround to gaining status that brings rewards through the deployment of cultural knowledge and creative endeavor without too much need for money. Moreover, engagement with such technologies can be—and often is—imagined within alternative, often creative frames, and while the resulting knowledge may remain niche, unlike other forms of alternative capital it also promises a future pathway for these families or their children that could be publicly valued.[98]

In this chapter we have drawn attention to the persistent challenges of the social reproduction of inequality, recognizing that, as Diane Reay emphasizes, it is families that "provide the link between individual and class trajectory."[99] It is too early to draw conclusions about the long-term consequences of embracing digital technologies by embedding them in homes, schools, and elsewhere. To those designing social justice–oriented interventions,[100] we highlight families' differential starting points and remind them that parents who appear "disengaged" may in fact be supporting their children through digital technologies and beyond in ways that are often invisible because they lack the cultural capital to make them legible within institutions; or familes that deliberately do not fit the normative expectations of institutions such as school because they are pursuing an alternative ethic. Additionally, we urge recognition of how seemingly similar efforts by parents have very different outcomes, because those with high cultural capital are able to ensure their distinctive advantage while those without it are left struggling. Cecilia Apau's now virus-ridden computer may be useless, but it should be recognized that she bought it "because my daughter [Esi, age 12] needed to use the computer for homework." Its now-blinking screen therefore symbolizes both her hopes for a digital future and her struggle to bring this about.

[98] We say "may" be publicly valued, for it is too soon to be confident that digital expertise can be "converted" into mainstream value. Consider the uncertainty over computer gaming, for instance: the United Kingdom has a highly profitable gaming industry, but many gamers will not gain employment in it, nonetheless, and neither parents nor schools are clear as to who will or will not.
[99] Reay (2004, p. 59).
[100] Ito et al. (2020); Watkins (2009).

4

Geek Identities in the Digital Family

We met Dani,[1] middle-income parent of Josh, aged 12, in a café after Josh's day at DigiCamp, an expensive, central London–based coding summer camp where we observed children and young teens, mainly privileged boys, White and Asian, learning Java, Python, HTML, *Minecraft*, 3D printing, and more. Dani kicked off our interview with enthusiasm, regaling us with her entire tech history, from learning Basic on a Commodore 64 as a child to her qualification in "ethical hacking" earned after-hours while working in technology sales. Dani had constructed a high-tech home to support her and her sons' digital interests, and might spend a happy evening tracking through the dark web to see how the latest high-profile hack was actually done while simultaneously setting coding challenges for Josh and his brother's *Minecraft* play. Her vision was to build an economically viable future for the boys, and perhaps herself, by doing something pleasurable—coding. Talking of a recent data breach on an online dating site for extramarital affairs, Dani was keen to explain how it happened:

DANI: Ashley Madison[2] told everybody that you can delete your profile for £12, like, completely delete it, and they [the hacking community] said it's not possible. . . . Ashley Madison refused to recant, so they hacked them and got hold of a load of deleted profiles, proving that it wasn't possible to delete a profile. It was a geek argument, basically.

JOSH: You just have . . . like, hard-down geeks have a massive argument over something and it's, like, what are they talking about? And then, it's just funny.

DANI: Yes, I normally understand them. I'm one of them, don't worry.

SONIA: I was wondering if I was going to use that word about you guys.

DANI: I'm quite happy to be a geek; there's nothing wrong with it.

---

[1] Family 56. Dani was divorced from Josh's mum, was called dad, and presented as female.

[2] In 2015, Ashley Madison, a commercial website facilitating extramarital affairs, faced a notorious cybersecurity attack, resulting in a huge breach of clients' personal details (Baraniuk, 2015; Victor, 2015).

Parenting for a Digital Future. Sonia Livingstone and Alicia Blum-Ross, Oxford University Press (2020). © Oxford University Press.
DOI: 10.1093/oso/9780190874698.001.0001

Over the course of the interview, the conversation sped up, words tumbling over themselves as Dani and Josh sought to display their interest in technology as much to each other as to us. We were struck by their sense of being secret explorers together in a dramatically changing world. For Dani, gaining "insider" knowledge was sure to pay off in what she was convinced would be a digital future:

> Once he's got the principles of [Java] he can move onto anything; he just has to learn a different set of syntax, it's just like, you know, it's like learning Latin, in many ways.

Not only had Dani invested in technology at home and by paying DigiCamp's high fees, but also, more important, she had embedded into her and Josh's relationship their mutual fascination with all things technological. Josh's animated geeky talk connected him with Dani as the parent he visited but no longer lived with since his parents had separated. He contrasted this himself with his classmates at his school, seeming to relish how his technological expertise set him apart:

> If I say Java, they'll know what it is. Loads of people in my class, anyway, most of them, if I say Java, they'll know what that is, but they don't know it. . . . Well, no, they know what it is; they know it's games [design] but they don't *know* it.

Dani and Josh illustrate an extreme case of "embracing" digital media, following—and going far beyond—the digital parenting advice so often given to parents, namely to share media use as a family, maintain good communication across the generations, and develop digital skills for the future.[3] But what exactly is involved in becoming a geek, what are the opportunities or risks for those involved, and what, if anything, can be learned from this experience for the benefit of the wider society?

As Brigid Barron observes, on the one hand, "the development of expertise goes hand in hand with a growing sense of one's self or identity as connected with the activities and roles this knowledge makes possible," and on the other, "an imagined future self helps motivate learning."[4] What if the

---

[3] Baggaly (2017); Bold Creative (2017); Heitner (2016).
[4] Barron (2006, p. 220).

imagined future is digital, and relished for being so? This chapter explores the learning, relational, and identity implications of repositioning the "geek" from the margins toward the mainstream of the digital age. We argue that although the opportunities are notable so too are the potential pitfalls, and the necessary level of commitment. This means that we must take with a grain of salt what might be applied more broadly from learning from geeks, given their path requires such a risky form of embrace.

The contemporary fascination with geeks

Type "geek" into Google Images and a host of earnest, pale, bespectacled faces appear. Usually White and male, some of these faces suggest that the traditional image of the clever, awkward loner persists, while another more "hipster" vision also emerges. Once an insult for the freakish, unsociable, and foolish, the term "geek" has been traced historically from the freak show through a largely masculine history of electronic tinkering—including ham radio hobbyists—to today's notion of someone who obsessively cultivates a narrow form of expertise specifically linked to the digital.[5] Gabriella Coleman articulates the geeky values of "craftiness, the cultural cultivation of antiauthoritarianism, and the sustenance of fellowship around labor in free spaces."[6] While such activity often remains under the radar and, arguably, inconsequential for mainstream society, geek culture's "crafty mindset" contributes to the more political activities of hacker culture, where hackers deploy what Coleman calls the "weapons of the geek"—the niche expertise, antihero politics, and confident risk-taking of privileged educated White men, who may inadvertently become mainstream (think of Edward Snowden or Mark Zuckerberg).[7]

Less cool but arguably more impactful are the efforts of public policy to support the mutation of geekiness from a personal (social, emotional) deficit to an asset in the digital age. Geekiness is repositioned as central to rather than a distraction from a national agenda concerned to keep up with changing expertise, future jobs, business innovation, and competitive success. Despite the radical and at times criminal nature of hacking, it has to some degree

---

[5] Bell (2013); Jancovich (2002). See also Dunbar-Hester (2014); Fuller (2017); Goriunova (2014).

[6] G. Coleman (2017, p. 95). See also Mako Hill (2002).

[7] Contrasting her analysis with Scott's (1985) anthropological account of peasant protest, G. Coleman (2017) explains: "While weapons of the weak embody tactics used by economically marginalized populations—small-scale illicit acts, such as foot dragging and vandalism—that do not appear on their surface to be political, weapons of the geek encompass a range of political interventions—recognized as such—and [are] exercised by a class of privileged and visible actors who often lie at the center of economic life" (p. S100).

been co-opted by a commercial culture seeking competitive advantage (as in now-ubiquitous so-called hackathons). Witness the rise of "cybersecurity" programs—growing in popularity in the United States, in particular—that teach young people how to harness hacker mentality and tactics to thwart security breaches.[8] Think too of the media's heroic narratives of the entrepreneurial founders of Facebook, Microsoft, and Google; its dangerous but romantic portrayal of hackers, or its bewailing of the fact that Europe hasn't produced its own Steve Jobs or Bill Gates.[9] Although the rise of the vlogger or "YouTuber" is less directly tied to the idea of the "geek," these stars also capture the public imagination in demonstrating how digital skills can bring fame and fortune, while other social justice activists like "nerdfighters" epitomize the interlinking of digital tactics and alternative values in contemporary geek culture.[10]

In this cultural effort to reimagine the geek, images of girls and women, often attractive, begin to appear—think of young adult books like *Geek Girl* or *Girls Who Code*—along with a few people of color. They all still wear glasses, however—the recognized symbol of unusual intelligence, while still carrying a whiff of outsider or potentially stigmatized status.[11] Along with the trope of the geeky computer whiz kid who saves the day in Hollywood blockbusters, popular TV shows like *The Big Bang Theory* or *The IT Crowd* poke fun at geeks while also conceding— even privileging, within reason—their identity as clever, satirical, or audacious. A popular David-and-Goliath narrative frames everyday such digital media engagement, proffering the valorization of geeky or hacktivist knowledge, a romantic antihero identity, a degree of anti-authoritarianism, and a warmly supportive peer community. As Henry Jenkins and colleagues have shown, youth from marginalized groups deliberately set out to gain digital skills to mobilize and express their collective concerns about social justice "by any media necessary."[12] More prosaically, echoes of this narrative can be heard in the everyday conversations of children and young people who, while far from radical, talk of "hacking" as a cool yet commonplace activity within their circles.[13]

In short, the current fascination with the idea of the geek is evident not only in the domains of academia, policy, or counterculture[14] but also among

---

[8] Brough (2016).

[9] Ensmenger (2010, p. 3).

[10] Kligler-Vilenchik (2013); Sugg (2016).

[11] Deutsch (2017); Goriunova (2014); Smale (2015). See also Broadnax (2018); Dionne (2017); Parks et al. (2018). Also consider the relative success of the film *Hidden Figures*, about Black women scientists and mathematicians.

[12] Jenkins, Shresthova, et al. (2016).

[13] For more on children's everyday accounts of hacking, see Livingstone & Haddon (2017).

[14] G. Coleman (2014); Jenkins (1992); Turner (2006).

ordinary families, as parents and children try to make sense of living in a digital age. At London Youth Arts (LYA) we met single mum Jen Pearson and her daughters Tegan (age 14) and Charlotte (age 11).[15] The family lived on a low income, for although Jen had a degree in art, she was now a full-time caregiver, home-schooling the girls. She relied on digital technology to research their curricula and find learning opportunities—we observed Charlotte in music technology and several other classes at LYA, as well as outside LYA at a Lego Mindstorms meet-up for home-schooled children.[16] Tegan studied film and photography through an online course offered by the Open University, among other learning activities, and had just heard she'd gained a place at film school as we ended our fieldwork. These activities represented a necessary workaround, given the failure of mainstream school to support Tegan's creative talent or Charlotte's special educational needs (SEN, in her case moderate dyslexia and dyspraxia) as Jen saw it. She said of Charlotte that school was

> trying to bang her in with a hammer into this shaped hole that she's not really going to fit into, which is really pointless, really, rather than finding what shaped hole she fits into and helping her fit into that really well.

At our first meeting, Jen told us how Charlotte was part of a group who had started "3D printing, and Minecraft groups with a bunch of geeky boys, and they sit and geek out together." When asked what "geeking out" looked like, Jen replied, "Sitting around talking about geeky things that no one else understands." Charlotte joined the conversation at that point, in the break between her classes, and a lively discussion ensued:

SONIA: Your mum was telling me about 3D printing and that you're becoming a bit of a geek.
CHARLOTTE: And a Minecraft geek. Nerd.
SONIA: Nerd or geek. I heard the origin of the word "nerd" the other day . . .
JEN: I think nerds are into different things, and they really know loads of stuff about loads of nerdy sort of stuff. Geeks are doers, and they are the ones who make the things. They're the ones who are the electronic engineers and the game designers, and the . . .

---

[15] Family 2.

[16] Lego Mindstorms is a build-and-program robotics tool set from the Lego group. It allows users to build, program, and command their own robots.

CHARLOTTE: It's the other way around, mum. Everyone thinks it's that way, but it's the other way around.

A fair few children in our fieldwork were keen to engage us in the geek-or-nerd debate, suggesting a popular fascination with what it means to follow a digital pathway: are you cool or irrelevant, leader or follower, alternative or mainstream, knower or doer? This debate engages not only self-declared "geeks" but also others who seek to negotiate their normality even when their behavior might appear geeky. When her daughter used social media, Daisy Bardem[17] compared her to her friend's children who were "really tech-savvy, they've got an older brother who's a real computer geek." Asked how she learned to blog professionally, Melissa Bell[18] told us:

> I'm still not, by any means, someone who's a natural technical geek or anything, but yes, it's quite a good feeling to know you've learnt stuff.

Even in this digital age, it seems that geeks remain "other," but saliently so, as they anchor in the imagination the extraordinary end of a scale of expertise in which many now share, as part of the "new normal."

Geek practices as learning

Central to the rehabilitation, even celebration, of the geek is a theory of learning. By contrast with traditional conceptions of a curriculum-based pedagogy, geeky learning is interest led, learner centered, grounded in practice ("learning by doing"), and sustained by a self-determining and specialized community of practice. This alternative vision of learning resonates with the theories long advocated by educational reformers, whether progressive or radical and whether offering a much-needed critique, tending to stereotype classroom practice or even arguing against school altogether.[19] For example, the framework of connected learning within which our project

---

[17] Family 30.
[18] Family 38.
[19] Gomez & Lee (2015); Ito et al. (2010); Sims (2017); Yelland (2018).

has been conducted echoes Coleman's three characteristics of geek culture, noted earlier, in recognizing how

> connected learning takes root when young people find peers who share interests, when academic institutions recognize and make interest-driven learning relevant to school, and when community institutions provide resources and safe spaces for more peer driven forms of learning.[20]

Generally committed to "craftiness" (among other forms of "tinkering" and self-paced, interest-driven learning) and collaborative "fellowship" (rather than individualized, even competitive, learning), these radical pedagogies are gaining mainstream attention in the digital age.[21] They seem in synergy with the competencies demanded by the specialized and fast-changing digital environment, and thus well positioned to meet the mounting concerns from employers and policymakers that traditional schooling isn't delivering the digital skills required by an innovative and fast-changing labor market.[22] While some parents and teachers feel particularly threatened by the antiauthoritarianism of geek culture, for others it is refreshing. Recall that Dani began our interview by telling us about her qualification in ethical hacking, revealing both her specialized knowledge and the antihero identity to which she aspired. She then detailed Josh's and his brother's learning through gaming and coding in *Minecraft*, neatly illustrating her theory of learning founded on the importance of child-centered, peer-supported, problem-focused experimentation:

> It's the social aspect that I like, the fact that they can chat with each other.... So they linked all their tablets together and were playing *Minecraft*, four of them, each on a tablet, sitting on the sofa, all collaborating with each other; and they were chatting about general stuff as well as, right, I'm going to build a house over there; ... to me, that's like Lego, but you're just using a tablet instead of building blocks with each other.

This form of learning can require significant resources, including from supportive adults (see Chapter 6). At first Dani tried to suggest Josh's interest in

---

[20] Ito et al. (2013, p. 8).
[21] Bevan et al. (2015).
[22] Nemorin & Selwyn (2016).

computers was spontaneous, drawing on the cultural narrative of the self-taught geek. But Josh was clear that Dani had showed him the way:

DANI: I don't know, no, you just got into computers, really, didn't you?

JOSH: Well, I got into Xbox, so that's my main thing, and then, and then you said if I have to go in at lunchtime, to go and code and program, at least—

DANI: Well, but, no, it was before that. It was before that, it was when in, it was when you first . . . I, no, I remember because I came home from that course and I said, hey, here you go, I've got Kodu,[23] why don't you go and have a quick play with this? Oh, we've had a little play with it at school, you said.

JOSH: Oh, yes, yes. That was, like—

DANI: And then I installed it on my machine and then you started playing with it at home.

JOSH: But I stopped playing it because on the tablet it was, like—

DANI: Yes, the tablet was a bit slow, but then I put it on the other machine and you'd play with it on the other machine.

JOSH: Yes.

DANI: But it was—

SONIA: On a computer then? Yes.

DANI: But you'd keep going on Kodu; you'd keep playing with it.

JOSH: Because it's fun; I like it.

DANI: But you're creating something at the same time.

JOSH: Yes.

DANI: You do realize that that's what people, essentially, do when it comes to creating a game?

JOSH: Yes.

In this exchange we see Dani's efforts to construct a pathway for Josh to learn coding, building on his interest in playing Xbox. For Josh, a willing participant in their shared geekiness, this may have offered a way of coping with some of the difficulties he was facing, including his parents' separation and his concern that he wasn't doing very well at his new secondary school.

---

[23] Kodu is a "Game Lab Community" where users create games on a PC or Xbox through a basic programming language (https://www.kodugamelab.com).

Jasper,[24] also age 12 and attending DigiCamp, thought himself as much a geek as Josh but, while similarly able to access resources, did not have a similarly supportive parent and was entirely self-taught. He started enthusing about his digital activity the minute we entered his house, saying:

I love it. . . . There's so many jobs I want to use it in that include digital stuff. I want to do graphic design and if I don't do that then I would like to become a professional gamer.

In a room strewn with current and discarded computer and game machine parts, he showed off his computer with pride—it had, he reeled off, a "NVIDIA GeForce GTX 870M graphics card" and "a Corsair K70 RGB keyboard." At the time he was learning Cinema 4D:

The most basic animations you can make tend to be in *Minecraft* so I learned how to put *Minecraft* files into my animation. And then I learned how to texture them and then I learned how to use rigs so you get a rig which is a character in the game and then it's got animating features. So, you can move its different joints, a different hand, like, you can move its fingers, pupils, eyelids, all of the rest. And then I just tried to make a simple intro with it. So, all he does, he walks in, it cuts to his shocked face, he goes, and then the name smashes in and he jumps backwards. And that takes, like, a whole day to do.

Asked to explain how he learned about technology, he summed up his approach as "try and try and try. And then you, kind of, get it and then you can just do stuff yourself." As fits the connected learning model, Jasper hoped for a digital career for its promise of autonomy—his talk was all about personal progress, fun,[25] searching for a tutorial or other resources, testing, and trying again.

Much of his effort went into constructing a professional-looking YouTube channel, populated with appealing videos that were gaining a modest number of views and even a few commissions for his intros and outros.[26] This had been achieved by melding his growing technical skills, his love for

---

[24] Family 61.
[25] See Goriunova (2014).
[26] Intros and outros, on YouTube, are the customized introductions and conclusions of videos—a way of branding one's channel.

art and sense of aesthetics, the tactics needed for commercial success in the online world, and participation in an informed community of peers:

> So, basically, there's a whole community in, kind of, games, and so, on my YouTube videos I'll often get someone saying, okay, add me on Skype, let's talk about something. So, they'll often give me shout-outs to publicize my channel or they'll. . . . Some sometimes pay me or that kind of stuff. And then in some way or another they will repay me. And I'll make them something. So, that's how basically that works.

Although he was having fun and learning a lot at DigiCamp, Jasper was critical of the educators for being only just ahead of the students. Generally, he was keen to share his knowledge, trying to teach digital skills to his mother—who, he said, didn't know what she was doing—and sharing expertise with friends and peers both online and offline. He was delighted that his art and information technology (IT) teachers at school admired his professional-looking YouTube intros ("I took a lot of appreciation of that"), while being frustrated—like Josh—that the school was still teaching Excel.

As proposed in Mizuko Ito and colleagues' account of connected learning,[27] "geeking out" is an interest-driven "genre of participation" that, for some young people, develops beyond hanging out and then messing around with digital technologies. As we have seen for the families discussed so far in this chapter, it involves "an intense commitment" to

> learning to navigate esoteric domains of knowledge and practice and participating in communities that traffic in these forms of expertise. It is a mode of learning that is peer-driven, but focused on gaining deep knowledge and expertise in specific areas of interest.[28]

It is also a mode of learning that contrasts with many children's experiences of school. Many children then find this pathway for themselves—as with Jasper—though in Chapter 6 we discuss the emergence of institutional alternatives to school that seek to support children's connected learning, including DigiCamp.

Far from individualistic—despite the misunderstanding of adults such as Jasper's mother, who don't understand why children spend so long alone in

---

[27] Ito et al. (2010, pp. 75–76).
[28] Ito et al. (2008, p. 28).

their room on their computers—"geeks" are dedicated to "producing know-ledge to contribute to the knowledge network," thereby "developing an identity and pride as an expert."[29] For sure, connected learning need not be digital, but both Josh and, especially, Jasper illustrate how well the digital environment supports geeking out in ways that produce value recognized at school and for the future. Other domains of interest-driven learning might include sports or music, as we explored in an earlier project, *The Class*. But insofar as niche interests are codeveloped with "fellow experts in far-flung networks," as Ito and colleagues put it,[30] it makes sense that digital technologies would afford children particular opportunities to connect with others.

How parents make sense of "geeking out"

From the parents' perspective, however, not all are ready or able to match Dani's enthusiastic support, in part due to the power of the pervasive (anti-) screen time discourse discussed in Chapter 2. Indeed, for some parents, their children's tech interests were a source of family conflict—with parents resisting rather than embracing. For many, they occasioned considerable anxiety about the future. For instance, it was something of a shock, after talking to Jasper upstairs in his elaborately equipped computer room, to go down and interview his mother. Natasha, who was recently widowed, immediately launched into an account of Jasper as "obsessed" saying "If I was to let him he'd be on there all day, all night." Natasha's ambivalence is shared by many parents. She worried that her child was wasting his time and was unhappy that he spent so much time upstairs and away from her, yet she had invested in the means for him to pursue his interests—in her case, buying a lot of expensive hardware and software, as well as the expensive web development class at DigiCamp. We asked her the critical questions: Is he happy? Are his school grades good? Does he have friends? She answered "yes" reluctantly, conceding that he also did ice hockey, art, and trampolining, and "is a very social creature." But when we asked, "How much of Jasper's world do you understand and enjoy?," her answer was plaintive:

---

[29] Ito et al. (2008, p. 29).
[30] Ito et al. (2008, p. 29).

I don't enjoy any of it pretty much. And I don't understand most of it. But I, sort of, want to understand what it is that he's posting on YouTube. We had a nice long big chat about what he can say. . . . I explained to him why, what my worries were and, you know, how these images can be used and misused and how once out there they're out there and so on. But I don't actually know and I don't check on him.

Despite managing significant professional responsibilities at work as an architect, she told us, of Jasper's activities, "I feel overwhelmed occasionally. I just think, how do I handle this?" Part of the anxiety was the challenge of the digital age, but part went deeper: the absent father was an ever-imagined presence—for Jasper, someone who shared his digital interests, and for Natasha, someone no longer able to support her parenting and no longer able to provide oversight for Jasper's digital interests.

Natasha's worries about the present gained added intensity from the implications for the future:

When he tells me, "I want to be a professional gamer," my heart just sinks. And I absolutely hate the idea of it, absolutely hate it, you know . . . because I just think it's a not worthwhile profession. And that's the truth, true and honest answer. . . . On the other hand, if it's going to make him happy, I keep on saying to myself, really all we want for our children are to be happy and healthy, you know.

The unspoken problem with the prospect of being happy as a gamer stems from a parenting culture out of step with digital culture. This may be because, even though the prospect of digital jobs has been co-opted by government and industry to a degree that did not occur for many previous ambitions, for instance of becoming a professional footballer or dancer, the pathway to success remains opaque (and, arguably, just as difficult). Certainly Natasha had not managed to override her fears of the imagined future by focusing on Jasper's actual strengths. Nor did she turn her conflictual negotiations over purpose or safety or cost into an active strategy of resistance.

In another comfortably off family, Sirash Rajan[31] had also enabled his geeky 12-year-old to attend DigiCamp, as well as learning filmmaking, acting, coding, app development, and more. As he put it:

[31] Family 58.

You can see how much life has changed in the last 20 years, so it doesn't take a genius to figure out what's going to happen in the next 20 years.

Complaining that "the way we teach is very industrial age. We're living in the information age and we're still using notebooks, handwriting," Sirash acknowledged that he lacked an understanding of his daughter Pranita's interests, but "we did encourage it because I was fed up being technophobic and I wanted her not to have that disability, as I regard it." He was certain that digital expertise will be vital for the future, but he endorsed little of the geek culture discussed earlier. Rather, he had appropriated Pranita's interests within the mainstream government discourse of the digital skills agenda, focused on gaining individual skills and an entrepreneurial mindset to succeed in a competitive context:

> She decided to do a mobile app [at school].... It was about career choices.... So she made a mobile app through AppShed or something; it was using what she learnt in DigiCamp and that was really well received. She got a distinction and that's just one example that she did and she's done a lot of creative projects.... [Since then] she hasn't done anything boring basically, if I can say that. She's always been quite innovative.

Sirash celebrated with Pranita when her YouTube channel helped launch her acting career (she appeared in a short film that did well on the festival circuit):

> YouTube was taking off and we were watching more YouTube than TV. And I thought . . . you know what I'd love? It would be really good to get her started at a young age. So we encouraged it and she loved it, of course.

The account that follows reveals a complex dynamic through which, on the one hand, Sirash encouraged, facilitated, and guided Pranita's online creativity while, on the other, she led, created, and taught him how the digital environment could be harnessed to meet her purposes:

> In less than a few hours she had created a brand name, a logo, and a YouTube channel.... I don't know how *Minecraft* works . . . but they [Pranita and her similarly *Minecraft*-crazy friend] apparently have videos and instructional

videos, or whatever, which they want to upload and they think they're going to get a lot of hits apparently.

Talking of "nurturing her entrepreneurial spirit," Sirash's approach to Pranita revealed his own worldview—of society, of his own life (with his day job as a dentist), and of his daughter's future:

> Correct me if I'm wrong, but nobody would choose to work nine-to-five, Monday to Friday, for other people if they had a choice. . . . Most people choose security over adventure and that's just a sad fact of life. . . . I feel very boxed in by a choice I made at 18 when I didn't know what I wanted in life. So now I would not want that for my child, no, no way.

Here, in some respects, is connected learning in action—Pranita's interest-driven learning, supported by sustained parental brokering of learning opportunities across formal and nonformal settings, resulting in the combination of innovation and creativity that gains academic recognition. Peer support is also part of the story. Pranita and a friend worked together, turning to the larger vlogger community for guidance as needed. But any deeper embedding in a geek culture of shared expertise was lacking. So too was the social justice ethos important for connected learning.[32] Sirash's talk was more competitive: "If technology's changing, I want her to be on top of it."

Arguably, without the collaborative practices and values of connected learning, interest-driven activities can be appropriated within a competitive framework more in tune with the wider policy and commercial context. This means leaving behind any association with the trial-and-error tinkering processes or the antiauthoritarian values of geek culture. In Sirash's case, then, embracing technology meant something different from its meaning for Dani. In few, if any, families did we find a wholehearted embrace of an imagined digital future grounded in collaborative, creative, sub for or inclusive values.

The case of parent bloggers

Leaving behind the polarized myth of "child as digital native" versus "parent as digital immigrant," research shows that parents have increasing digital

---

[32] Blum-Ross & Livingstone (2016b).

expertise, often gained through work or through pursuing their own interests.[33] This influences how they variously balance the risks and opportunities associated with their children's digital activities, also opening up new forms of the mediated family, as we saw in previous chapters.[34] At the time of our research, parent blogging had gained public visibility (which it later lost—ceding ground to newer forms of "influencer" parents like vloggers and "Insta-mums") . This demonstrated parents' digital interests and facilitated new kinds of remunerated labor but also raised new public anxieties about parents sharing images of their children online and, in some cases, "monetizing" those images.[35] To explore how parents, themselves born into the digital age, are now taking up these opportunities, we recruited some bloggers for our research by visiting parent blogging conferences and contacting parents via popular blogging networks.[36]

To our surprise, we found few such parents who had, like Dani, sought solidarity by drawing their children into their own digital interests. Rather, they sought to construct symbolic boundaries within the home, by which their own digital activities—some more "geeky" than others—were kept separate from their children. In relation to their children's digital activities, they seemed as much, if not more, wedded to the idea that good parenting means restricting screen time, and indeed that digital activities were the domain of the parent—not to be shared with the child.

This combination of parents embracing technology while resisting their children's digital activities occasioned some problematic family dynamics. Recalling the child's plaintive exhortation to the parent to "look long" in Chapter 2, we noted many cases of the parent rather than the child being accused of absenting themselves, spending too long staring at the computer or phone, or being hypocritical in controlling their children's technology use. While blogging parents are exceptions to the norm, they illustrate the tensions visible in many families now that—like their children—parents are increasingly absorbed by the digital world.[37]

There is a strong gender dimension at play here, for although we did interview a couple of "dad bloggers," most bloggers were mothers of small children. It seems likely that, as for the teenager held at home in a city of unsafe public places, so too for these mothers often stuck at home does technology provide a supportive community and access to the wider society.

[33] Blum-Ross & Livingstone (2017).
[34] Livingstone et al. (2017).
[35] Bessant (2018).
[36] Blum-Ross & Livingstone (2017).
[37] Radesky et al. (2016).

The popular press's castigation of parents for supposedly preferring their phone to their toddler, for "sharenting," and, in some cases, for gaining financially from their blogging can, similarly take its place in a long history of mother-shaming. All this adds to parents'—especially mothers'—complex balancing of personal pride and opportunity with concern for and about children's digital activities. But as we discussed with "mum blogger" Melissa Bell, who (like Nicole Saunders[38] in Chapter 2) had recently launched a new career in social media management, blogging had brought real advantages:

> I've learnt loads of things, on the technical side of things, like code, and, made some really nice friends. My photography skills have improved. It's really like having your own magazine and you're the editor of it, and getting paid to do it without anyone telling you what to do. It's great, and it fits in around the children.

Here too we see the elements of connected learning: interest led, creative, with learning self-paced through trial and error, as part of a supportive community, and recognized in the wider world (now, through gaining an income rather than, as for children, in academic terms). Yet Melissa expressed a sense of "terror" when thinking about children using technology in the future, having felt firsthand the addictive pull of the blogging world:

> It's ironic, considering my job and stuff I do now is so technology focused, but actually, I'm very against small children [using technology]. . . . I just think, let them be children. I think it can be good. I mean, the iPad, he liked to watch YouTube videos, sometimes, of trains on it, you know, so that's sometimes a bit of a treat.

Indeed, Melissa was conflicted, talking of technology providing the jobs of the future ("we're growing up in a technological world"), glad that she herself was beginning to make money from her blogging, yet worried that "it can take away their childhoods" and "afraid for my grandchildren" as "it makes the world not a very innocent place for children." Since her being at home with the children and an uncertain income put pressure on her husband's earnings, she also "feels the fear that if I haven't blogged for a bit, my

---

[38] Family 37.

ranking's going to go down," reflecting the individualized risk and, as Angela McRobbie makes clear, the often-gendered experience of the precarious creative worker.[39] Yet Melissa loved belonging to a generally supportive (though sometimes competitive) community, helping her overcome the isolation of parenting and the perception of bloggers as antisocial.

Consonant with the pathway from messing around to geeking out described by Ito and colleagues, several parent bloggers told us how they began with various tinkering activities before gaining sufficient expertise to embrace the identity and find ways to contribute to, as well as draw from, the parent blogging community. This was not always a planned process. Some parents had an early post "go viral," launching them into the spotlight and establishing their success earlier than anticipated. For some the push factor— needing to "use their brain" as a stay-at-home mum, to carve out some space for agency independently of their parent status, or to gain peer support when isolated at home with a child who doesn't sleep or with special educational needs—was more significant than the specific appeal of becoming a blogger. But the benefits for their family—new clothes or toys (often given by companies free in exchange for promotion on the blog), feeling more confident and supported, a contribution to the family income—also counted.[40] Yet belonging to a community brings its own pressures, as Melissa explained:

> You only have to see or hear things other bloggers have written, the ones which aren't so confident, and they say, oh, you know, everyone seems to be having this perfect life, where it makes your parenting skills feel rubbish when you're seeing people with this amazing home, or these, like, amazing children, and experiences, and I think it's not good for your soul, I really don't.

And yet, for the benefits of confidence and competence, both arguably necessary "currencies" to succeed in the world of blogging, she added: "I'd be more than happy for the children to start a blog if it was supervised. Yes, I think it can be great." Three-year-old Ella had already learned that mummy did "everything" on her laptop, yet four-year-old Milo had been having tantrums over YouTube, "so it's now not working." Here again is the tension—the digital world brings heightened opportunities, but it demands parental

---

[39] McRobbie (2015).
[40] Blum-Ross & Livingstone (2017).

restrictions too. Yet when Melissa looked back at her own childhood she relaxed, recalling:

> My mum didn't really monitor it at all. I'd often, during the day, when I was around, have the telly on in the background, but again, I would be playing and doing, you know, like, building my Lego whilst it was on. And, you know, and I used to read loads; I was a big reader, so maybe it didn't bother my mum as much. But, yes, she certainly didn't care, so I almost don't know why I care so much. I think possibly because we've got so much information now, about screen time is bad, or just stuff pumped at us; you sort of feel guilty if you let them have too much.

Long-time blogger Jack[41] was trying to resolve these dilemmas by deploying his digital skills proactively to manage his children's first steps on the path to a digital future—for example, by opening email and Facebook accounts for his children aged seven, five, and three so that when they come to need them (not yet!) he will have the passwords and "a light hand on the tiller." For now, though he appreciated that "they're basically very tech-savvy," he was limiting their time on the family tablets, computers, and TV. Talking of the older two, he was ambivalent about how the digital future puts pressure on the present, and about his capacity to manage this:

> Both of them learned to use my iPhone at pretty much the same time they learned to walk. I find it sometimes scary how, and I'm conscious about the fact that they're in a world where all this stuff matters to them and I'm reasonably, I'm fairly technical, but I'm also conscious of the fact that they're assimilating so fast I'm now getting to the point where I'm finding it a little bit more difficult to change my ways. And that creates a challenge for me in terms of as they get older, not monitoring, but being aware of what they're doing and almost like trying to keep up with them.

Although these parents reveled in their own digital interests, they carefully balanced the digital interests—and in some cases growing autonomy—of their children. Dad-blogger Harvey Simon[42] had experienced this firsthand, when six-year-old son Archie had started objecting to Harvey taking

---

[41] Family 50.
[42] Family 49.

so many photos on family outings to populate the home-schooling family's blog. Unbeknownst to Harvey, Archie got his revenge by taking an unflattering picture of Harvey and sharing it to Harvey's Instagram without his consent. Somewhat reluctantly, then, Harvey had to learn to share his geeky interests with Archie by begrudgingly involving him in deciding, as Harvey described, "what he wants me to write."[43]

Therefore, even among families that had most strongly embraced digital technologies, judicious efforts to manage and resist problems were part of the daily repertoire of practices and sometimes presented unique problems that even technologically savvy parents had to find ways to fix. Harvey Simon found that resolving his specific digital dilemma had a nondigital component—talking to and involving his son in decision making. Dani Sykes, the digital enthusiast who set her sons complex building challenges in *Minecraft*, had created a system where her sons had to ask permission to add a friend and use her password to log in so that she could keep an eye on what they were doing. Dani made sure that when Josh poked fun at the "online safety chat at school," the messages still hit home, "drumming that into him every single time." So while Dani had done everything she could to support Josh, who had "been online ever since he's been young," her embrace did not mean she did not try to balance too.

Inequalities in geek culture

Be nice to nerds. You may end up working for them. We all could.

—Charles J. Sykes

This much-quoted prediction, widely misattributed to Bill Gates, captures a view among families who embrace digital technologies that once-niche or even disparaged knowledge brings valued status, with geeking out marking a route to a successful future that many will and should follow. As Dani put it:

---

[43] We discuss the issue of "sharenting" and how parents negotiate tensions around what is theirs to share (or not) in Blum-Ross & Livingstone (2017).

I'm excited about the digital future. . . . I think work's probably going to become a lot more fluid. . . . But, I think coding is going to fast become a bit
like having Microsoft Office skills.

Significant questions arise as to who will manage to gain this knowledge,
and for whom it will prove advantageous. In other words, if more follow a
digital pathway, what inequalities of gender, ethnicity, generation, and class
will influence who benefits? Proposals to reform education by learning from
alternative pedagogies—including connected learning—although generally
motivated by social justice ambitions, have been criticized for romanticizing
the self-taught and self-motivated "geek" without sufficient attention to the
often-classed resources required to facilitate the transition from hanging
out to messing around to geeking out.[44] The parents of geeky children, we
have shown, find themselves investing heavily in their children's self-chosen
interests, while, as Coleman observes, the weapons of the geek are traditionally associated with highly educated White men. Sarah Banet-Weiser notes
that the more that geek culture gains mainstream status, the more, not less,
likely it is that girls and women will find themselves sidelined.[45] Put simply,
promoting geek culture more widely—say, through schools or government policy, or in the popular media—is likely to extend inequality unless
countermeasures are taken. Not only do poorer families lack the resources
to support and sustain their geeky interests—as parents and/or children—
but also few poorer families can afford to take deliberate risks with their
children's learning,[46] and there's no doubt this route to a successful future is
yet to be securely established.

We do not, however, draw straightforward conclusions regarding social
class, for the reasons explained in the previous chapter. Some of the families
discussed in this chapter as "geeky" can be characterized as middle class—
Pranita's, for sure, and also Melissa and Jack, the bloggers. Dani, Jen, and
Natasha were all educated women, and Natasha had a professional job, but
they were also single parents, which diminished their financial resources and
perhaps added to their determination to provide whatever their children may
need. Nonetheless, while in Chapter 3 we identified a range of ways in which

[44] Ames (2019), Livingstone & Sefton-Green (2016). Other critics include Loveless & Williamson
(2013); Pelletier, Burn, & Buckingham (2010).
[45] G. Coleman (2017); Banet-Weiser (2018). See also Lange (2014); Warschauer & Matuchniak
(2010).
[46] Livingstone & Sefton-Green (2016).

poorer families tried hard to provide their children with digital as well as other opportunities, it appears that those families were not particularly geeky, at least in our fieldwork. Embracing the digital is, we conclude, a relatively privileged phenomenon, requiring considerable educational and some economic capital and, as suggested earlier, also requiring the confidence to take a risk with the future.

A few of the parents in our fieldwork, however, felt they had little choice but to embrace the digital opportunities on offer. Specifically, for some families struggling with their children's special needs, the label of "geek" or "nerd" offered a positive account of otherwise problematic characteristics such as obsessive behavior or social struggles (as we discuss further in Chapter 5). Susan Scott,[47] the wealthy American mother who we met in Chapter 2, hoped that her youngest son, Sean, who had attention deficit hyperactivity disorder, might embrace this identity to "realize that nerds are cool, right? I mean I'm a nerd, my husband's a nerd, his brothers are nerds. . . . Nerds are awesome." By co-opting this oft-disparaged label for its positive characteristics, Susan asserted a positive identity for her son, and one that resonates with the digital age. Sandra and Jonno Stubbs[48] were delighted when, in recognition of their low-income status, they were awarded a scholarship at DigiCamp for Lucas (age nine), who was on the autism spectrum:

SANDRA: For us or for Lucas's understanding of a geek, it's a good word, and it's something positive, it's somebody who cares about their work, who understands that hard work will get the results and that you need to apply yourself. He's only just getting this.

JONNO: Just getting that. Well, it's going to be his career as well, I think that's, you know, kind of being a geek is what's going to earn him money and a livelihood, because if he didn't have the world of computers to go into . . .

SANDRA: He would have nothing.

JONNO: Well, I wonder where he would go, to be honest.

SANDRA: There's nowhere for him to fit.

JONNO: Computers are kind of his way out and his way ahead in life, because he's so good at maths, and he's so good with computers, that is going to be his saving grace.

---

[47] Family 59.
[48] Family 62.

Fully aware of how hard it was to catch Lucas's interest but recognizing that once interested in something he'd pursue it passionately, even obsessively, Sandra and Jonno were ready to try anything—father and son spent a lot of time gaming together, another activity commonly linked to geekiness (and, more contentiously, to learning[49]). Indeed, Sandra and Jonno *needed* Lucas to be a geek, for they could imagine no other future for him.

Finally, as regards gender inequalities, the situation is complex. Insofar as digital expertise is concentrated among—or, at least, particularly claimed by—men and boys, it is noteworthy that our fieldwork included Pranita and Charlotte as well as Jasper and Josh. But there is no doubt: we had many more boys to choose from for our fieldwork, but only a few girls who had embraced a geeky identity. For some parents of these girls, it was important deliberately to counter gender stereotyping. For instance, Anne Reynolds,[50] now a company director, recalled how at one of her early jobs,

> our company had a network and I didn't know how to turn it on and use it at all. I was humiliated by my office mates, two young men who'd been there for some time who thought it would be really funny to, like, you know, laugh at me, and they wouldn't help me. And in the end I managed to figure it out, but, you know, it's part of the future.

It's no accident that we'll meet Anne's 12-year-old daughter, Esme, taking a rapid prototyping class at DigiCamp, in Chapter 6. As Anne said: "I think it's empowering, and if she chooses to pursue that, I think that's absolutely wonderful."

We discussed the question of gender explicitly with Giovanna (age 13),[51] after watching her spend several Saturdays in a roomful of boys at LYA, usually with her headphones on to blot everyone out as she concentrated on her work:

SONIA: One reason I wanted to talk to you was I thought maybe there aren't very many girls in digital animation and video production.
GIOVANNA: Yes, only one.
SONIA: Okay, you really are the only one. Why do you think that is?

---

[49] Ito et al. (2010); Jenkins, Ito, & boyd (2016).
[50] Family 53.
[51] Family 15.

GIOVANNA: I don't know. I think there was one last year and one the year before, but they, kind of, go off. . . . The Photoshops are, like, between superheroes and blah, there's not a lot of girly stuff to Photoshop, but I don't think it's supposed to matter, because you can just Photoshop, like, animals and stuff.

SONIA: So it's something about the images that they pick? Because you could have a girl superhero, couldn't you?

GIOVANNA: Yes, but it's not, like, the type of thing, it's not, like, stereotypically a girly thing to do.

SONIA: Yes, but you don't look like a girl who cares about the stereotypes?

GIOVANNA: Yes, because I enjoy it so that's why I do it.

Giovanna expressed points often made in the academic literature—the examples (here, the superheroes) are tacitly gendered, as are the practices (not "a girly thing to do"), though she appreciated that the educator, Diana, was a Black British woman determined to model digital competence equally to boys and girls of all backgrounds.[52] But while Diana's effort was political, to play her small part in the wider effort to get more women into the film industry, or Giovanna, gender is—or should be—irrelevant. Contra Elin Kvande,[53] she didn't wish she were "one of the boys," saying, "it's not that I'm one of the guys, but it doesn't really matter." Thus, she tried to sidestep the seeming choice between embracing the digital and being a girl.

Whether she can sustain this through her teenage years we cannot know, but it did seem to us that some of the boys too embraced their "geekiness" as offering an escape from traditional gender roles. For instance, while Dani worried a bit that Josh did not "fit in," given that "there's still that stigma around geeks," Josh was disdainful:

Most people in my form . . . they think they're so cool and they've got, like, they've got 87 friends, and they just talk about football and rugby and sport; I wouldn't be able to fit in with any of that because I don't know about sports or rugby or anyone.

So although technological mastery itself is, in Ruth Oldenziel's words, imbued with a "masculine mystique,"[54] and although the digital learning spaces we

---

[52] Westman (2007).
[53] Kvande (1999).
[54] Oldenziel (1999); see also Kerr (2011).

visited were certainly more populated by boys than girls (see Chapter 6), we hesitate to conclude that geeky digital activities are straightforwardly gendered. Indeed, it seems possible that if boys invest too much in their geekiness they risk being "feminised and socially marginalised" by others.[55] The cases of both Giovanna and Josh suggest young people exploring the potential of creative digital identifies as an alternative to the binary gender roles broadly accepted by their classmates.

Are things changing? Patricia Lange argues, of girls "geeking out" as YouTube creators, that as the digital world extends its embrace and gains more recognized value, with gender on the "digital agenda" both at school and in the world of work, participation in geeky activities will widen and diversify.[56] However, as feminist scholarship on the history and culture of computing has observed, a long history of structural discrimination in the computing industry mitigates against simple hopes of improvement.[57]

Apart from instructor Diana—who one day asked the class to discuss why there are so few girls in the games industry and why there are so few games made for girls—we saw little attempt to politicize these issues explicitly either at home or in learning sites. For instance, although the increasing digital expertise of parents, especially mothers, might be expected to challenge stereotypes, even our more successful mum bloggers did not reflect critically on the conditions that led to their precarious incomes and a degree of isolation for example, inflexible workplaces or the lack of state support. Indeed, the fact that the mum bloggers chose *not* to claim the "geek" label reminds us that digital jobs are themselves gendered—with often female "influencers," seemingly valued more for their feminine craft skills and "style" than their digital skills (although surely, to be successful, these must also be substantial).[58] However, we heard little politicized discussion from them regarding the possibilities for improving their recognition or security in the technological workplace, although several bloggers were sensitized to the politics of making visible the formerly silenced experiences of mothering.

---

[55] Ward (2014).
[56] Lange (2014).
[57] Wajcman (2004); Kerr (2011); Miltner (2018); Banet-Weiser (2018).
[58] Luckman & Tomas (2018); L. K. Lopez (2009).

Conclusions

It seems that the state, industry, and popular media are combining forces to rehabilitate the long-stigmatized "geek." The widely felt policy imperative that children should learn to code—to be content producers, not just consumers, and to prepare themselves for jobs that are just emerging or haven't been invented yet—is leading many countries, including the United Kingdom, to pour public funding into refreshing, if not reinventing school for the digital age, as well as supporting out-of-school and online opportunities to learn digital skills, especially coding.[59] In addition to the incorporation of previously specialized computing knowledge such as coding into the UK national curriculum, a growing number of schools are creating makerspaces and code clubs or hosting "game jams" or hackathons.[60] The triumph of the socially awkward characters in films like *Revenge of the Nerds*, who use their proficiency to "get the girl," seems almost quaint in the face of today's claims that, with the advance of robotics, algorithms, and artificial intelligence, we had better *all* become "geeks" or lose our autonomy, as Matthew Fuller describes.[61] Or as Dani foretold, more optimistically, "the geeks will inherit the earth, you know."[62]

But is becoming a geek worth it? In the research literature, there appears to be little disagreement over the nature of geek learning and participation.[63] As advocated by the theory of connected learning,[64] the productive synergy between the affordances of the digital environment and interest-driven, trial-and-error collaborative learning could be beneficial for many, even if they stop short of the full-on identity commitment made by some of those discussed in this chapter. There is disagreement, however, about the politics of the geek. Whereas geeks have long been antiauthoritarian, critics of their current mainstreaming are concerned that their values are increasingly neoliberal. Fuller dubs this a modern "geek tragedy."[65]

---

[59] Department for Education (2018); Dredge (2014); Selwyn (2014); Royal Society (2017); B. Williamson et al. (2018).

[60] Makerspaces are spaces where participants meet to create different artifacts with the combination of digital and nondigital resources (Blum-Ross et al., 2020; Marsh et al., 2017).

[61] Fuller (2017).

[62] Mako Hill (2002); Robbins (2011); Roeder (2014).

[63] Fuller (2017); Gibeault (2016); Ito et al. (2010).

[64] Ito et al. (2010); Ito et al. (2013).

[65] Fuller (2017).

Ben Williamson argues that geeks are being co-opted by the very system they seek to escape:

> A "cultural resonance" has therefore been established between the culture of the designers of the Internet and the rise of a culture of networked individualism and creative audiences that finds its way into the minds of millions of Internet users. Networked individualism, with its focus on personal choice, projects, and self-entrepreneurial behaviour, is the globalized cultural expression of a set of Silicon Valley cyberlibertarian values.[66]

Some of the parents we interviewed embraced such a normative market logic—as did the educators at DigiCamp and other tech sites, as we explore in Chapter 6. While most families valued collaborative learning as part of their technological engagement, this neither ruled out embracing a competitive ethos nor extended far beyond their immediate circle to constitute a political commitment—although for some, digital technologies allowed them to engage a community of people facing similar life circumstances (as we will see in Chapter 5, for some parents of children with special educational needs).

Rather than opposing social justice and neoliberal value commitments, Lars Konzack sees tech geeks as forging an alternative to what he calls the "hippies" and "yuppies" that preceded them.[67] Thus, he tells a history of how the geek generation was born when Silicon Valley met 1960s hippy counterculture to shape the conditions under which the (micro, domestic) computer was constructed as a means of liberation. Concurring with Coleman's linking of geeks and privilege, he argues that "by using the Internet as if it was their own playground, they are in fact manifesting their cultural power and progress in society."[68] However, they do so not by being antiestablishment but, rather, by forging a hybrid ethos that stands apart from normative traditions on either the right or the left. Reflecting on the families we interviewed, we are inclined to agree with Konzack. Yes, the families we have discussed in this chapter had educated backgrounds, and though they varied in income, none was truly precarious. To support a geeky child takes a considerable commitment from parents, which not all are able to provide, and it is important to recognize

---

[66] B. Williamson (2013, p. 88).
[67] Foer (2017); Konzack (2006); Turner (2006).
[68] Konzack (2006, p. 4).

that many of the families who embrace geekiness, in one way or another, are able both to invest as required and to accommodate a degree of risk in terms of ultimate outcomes. Beyond this, we can hazard two linked generalizations.

First, we suggest that the emphasis in the families discussed in this chapter has been on the search for agency and recognition. Each of the children and adults we have dubbed "geeky" was committed to learning about and using technology for its intrinsic pleasures, for self-actualization, to gain expertise, and, sometimes, to share these pleasures and expertise with a community that offered recognition. We have analyzed their activities in terms of the mode of learning involved (akin to that proposed by connected learning theory), the forms of relationship pursued (egalitarian, collaborative, peer based), and the identities thereby constructed. Of course, the families discussed in this chapter were different from each other in many ways, but they had each made a considerable and effortful commitment to their chosen way of life. Taking on a geeky identity is not a casual or occasional activity, but it absorbs the whole way of life. The result, as we have learned from our fieldwork, is a strong sense of motivation and direction, considerable confidence in one's capacity and expertise, and active solidarity with others who share one's interests.

Second, embracing the identity and the lifestyle of the self-proclaimed geek is a high-risk strategy, creating a sense of being apart from the majority of one's peers. So while they may have benefited from particular connections in informal learning settings or through niche online networks, the "geeks" we interviewed also experienced problematic disconnections in relation to school learning or wider social acceptance. Some of the families' experiences also hint at some sadness, and a measure of defiance too, in relation to their outsider status. Nor can one reassure parents such as Natasha who—when they looked at their child in the here and now, "obsessed" with what's on the screen—worry the costs will outweigh any future success. However, in families where a parent was frustrated or where a child seemed not to "fit in," the identity of the geek seemed to offer a solution, especially now that this identity is increasingly recognized and valued by mainstream society.

It is intriguing that many of those who embraced technologies in our fieldwork were motivated in part by looking for a sphere of positive engagement to overcome or compensate for some very real offline problems. As we have mentioned, Josh's parents were recently divorced, Jasper's father had died two years ago, Pranita's mother had a terminal illness, Charlotte had multiple special needs, and Melissa felt isolated as a young parent at home. For some, personal beliefs seemed to be the main motivation. Giovanna's mother, Luisa, had—rather dramatically—taken her away from her father, wealthy home, and country of origin to live in cramped circumstances in order to benefit from new opportunities in London, telling us: "I think this is the future; I wanted my children to be prepared for the future."[69]

Our fieldwork does not permit us to generalize beyond these individuals. But it seems not far-fetched to suggest that personal choice, absorbing projects, and a growing expertise shared with others has considerable appeal. Equally, it seems that, as each had had reason to find the offline world risky. This made the considerable investment twinned with a highly uncertain payoff associated with choosing a geeky path to a digital future may have seemed relatively less risky. And there is the possible advantage of feeling in tune with a tech-optimistic public discourse, of knowing that one is doing all that can be done to prepare for the imagined digital future.

As regards family dynamics, we have found that where the parents and child(ren) *both* embraced technology by making significant identity commitments, this could enable a constructive discourse among equals in which each could value and learn from the other, thereby avoiding some of the conflict around tech that bedevils families where digital interests or expertise are not shared. We can even interpret this as implementing a particular version of Giddens's democratic family,[70] with the parent–child relationship partly reconfigured away from the exercise of authority toward a peer relationship centered on mutual learning and shared pleasures. But even in these families, parents did not entirely relinquish their authority: the interview with Dani was punctuated by moments of slight frustration at Josh's criticism of her lack of knowledge as well as parental reprimands when he took the geeky talk too far; we saw a similar dynamic with Jen and Charlotte, with Jen shifting between the roles of peer, mentor, and parental authority as she thought necessary.

However, when only one of the parents or children identified as a "geek," this could generate significant discord, as we saw with Natasha and Jasper, or to a lesser but perhaps growing extent with Melissa and Milo. Geeky children's absorption in their digital practices was worrying to parents who

---

[69] This resulted in some family tensions. Luisa told us that Giovanna "is going to be into all movies . . . because have you ever seen her drawing? She has fantastic. . . ." But Giovanna told us she hoped to be a scientist, having little interest in her mother's creative passions. Nonetheless, she too saw the potential benefit of learning digital skills in her animation class, whatever her future might hold.

[70] Giddens (1991).

didn't understand the pleasures but who felt the burden of society's warning that they should limit screen time. Society's warning about screen time even influenced some geeky parents who, while themselves digitally skilled and, thus, aware of possible benefits, nonetheless restricted their children's digital activities.

In this chapter we have argued that "geek" families are often self-motivated and confidently self-reliant learners who enjoy learning for its own sake, benefiting from a conception of learning as iterative and reflexive, on the one hand, and collaboratively peer supported, on the other. But all this takes considerable resources and commitment, and the identity of the geek can occasion tensions both within the family and with others beyond it—notably with peers and teachers. Perhaps for these reasons, they tread a path that few follow, despite growing public approval, for reasons that concern both the causes (often very personal) and consequences (riskily unknown) of being a "geek."

5

(Dis)abilities

When Lucas Stubbs,[1] aged nine, got a scholarship to attend a summer session at DigiCamp, his parents, Sandra and Jonno, told us they'd felt like they'd won the lottery. Although for many families who attended DigiCamp, like the Thiebaults,[2] whom we met in Chapter 3, the £500 tuition fee was no problem, without this scholarship the Stubbs "never could have afforded" it.[3] Sitting in their dilapidated 1960s house on a South London council estate, surrounded by pictures of their extended, multicultural family, Sandra and Jonno poured out their hopes and fears for Lucas.[4] They described him as a "unique little boy" who "loves maths, has been playing chess since five years old, and is obsessed with computers, football, and Pokémon." In recent years he'd started to seem out of sync with his peers—fixated on video games, withdrawing socially or overly invested in particular friends, pestering them until they moved on. His parents characterized Lucas himself as "nonplussed" about his increasing social isolation, but Sandra felt "really bothered by it" and so Sandra and Jonno had him evaluated by a learning specialist. By the time he enrolled in DigiCamp, it had been about a year since Lucas was diagnosed with autism spectrum disorder, and Sandra and Jonno were still making sense of this diagnosis, sometimes referring to him as having "high-functioning ASD," sometimes as having "Asperger's" (which Sandra thought "sounds nicer").[5]

Sandra, who ran a small business doing graphic design and entertainment at children's parties (she ambled into the interview wearing bright pink lipstick and a furry cat tail), hoped that DigiCamp might help Lucas figure out

[1] Family 62.
[2] Family 57.
[3] Founder Susanna had worked hard to provide scholarships, finding corporate sponsors to subsidize places for low-income students.
[4] The house was owned by Sandra's grandparents, who had raised her when her own parents fell on hard times.
[5] Terms such as "Asperger's" and "high-functioning autism" are contested for various reasons, but perhaps the most pressing issue is how the different labels have profound implications for the public services offered to families and individuals who have been diagnosed. For example, children diagnosed with autism generally receive much more school support than children with Asperger's disorder, who typically go without the help they need (Sheffer, 2018).

Parenting for a Digital Future. Sonia Livingstone and Alicia Blum-Ross, Oxford University Press (2020). © Oxford University Press.
DOI: 10.1093/oso/9780190874698.001.0001

how to move from playing video games into being a games designer. Jonno (who described himself as "working-class Northern through and through") felt this could be "the first step, could be what really gets him on the run towards doing this in his life." Lucas already knew a bit about coding, having learned Scratch in his school's code club, and he had worked with a tutor that Sandra found over Skype (along with joining a local football league and a drama class, again supported by a scholarship, all forms of "concerted cultivation" as theorized in Chapter 3). Although the family struggled for money—Jonno was a trained nurse but was at the time unemployed—they decided these costs were worth it because when they had received the autism diagnosis Lucas's headmistress had encouraged them by saying that if they could "keep Lucas on track, you will have a lovely little computer games designer who, you know, is happy in his life."

When Sandra discovered DigiCamp, it seemed to offer a way to step up their efforts. DigiCamp was based at an elite London university with tutors with industry experience, all of which Sandra felt was deeply "inspiring" for Lucas. She showed us a picture of Lucas on his first day, grinning while wearing his DigiCamp lanyard and hoodie and holding a Starbucks cup with his name scrawled on it (hot chocolate inside), looking to all intents and purposes like a miniature version of a start-up "geek" character from a show like *Silicon Valley*—although unlike the majority of the characters, given Lucas identifies as Black.[6] Sandra described how he'd stayed after class to look at the games the tutor himself had made, and how that night he'd come home and announced, "I'm really proud of myself."

Yet Sandra and Jonno's celebration of Lucas's "geekiness" was tinged with some desperation, as noted in Chapter 4. Jonno saw computers, wistfully yet not without mixed feelings, as Lucas's "way ahead in life, his saving grace." The parents embraced technology as key to Lucas's future, but this did not exempt them from challenges in the present. Sandra noted that when playing games Lucas had "endless amounts of fun and can join in . . . in that environment he's just normal" but said there were "unbelievable tantrums" when his parents tried to get him to turn off, as he would "play it to all detriment of toilet needs, drinking needs, anything needs, he may have a blinding headache and he won't notice until he comes off." Whether his "obsession" was attributable to his autism or not was hard for the parents to say, given how

---

[6] *Silicon Valley* is an American sitcom about a computer programmer and his "geeky" friends, who try to capitalize on the Silicon Valley start-up market (*Silicon Valley*, 2018).

mysterious his diagnosis still seemed to them. They were also unsure how much to talk to Lucas about autism, as Jonno described:

> I don't want him thinking he's abnormal or anything like that, because it's not that. . . . Nobody is abnormal anyway, we're all unique, but the kind of illness it is really, it kind of allows kids to have such gifted areas, have such benefits from that particular illness as well as drawbacks.

Sandra and Jonno had thus begun to develop a language shared by many other families we interviewed, in which Lucas's autism was as much of a "gift" as it was an "illness." When they considered Lucas's skills and his challenges, digital technologies promised great potential despite the very real challenges, and so were embraced as a way to channel his "gift" toward future employability, social connections, and happiness. These hopes were keenly felt even though Lucas was only nine.

Defining disability

In this book, we have sought to group families who share similarities while also acknowledging the significant differences among them. This is tricky in this chapter insofar as labels like "disabled" or "special educational needs" can be used to point to a monolithic "other" or outsider group to be *treated* (the medical model), *pitied* (the charity model), or *inspired by* (the noble hero model). On the other hand, labels help us understand similarities within the diversity of family experience, and we also saw how labels and diagnoses unlocked practical, financial, and emotional support for families.[7] To avoid essentializing families of children with special educational needs (SEN) and disabilities, we have included a diversity of families throughout the book where they match the relevant topic, as well as according them focal attention in this chapter. We should note, however, that our focus is on the *parents* of children with disabilities rather than on those children directly. While children with disabilities undoubtedly lack sufficient attention in academic work, so too do their parents, with parents also often overlooked in official discourse and in the design of services that are meant to help them and their children.[8] By focusing on parents rather than children,

---

[7] Briant, Watson, & Philo (2013); Kapp et al. (2012); Shakespeare (2010).

[8] For work on the perspectives of children and young people with disabilities see Fleischmann & Fleischmann (2012); Higashida (2013); Resch et al. (2010). We acknowledge that parents may focus more on a child's impairment than the child may feel is warranted.

however, we acknowledge that this may mean a more disproportionate focus on particular diagnoses or disabilities than a child might feel is warranted.

The terms "*disability*," "*disabled*," and "special educational needs" remain contested for implying variations from a presumed "norm." Popular definitions center on "disadvantage, deficiency, especially a physical or mental impairment that restricts normal achievement, something that hinders or incapacitates."[9] Critiques of this view and the dominant medical model that underpins reject how it defines people by what they purportedly lack, making disability an individual "problem" rather than grasping the wider social and relational context. By contrast, the social model of disability argues, in disability and media scholars Elizabeth Ellcessor and Bill Kirkpatrick's words, that the "social, physical, economic and ideological conditions of disability and able-bodiedness" are constructed.[10] So, rather than asserting that it is the individual who *has* the disability, the social model asserts that, in failing to accommodate a range of experiences, society *disables* people who do not fit within an anticipated or normative range of expectations. Thus it refocuses attention away from the person with an "impairment" toward the institutions that fail to create conditions in which everyone, inclusively defined, can access opportunities to participate.[11]

While acknowledging the value of the social model in disrupting the presumed equivalence between disability and deficit, others have noted that focusing on social constructions risks underplaying the ways in which disability is "complexly embodied" in ways emergent from the interplay between the body and the social context.[12] As described later, many parents we

---

[9] Linton (2006, p. 162). See also Ellcessor & Kirkpatrick (2017); Tirraoro (2015).

[10] Ellcessor & Kirkpatrick (2017, p. 5). The disability rights movement, from which the social model of disability emerged, rightfully privileges the perspectives and experiences of disabled people, who have too often been silenced in decisions about their lives—this is doubly so for children and young people with disabilities (Alper, 2017; Oliver & Barnes, 2012).

[11] Osteen (2008, p. 3). The use of the term "disabled young people" is common in writings on the social model of disability. However, we have used "people first" language, as in "young people with disabilities," unless the family identified otherwise. Some people we interviewed described themselves by their impairment (e.g., Iris, later, calls herself an "Aspie"). Some argue that "people first" language decenters the social realities of disability by making disability something that an individual "just happens to have" (Alper, 2017; J. D. Brown & Bobkowski, 2011; Fleischmann & Fleischmann, 2012; Titchkosky, 2001). The social model of disability is vital in challenging the limited ways disabled people have been portrayed in the media (Ellis & Goggin, 2015).

[12] Alper et al. (2015). The "neurodiversity" movement rejects the goal of "normalization" (Siebers, 2008, p. 14; Thomas, 2013, p. 9), helping parents understand children as part of a spectrum of experience, tied to physical "hardwiring" and therefore not a result of their personal responsibility (Blum, 2015). Such brain talk or "cerebralization" tries to turn difference into a positive attribute (Kapp et al., 2012; Ortega, 2009)—although see Macvarish (2016) for a critique of the rise of "neuroparenting."

interviewed were attracted to the social model of disability for offering a language that supported their view of their child as not being *less than*, along with its critical lens on "mainstream" society's inability to provide the support they and their child needed. At the same time, they drew on the "medical model" because this is the language typically employed by support services, and parents were often preoccupied with juggling appointments with medical or learning specialists in ways designed to manage or mitigate the effects of their child's disability.

In Sandra and Jonno Stubbs's account we saw many of these contradictions playing out. They explicitly rejected the label "abnormal"[13] but, like many other families of children with "invisible disabilities,"[14] were immensely relieved when Lucas was diagnosed as that gave them access to much-valued (and expensive) resources at school and beyond.[15] Tending to Lucas's medical and social needs had become a preoccupation for both parents as Lucas entered his "tween" years with their sometimes fraught social interactions. While they were relieved that Lucas had "been statemented" (itself a popular but troubling phrase), Sandra and Jonno were fighting hard to ensure he got the resources he needed at a time in which the politics of "austerity Britain" had led to social services cuts that deeply impacted people with disabilities, especially youth, rolling back provisions that helped decrease social isolation and marginalization, including support at school.[16]

Although Sandra and Jonno had a good relationship with Lucas's school, other parents of children with disabilities that we interviewed felt themselves let down by "the system," and many had had to leave work to become full-time caregivers or home-school their children, as we explore later.[17] For all parents, identities are relational and co-constructed along with those of their child or children.[18] For parents of children with disabilities this is often described as more intimate, intensely emotional, and seemingly

---

[13] Lester & Paulus (2012).

[14] Blum (2015).

[15] In England, the term "special educational needs" (SEN) came to replace "handicapped" in the late 1960s (Gulliford & Upton, 1992), so that rather than categorizing children by an impairment or "handicap," they would be characterized by the "special educational needs" that impairments may give rise to.

[16] Goodley, Lawthom, & Runswick-Cole (2014). Merry Cross (2013) states, "by 2018 disabled people are set to lose an astonishing £28.3 billion worth of financial support" (p. 719). The National Audit Office (NAO, 2018) documents the rising need and reduced expenditure on local services during the second decade of this century.

[17] Kendall & Taylor (2014).

[18] Blum-Ross & Livingstone (2017); Gergen (2009).

unending—consider the embodied reality of the care parents provide, in some cases physically carrying teenage children, changing colostomy bags, or staying up all night with children whose impairments mean they sometimes cannot sleep. In short, for many parents, battles with institutions to obtain funding and thus secure present and future chances, were central to their experiences of parenting and to their relationships and identities.

Disabilities and technology

Digital technology are often seen as a liberating tool, offering the potential for people with disabilities, to communicate their needs and experiences, joys and frustrations. There are myriad studies exploring how "assistive" technology such as voice output communication aids or picture exchange communication systems or even emergent tech like artificial intelligence (AI) and robotics might help children and young people with disabilities, participate in their communities and families—although it is important to note that access to these technologies is not evenly or equitably spread. In addition to the technological properties of digital media, the particular affordances of online communication—for example, that it is *not* face to face and is often more amenable to asynchronous ways of interacting—can relieve some of the pressures that young people with autism feel in other forms of communication.[19]

But such techno-utopianism is problematic, for even with the growth of "accessible" technology and hopes of technology being an "equalizer" for people with disabilities, many remain excluded.[20] One reason we were interested in interviewing parents of children with special educational needs and disabilities was the particular ways in which some turn to digital technology to mitigate the social impacts of disability, even though the risk is that it also that it may exacerbate them. As media and communication scholar Meryl Alper has observed, new technologies, especially touchscreen devices, are often

---

[19] Alper (2017); Pinchevski & Peters (2016).
[20] There is a growing body of literature on the design and development of interactive technologies as well as robotics for rehabilitative and therapeutic use by children with disabilities (Alper, 2017). Robots are used as assistive technology for children with autism to help with communication and improved social behavior (Alper, 2018; Besio & Encarnação, 2018). However, digital media are not inherently "equalizers" for people with disabilities (Borchet, 1998). For example, a study of children with sensory impairments found both that they felt positive about digital technology such as tablets to support their learning and communication with their peers and that these same "technologies could sometimes make young people feel self-conscious and stigmatised" (Cranmer, 2017, p. 6).

promoted to parents as a way to help their children learn, express themselves, and thereby participate in the world.[21] Some digital discourses are straightforward and compensatory—talking books for people with visual impairment, for instance. Or as Esme Skelton's[22] parents told us, as we explore further in Chapter 6, Esme's use of such technologies as the spellchecker eased the impact of what her parents called her "mild dyslexia," so that at school she could "find things a bit easier on the computer and she can feel more confident."

Some of what we heard from parents was more complex, even creative in its imagining of new digitally mediated pathways. In Chapter 4 we met Jen Pearson and her daughters, Tegan and Charlotte,[23] whom she was home-schooling after difficult experiences in state schools—especially for Charlotte, who had mild to moderate dyspraxia and dyslexia. Jen's optimism about technology was founded on her theory, drawing on the research literature she avidly read, of a productive intersection between special educational needs, digital affordances, and the changing labor market:

JEN: I let her do a lot of *Minecraft*. She does a lot of that and it's really good for her, being dyslexic. She's very 3D aware. She already thinks in a 3D environment.

ALICIA: So what do you think is helpful about *Minecraft* to her?

JEN: Well, it's a, kind of, good start-off for things like CAD [computer-aided design] and a lot of other things, skills that are new, that children are going to—it's going to become more and more important in their work environment, and it's also very creative and she's very good at it, so it's great for her confidence.

Indeed, Jen believed the digital future would make dyslexia obsolete:

I've said to people, dyslexia is going to be a condition which only appeared for a short time in history. Because before we had writing, she probably would have been a leader, master, brilliant textile designer, anything. . . .

---

[21] Alper (2017). Myriad studies explore how "assistive" technologies like voice output communication aids and picture exchange communication systems (Faucett et al., 2017; Flores et al., 2012) or even emergent technologies like artificial intelligence and robotics (Besio & Encarnação, 2018) might help children and young people with disabilities, including autism, to participate in their communities and families, although noting again that access to these technologies is not evenly or fairly spread.
[22] Family 53.
[23] Family 2.

And at some point, we're just going to talk to computers. In this bit in between, she's got a learning difficulty which only exists now, really.

For other parents, technology introduced worrying risks to already-vulnerable children—our survey showed that parents of children with special educational needs and disabilities report more online harms for both themselves and their children. Technology is thus to be resisted or at least carefully balanced with other, nondigital, activities, as parents see it.[24] At London Youth Arts (LYA) we interviewed Robert Kostas,[25] father of 15-year-old Jake, whom we met in a digital apps class, and who had autism. Robert worried constantly that Jake had become "too addicted" to his iPad and this led to acrimonious arguments with his wife, Constance, a stay-at-home mother, because Robert felt she was too permissive, using the iPad as a "sort of babysitter, so she could get some peace and quiet . . . [but now] the horse has bolted and we're trying to close the stable door." Jake had always had trouble sleeping and now, at Robert's behest, they were trying to wean him off "screen time" by reducing his iPad time by 15 minutes each day.[26] On the other hand, Robert hoped that technology might be the key to Jake's future, a concern weighing on Robert's mind as Jake approached the age at which educational and state support would cease—something that Mia, SEN educator at LYA, called a "cliff edge." Like Sandra and Jonno Stubbs, Robert fantasized about

a career path that [Jake] could choose and his condition probably would be an asset . . . because he thinks outside the box . . . he's got brilliant attention to detail. So there must be instances in terms of jobs where that is really good.[27]

[24] Unsurprisingly, therefore, they also report doing more parental mediation in the majority of the activities we asked about, ranging from suggesting ways to use the internet safely to doing shared internet activities together with their children (Zhang & Livingstone, 2019).

[25] Family 3.

[26] Studies have documented sleep problems as a prominent feature affecting daily life for those with autism spectrum disorders (ASD) and their parents (Krakowiak et al., 2008; Richdale & Schreck, 2009).

[27] That Jake or Lucas might potentially enter the digital gaming industry is not so unreasonable, given that they live in London. The UK video game sector is the largest in Europe, contributing over £1 billion to the United Kingdom's overall gross domestic product. The gaming industry falls within the creative economy, which outperforms the rest of the UK economy and is expected to increase exports by 50% in the next five years, creating an estimated 600,000 new jobs (Department for Digital, Culture, Media & Sport, 2018).

Robert's framing of Jake's abilities (rather than disabilities) as his "asset" was echoed by Nina Robbins[28] and Jen Pearson, among others. These parents were naming, in their descriptions of their children, a way of thinking of them not as incapable but of having "special" skills and aptitudes that could match to opportunities. Technology-enabled or -focused jobs, especially for parents of children with autism, were often seen as offering this potential and therefore were aspired to, overriding other concerns about technology. In part, the intensity with which some parents clung to this vision speaks more about the narrow options that society presents as avenues for independence for people with disabilities than it does about technology itself.[29]

At our field sites we met families with children with a variety of impairments (mostly intellectual rather than physical), most often children with autism.[30] We found the parents of children with autism keen to discuss both the benefits and the harms that their children had experienced—or that they hoped or feared that they might experience. It seemed that these families often gravitated toward digital learning opportunities, focussing on the idea of a *digital* future as both welcome and worrisome. Often, these reflected a potent archetype in the popular (and professional) imagination that equates autism with technological proficiency. In writing about the mythology of the "computer boys," social historian Nathan Ensmenger describes the stereotype of the (male) engineer as

curt, antisocial, and more concerned with maintaining the integrity of the "system" than in being truly helpful to the end user. So recognized is this stereotype that a high degree of proficiency in computer programming has been linked with mild forms of Asperger's syndrome and autism—the so-called geek syndrome or engineer's disorder.[31]

[28] Family 65. The nature of such assets tends to remain unspoken, but parents seem variously to be thinking of the ability to concentrate, perhaps even obsessively, to focus with great accuracy and eye for detail, and to think in creative, non-standard ways.

[29] Disabled artist Sunny S. Taylor (2004) writes, "In actuality, the only reason that many people [people with disabilities] are a burden on their family and friends is that they have such limited options.... In our society it is not the impairment that is the only reason for dependence; it is our impaired system of social services" (para. 18).

[30] As described in the appendix, our approach to recruitment was purposive: we had identified certain thematic categories from our literature review that led us to seek out families who allowed for the exploration of particular lines of inquiry; we also recruited families who were diverse according to socioeconomic status, ethnicity, and age of child.

[31] Ensmenger (2010, p. 2); Jack (2014); Silberman (2001).

Thus, it is no coincidence that some of the "geek" families discussed in Chapter 4 had children with autism, nor that, according to the founder of DigiCamp, children with autism were overrepresented in the classes.[32] In our survey, more parents of children with special educational needs and disabilities than without agreed that "When it comes to new technologies, my child likes to be ahead."[33] Nina Robbins, who lived with her husband, Chris, and eight-year-old daughter, Iris, in a large house in a leafy outer South London suburb, told us about an employment initiative at Microsoft that proactively recruits people with autism through an alternative hiring process precisely because they are seen as assets to the company.[34] Nina saw this as a potential pathway to employment for Iris, who had autism and sensory integration disorder so severe that she would often go for days without being able to get dressed. Nina imagined that Iris might benefit from the ways that "the world of work is changing anyways, so chances are that she may tele-work or whatever the latest work-from-home" technology might be.[35]

Media and communications scholars Amit Pinchevski and John Durham Peters reflect on what they call the "elective affinity" popularly asserted between people with autism and digital technology. Noting that such people are "often said to be the fittest to cope with the strains of the new media age, a view common among autism activists themselves,"[36] their concern is that by positioning technology as a workaround for those who struggle with face-to-face communication, face-to-face communication is reaffirmed as the standard against which those with autism, and sometimes also teens in general, are reaffirmed as deficient.[37]

---

[32] This connection was discussed in the best-selling novel *A Boy Made of Blocks,* about a father who only connects with his son with autism through playing *Minecraft* together (Stuart, 2016). Also pertinent to this stereotypical conflation of computer "geekiness" with autism is the fact that White boys and men are more likely to be diagnosed with autism and to be overrepresented in technological fields (Jack, 2014).

[33] Zhang and Livingstone (2019).

[34] Bach (2017).

[35] Iris had struggled in school, in part because she found the sound of a pencil on paper distracting and upsetting, preferring to write on a keyboard—which she described as feeling "quite bouncy, it is stiff and smooth, that feeling is nice to me." Iris had made it through year 2 in the local state primary school, but being in a rowdy classroom had put a huge strain on her. She could cope at school (and indeed had done well academically) but would then fall to pieces at home, throwing tantrums that lasted for hours.

[36] Pinchevski & Peters (2016, p. 2508).

[37] Thus, a seeming admiration of children with autism's facility with technology harbors a trap insofar as it sustains a conception of "normal" to which they will never match up. Indeed, some autism researchers have expressed concern that the popular equation of autism and computers may serve the reverse purpose—to render people with autism as "inhuman" or "cyborgs." See Nadesan (2005, p. 131).

These dilemmas played out uneasily among our parents who, while optimistic that digital technologies may facilitate social connections for people with autism by providing an alternative to the pressures of face-to-face communication, still prized face-to-face forms of communication and worried that digitally mediated forms (texting, playing games together, asynchronous messages) were less ideal, indeed perhaps less human.[38] Their effort to strike a balance—made more difficult by the heightened aspirations but also by the more pronounced concerns of parents with children with autism—is the reason we have chosen to focus on these families next.

Connected present, uncertain future

Sandra and Jonno had pinned all their hopes on Lucas's future as a games designer, but other parents were far more absorbed in present challenges. We met Kyle Campbell[39] (age 13) at LYA in a multimedia/app development class for young people with mild to moderate special educational needs and disabilities.[40] Kyle, the youngest in the group, had been given special permission to join for, although he was categorized as having moderate to severe autism and was largely nonverbal, he was especially passionate about digital design. His father, Ryan, described his "understanding of computers as very innate," as was his "sensitivity to the visual structure of language and words." From the age of two, Ryan explained, Kyle had shown an interest in graphics, especially letters and fonts—painstakingly drawing and redrawing logos from the sides of DVDs and appliances he found around the house. Having always worked with pen and paper, more recently Kyle had started translating his interests into computer art. Although Ryan had no idea where he found it, Kyle had "downloaded, miraculously, professional architectural software"—the program SketchUp.[41] This had instigated Kyle's new interest in designing shopping malls and urban infrastructure.

---

[38] Benford & Standen (2009). An example of digital alternatives to face-to-face communication designed specifically for children with autism in mind is *AutCraft*, a *Minecraft* virtual world played by those with autism or their friends or family (Ito, 2017; Ringland et al., 2016).

[39] Family 4.

[40] See Ito et al. (2020).

[41] SketchUp, a free application is a basic 3D modeling program used to facilitate video game design, architectural drawing applications, and civil and mechanical engineering design (SketchUp, 2018). Cheryl Wright and colleagues (2011) explore specifically how SketchUp can facilitate intergenerational learning between children with autism and their parents/grandparents.

Kyle's mother, Amy, though somewhat baffled by Kyle's interest in urban design, had embraced it by taking him on local outings to retail outlets and helping him take pictures on their digital camera that he could use to inform his designs. They also bought an Apple desktop so he would have a powerful machine, but when we visited the family at home we saw him playing on an old laptop using PowerPoint instead of the modeling program that had so impressed his parents. We sat with Kyle for a while; he was clearly adept at cutting and pasting images and sizing and resizing graphics, but PowerPoint is not a sophisticated graphics program and Kyle moved so quickly between screens (he had dozens of windows open at any time) that it was hard to ascertain whether what he was doing was especially creative or advanced. After a while we asked him to show us what he'd been working on in SketchUp. When Ryan powered up the desktop, which had sat unused for some weeks, it became clear that not only had the free trial of SketchUp ended but also that the desktop now had a virus—problems Kyle hadn't been able to express to his parents and that they hadn't noticed until prompted by our visit.

Ryan and Amy Campbell signed Kyle up for the class at LYA because they felt it was important to help him find the "satisfaction that can come from creating things rather than just wandering the internet."[42] Although they judged him to already have the "ability and the skills," they also hoped the digital apps class would build on "something that he enjoys" to help him get on with other young people through the "socializing aspect of it," rather than particularly focusing on digital skills valuable for future employment. The LYA staff had years of experience of working with young people with special educational needs and disabilities, but they were not autism specialists—so Ryan and Amy hired a trainee teacher from Kyle's school to attend the sessions with him as an aide and help him focus. Unlike most of the other extracurricular learning sites we visited, including the "mainstream" classes at LYA, the class for young people with special educational needs and disabilities involved much more detailed communication between program staff and parents, with a dedicated member of staff whose sole responsibility was to act as liaison. Mia, his facilitator at LYA, said of her hopes for Kyle:

---

[42] This was, in part, because of a memorable incident a few years before when, searching for Winnie the Pooh, Kyle "wrote in Pooh and he got the most gross sites you could imagine." As Ryan went on, "he didn't go back for a long time. He was somebody who would, you know, he'd spend four or five hours a day on his computer, so it was a really big break."

It would be great to see if he could really build upon his communication and listening skills. I would like him to be able to be part of the group and be more engaged in it, that he's not walking around so much. . . . That would be a massive achievement for him, and it would be so important for his independence as well, that he's not relying on someone one to one all the time.

While well meaning, Mia's comment revealed her limited specialist knowledge of autism. Kyle's movement in the room—or what to Mia seemed like fidgeting and not paying attention—a key to how Kyle related to the space and tasks at LYA. His more specialized aide supported him to move in the room, recognizing his behavior as sensory-seeking, and simply redirected him or moved with him as needed for him to feel comfortable in the environment.

Although the sessions incorporated activities like drama—which Kyle found challenging—they also included drawing and time spent on the LYA tablets designing a music app using the software Max.[43] Eventually, the group combined Max, an Arduino circuit board, and physical gestures—holding hands to create circuits, touching a banana hooked up to the Arduino—to make sound effects and music.[44] Gus, an LYA "inclusive technology officer" (which he described as "the best job in the world," being also a self-described geek), had thought carefully how to design this program, building on his experience that "nonverbal young people . . . are the most adept users of technology I've encountered." Certainly it seemed to us that when the sessions focused on using the tablets and the Max software, Kyle seemed most engaged, connecting the physical wires to the fruit and tapping it rhythmically to make sounds emerge on the tablet via Max and Arduino.

When they looked into Kyle's future, Ryan and Amy did not share Lucas Stubbs's or Jake Kostas's parents' optimism about the role that his interest in and aptitude for technology might play. Although they felt that Kyle was talented and could perhaps work at a professional level in graphic design, Amy knew this would be "totally inappropriate for him because he just loses

[43] Max is a visual programming language developed by software company Cycling '74 (Cycling '74, n.d.).
[44] Arduino is an open-source hardware and software system that makers, designers, engineers, and students utilize to create a variety of products (Arduino, 2018).

interest." Ryan added that he lacked the "motivation" to work to a brief or with clients, although he expressed this positively as an enviable lack of self-consciousness—he "doesn't care if there's anybody who thinks [his work] is great or useless." So while Amy and Ryan loved and valued Kyle's experimentation, when it came to his future employability, they knew his skills would be "of no use if you can't work with people."

Ryan's respect and indeed admiration for Kyle's self-direction recalls our discussion of "geeks" in Chapter 4 (although Ryan and Amy did not use this term)—as people engaged in fostering their own expertise, free to be creative irrespective of conventional or mainstream views. While they seemed at home with their caregiving roles and in awe of Kyle's interest in technology, when they looked to Kyle's future, they were pessimistic. Their daughter Pia (age 20), who was excelling at her top-tier university, had been eight when Kyle was diagnosed with autism. Amy recalled

> when she was 10, she said to me, "it's okay for you, you're going to die. I'll be taking care of Kyle all my life. . . . I have to make money so I can cater for him."

Ryan felt "huge guilt" in consequence, while "encouraging her to follow her heart." He also saw her as "ferocious," because being Kyle's sister "had made her a very high achiever." Here we see again how, for many parents of children with special educational needs and disabilities, the future was hard to contemplate, and while some turned to technology as a means of shoring up their child in the present, for others this was overshadowed by deeper concerns.

Kyle's parents therefore had hopes that technology might help him create, connect, and learn in the present, to instill social skills and foster connections helpful for the future, even if this wouldn't lead to independence. This was in part attributable to his age. Now that he was 13, his parents were largely focused on helping him relate to others socially, knowing that he needed more support to do this than typically developing peers.

For some parents, their child's prowess at game play facilitated their relationship with siblings and peers and won social accolades that otherwise eluded them. The parents of both Jake Kostas and Lucas Stubbs noted that their sons' skills as gamers helped them connect with their typically developing peers and siblings. Despite his worries, Robert appreciated Jake's gaming, saying, "Because of the type of the child he is, he's not comfortable in social situations, finds it difficult to make friends."[45]

Technology had also proven a lifeline for the Stubbs family when the parents had separated. While limited incomes necessitated that they remain living together with Sandra's grandparents, Jonno had gone back up north for a while, staying in touch with Lucas by playing games together, "talking to him over the headset, you know, trying to link with him because he missed me a lot." No less poignantly, several families with children with autism and attention deficit hyperactivity disorder (and, indeed, typically developing children) talked of "screen time" as offering a valued opportunity to really *cuddle* their children—so dispersed was much of family life.[46]

For Nina Robbins, technology connected Iris to the world, for

[even when her] sensory problems are really bad, she can still virtually travel the world, interact with different types of people. She isn't just peering out through the curtains wondering what's going on out there.

Nina and Iris used technologies like Google Street View or virtual tours to ease Iris's anxiety before traveling to new places, as it helped her "check out environments where she's going."[47] Before Alicia visited their home, Nina and Iris had googled her to see her photograph and prepare Iris for the visit. For these parents, digital technologies constituted more than a simple work-around: they were a means for their children to build relationships and participate using a medium that played to their particular strengths and needs.

Digital technologies also provided, perhaps paradoxically, valued ways of *dis*connecting in families that ultimately supported their relationships. For example, when we spoke to Andrea Foster,[48] she described how oldest daughter Elsie (age six) struggled with the chaos of having two younger siblings. Elsie, who had autism, was often unsettled by the mess and noise

---

[45] Pugh (2009); Seiter (2005). Although many young people with autism spend significant time with digital media, they make less use proportionally of social networking sites (Mazurek et al., 2012). While digital media may enable young people with autism to foster "supportive relationships," they also introduce issues of who to trust, how to assess information, and what to disclose that may be more difficult for young people with autism to navigate (Burke & Hammett, 2009).

[46] Alper (2018) calls for the use of "sensory ethnography" to help "account for greater neurodiversity in how humans process sensory input, as well as a fuller range of multi-sensory encounters with new media" (p. 1).

[47] Launched in 2007, Google Street View is a feature of Google Maps and Google Earth displaying panoramic street-level views of many streets around the world (Google Street View, 2018).

[48] Family 64.

having two toddler siblings introduced into their open-plan home. Her iPad had become a way for her to retreat into a calmer, more manageable environment without stigmatizing her need for "time out" from her siblings. Her mother, Andrea, explained:

> Sometimes she needs it. . . . It can be very difficult to coax her towards some time on her own, and a quiet activity. That can be really hard, and it kind of feels to her like she's being punished, whereas if she has the iPad, she knows she's not being punished.

On the other hand, this strategy raised concerns about "screen time," which Andrea thought was not a "good thing for any child, but especially a child with autism." Andrea described Elsie as becoming "violent afterwards"[49] if she'd watched the iPad for too long but found trying to "strike the balance . . . really tricky." As Elsie was only six, Andrea's weighing of digital risks and opportunities was focused on the present. These balancing acts shift as children get older and as wider concerns about their navigation of social worlds beyond the family come to the fore.

Intersecting Identities

Parents of children with autism especially often told us with pride how their children navigated the online world. But as well as their stories of conflict when it was time to "disconnect," parents also faced fears of exploitation, given the distinctive communication affordances of virtual spaces.[50] While we have argued in previous chapters that parental strategies towards and practices regarding digital technologies—whether strategies of embrace, balance, or resist—are pursued in accordance with parents' values and imaginaries, the focus of this chapter reminds us that parents must also take into account their child's desires and their understanding of the difficulties they might encounter.

Sana Kader[51] (age 16) was in the same class at LYA as Jake Kostas and Kyle Campbell and was one of the most social members of the class. In

---

[49] Andrea used the term "violent," although it wasn't entirely clear what she meant by this. However, it was clear from the interview that she felt overwhelmed by her daughter's strong reaction, and that this reaction was physical and, Andrea felt, aggressive.

[50] Livingstone & Palmer (2012).

[51] Family 9.

our interview with her father, Ali, we told him how Sana had shown us her notebook—painstakingly filled with collage cutouts of characters from the *Twilight* film series—and she had told us of her feelings about the characters Edward, Jacob, and Bella. Although he nodded in acknowledgment, it was also clear that this story had touched a nerve. He worried that Sana had "started getting completely mixed up between reality and movies" and that "she loved these characters and she wanted to be like them; she thinks it's a role model for her." Ali's concerns centered on the sexualized content of the *Twilight* films and the other "tween" media she loved, such as Taylor Swift music videos. On the positive side, since she was "very naïve," she would readily tell her parents when she'd watched something where "somebody is killing or something like that," which Ali saw as being to his "advantage" in controlling her media access. Mia, the tutor at LYA, knew about Sana's interest in *Twilight*, saying, "She'll have a tendency to be obsessive about certain programs." Although Mia described drama as a great way of engaging Sana, she said the tutors had to be aware of these "obsessions" and guide her away from relying on them in the sessions. Her parents took a stronger stance: after trying unsuccessfully to wean Sana off of her *Twilight* fixation, her parents simply took away the iPad and the computer they'd bought for her, telling her "there's a virus and it doesn't work. Every time she asked the question and got fed up but she's not asking about it now."

Not all the struggles around technology in this family were directly due to Sana's autism. Some of her parents' concerns were typical of those with teenage daughters, while others echoed the general discourse around "screen time" we heard from many parents. For instance, when she did have access to the iPad, Ali said, "she doesn't last more than two hours, that's the rules" (see Chapter 2).[52] He also mentioned watching a program about how "people really involved in high technology, especially the cutting edge, they don't let their kids use the iPad or the digital technology"—presumably a reference to the now-infamous story that Steve Jobs himself was a "low-tech parent."[53] But Ali did see some concerns as specific to her autism, such as her difficulty

---

[52] In this, Ali seemed to echo the now-superseded American Academy of Pediatrics (AAP) screen time rules, although we can't be certain that this was the origin of his rules (Blum-Ross & Livingstone, 2018). Notably, SEN considerations are largely absent from "screen time" advice for parents, with exceptions being guidance from Common Sense Media (CSM) and Parent Zone (Kamenetz, 2018, p. 46), although Alper (2014) discusses how screen time rules may appear very different for families with children with disabilities, given that assistive technology or other uses of technology are an essential part of daily life and therefore difficult to fit into narrow, time-based restrictions.

[53] Bilton (2014).

in interpreting *Twilight* content as "just a fantasy"; thus, Ali characterized her media use as "really dangerous stuff for her." Also specific was how media concerns were part of a larger set of worries about Sana's ability to independently navigate both digital and physical landscapes. Her parents questioned whether she would ever be able to travel independently on a London bus, for instance? Relatedly, the solutions they found were both distinctive and routine too—the family went to the cinema together (Sana loved Disney movies and Will Smith) and Sana was allowed access to her parents' phones "as a reward" for good behavior—this worked for her, but might not for many 16-year-olds.

In this chapter we have discussed families of varying economic means and cultural circumstances, and children of different ethnicity, gender, and nature of impairment. We have also attended to the interrelations among these factors, often serving to compound advantage or disadvantage. For instance, Ali Kader's worries for Sana were due not only to her autism but also to her being a 16-year-old girl, and he therefore worried about her interest in sexual behavior. Relatedly, Sandra and Jonno Stubbs's worries for Lucas were partly about his autism and its social isolation costs, but they also arose because he was a young Black boy growing up in South London. Although Sandra and Jonno admired Lucas's prowess online, where he was more independent than in "real life," they also thought him a "bit of a sheep," "easily manipulated." When his older cousin taught Lucas how to use Instagram, Lucas's very first picture was a selfie, egged on by his cousin, of him "holding up his middle finger with the text caption 'Bitch Ass Skills.'" Though Jonno privately thought this "hilarious," Sandra sat Lucas down and said:

> You are a young Black man, is that what in 10 years' time when people search your name on the internet, you want to come up? Like you're some gangster street crappy hood? Like a drug dealer?

While many parents will (or should) discuss their "digital footprint" with their children, the fact that Lucas was Black and had autism added to the urgency Sandra felt. Thus, as for all of the families in this book, understanding these families necessitates an intersectional approach that attends to how their hopes and fears are inflected through the diverse ways in which their identities, experiences, and society's expectations, interact.

Access (or lack thereof) to economic and cultural resources and privilege underpins families' opportunities and risks, as discussed in Chapter 3, including families with children with special educational needs and disabilities. For example, the Campbell and Robbins families were middle class, White, and living in comfortable semisuburban homes. This allowed the Campbells to provide Kyle's individual support worker. It also enabled Nina Robbins to stay home to home-school Iris, not only financially but also in terms of her confidence in researching and emulating the experiences of the "unschooling" movement. After all, it took considerable cultural capital for Nina to build on Iris's love of "open world" games like *Roblox*, *Minecraft*, and *Terraria* to conceive of *Minecraft* as a hook for Iris's "unschooling."[54] "For months," Nina said, she and Iris

> played *Minecraft* all day, every day, we did ores and minerals and smelting and furnaces. Through *Minecraft* we bought iron filings, we looked at magnetism, and that led on to looking at chemical solutions, so we had loads of fun with vinegar and baking soda and acids and alkalis.[55]

Similarly, Jen Pearson deployed her high cultural capital in her reading of research papers to support Charlotte's home schooling, though her financial resources were much more limited. But while privilege eases the lives of families of children with special educational needs and disabilities in considerable and much-valued ways, it does not erase the realities of disability. And while technology too can ease these families' lives in some ways, it cannot overcome structural problems of disadvantage. In fact, technology may compound prior disadvantage in some respects, though the picture is complex. Our survey showed that parents of children with special educational needs and disabilities said that they (the parents) used the internet less often and faced more barriers to use compared with other parents.[56]

At one point we visited single mother Laura Andrews and her 17-year-old son Zachary,[57] who attended a class at LYA focused on communication skills

---

[54] Unschooling is an experiential education philosophy that eschews formal levels and progression in favor of using a child's own interests to drive learning (Holt, 2017). Open-world games have non-linear, open levels with various pathways toward the objective (Sefton, 2008).

[55] Similarly, they had recently collected elderflower blossoms to make cordial, another way of exploring chemistry, in part inspired by their love of a YouTube channel called The Spangler Effect, which teaches kids how to do science experiments with everyday household materials (Spangler Effect, 2018).

[56] Twenty-one percent of parents with a child with SEN reported the "internet being too time-consuming" as a barrier for internet use, compared to 11% of those with a non-SEN child. However, they reported using a wider range of devices and offered more overall online support to their child, such as seeking information on their child's health or helping their child with his or her studies (Zhang & Livingstone, 2019).

[57] Family 46.

for young people with severe impairments. They lived in a cramped flat in a council block in North London, ill-equipped for a boy who largely navigated in a wheelchair, and with no funds for updating their frayed furnishings. Throughout the interview with Laura the TV was on for Zachary, who watched intently while vocalizing and rocking back and forth. He was dependent on his mother, who cared for him full time and seemed to be worryingly close to her limit, also facing her own physical and mental health problems and with little social support. For Laura and Zachary there were no great ambitions about technology as a means of communication or employment. Along with his participation at LYA, the time in front of the TV offered much-needed respite for Laura as well as pleasure and comfort for Zachary. At age 17 he would soon be too old for many public services for young people with disabilities—including access to LYA (and the bus that took him there). Laura and Zachary were profoundly devoted to one another, yet they seemed isolated from the community around them. Digital technologies presented valued ways of spending time in the present, but looking into the future posed problems significantly greater than anything digital technology might be able to fix.

Dilemmas of voice and support

Laura described how the severity of Zachary's impairments impacted the breakdown of her relationship, isolation from her family, and, as she was a full-time caregiver, her poverty. For her, technology was not privileged for its learning or connection opportunities, though it was valued in other more quotidian ways. Other parents we spoke with had begun to use technology, notably social media, to develop a "community of practice"[58] that provided practical and emotional support in negotiating life as the parent of a child with special educational needs and disabilities. For example, Constance Kostas was a heavy social media user, participating in groups for mothers with children with autism and a particular, active WhatsApp group for her "real life" mum-friends of children with special educational needs.[59]

But the use of social media, blogging, messaging groups, and other forms of online communication, though popular, was not without its problems.

---

[58] A "community of practice" is a group of people who possess a "shared domain of interest" and engage in collective learning (Hoadley, 2012; Wenger, 2000).
[59] Jordan (2016).

Robert Kostas struggled to find good connections with other parents of children with autism: he'd visited forums online, but there were thousands of blogs written by parents (more mums than dads) and sometimes by children, including many with an agenda to push (including diets, advocating for particular behavioral interventions, or antivaccination). He described trying to find answers online to his deep questions about what was right for his son as making him feel "like a fisherman trawling for a specific fish . . . how are you going to find the one fish that you're looking for in an entire ocean?"

One parent's story captured the potential and risks of today's "sharenting culture."[60] Nina Robbins had had a creative and well-compensated career working in "fashion and trend-prediction and media" before leaving to stay at home with Iris. At the time of the interview Iris was turning eight; her long, curly hair spilled down her back, and although it was a cold day, she wore only her dad's stretched, oversized T-shirt to avoid constrictions that would make her itchy and anxious. She was precociously articulate—calling herself an "Aspie" with pride and explaining her autism and sensory integration problems in evocative detail. Sometimes, when Iris's sensory problems were less severe, the mother and daughter were able to attend classes together, digital and not. But at other times, having left both work and a "community at school" that she had been "proud" to be part of, Nina too was searching for connection. One way she sought to connect with other parents of children with special educational needs was through her self-described "snarky" blog about her life, harnessing her wicked sense of humor to reflect on her struggles in mothering Iris. She'd started the blog when she became "suddenly housebound" and found it "quite difficult to process the 'I don't want to' feelings." The blog was heartfelt and sometimes raunchy. Nina described it as

one of the bits that's just me, the one that sits in a bar with a glass of—no, a bucket of wine and a packet of fags [cigarettes] . . . who doesn't exist in someone else's world.

---

[60] As we have discussed elsewhere, for some parents, "sharenting" (sharing images and information about children online) has become a vital part of expressing their experience, building community, and accessing much-needed sources of advice and support (Blum-Ross and Livingstone, 2017).

This description was as poignant as it was evocative, since Nina rarely left the house without Iris, so necessary was she to Iris's care—so the blog took the place of "blowing off steam down the pub."

Not long before our interview, Nina had penned a different sort of blog post for Autism Awareness Week.[61] It was a poem about sitting beside a daughter who struggled mightily with the world but also had profound gifts, whom Nina found hard to comfort but who desperately needed comforting, whom doctors and specialists agreed needed help but couldn't provide it, whom strangers and loved ones alike offered suggestions for "fixing." Nina linked her poem to a fundraiser, shared it on her Facebook page, and imagined her aunts and a few other readers donating to it. Overnight the post went viral. Nina described it as

> almost like an out-of-body experience with all these people discussing it on forums. . . . It didn't feel like it was anything to do with me anymore, it was just out there.

Suddenly there were over a million hits on Nina's small blog. She quickly went back and deleted old photos of Iris and Chris and herself, removing identifiable information and trying to process what had happened. Some laudatory emails told her "you're an amazing mom and gosh I couldn't do that," some were "heart-rending pleas for help," and some were horribly offensive, suggesting she give Iris bleach enemas or take her to an exorcist. All these responses were hard for her to make sense of; some were overwhelming and others intrusive and upsetting. Clearly blogging poses a dilemma over *what* can be said and *how*—for instance, how to strike a tone between humor and complaining without being misunderstood or triggering judgmental or downright hostile responses.[62]

---

[61] There's some debate about whether the focus of advocacy should be about autism awareness (medical model) or acceptance (social model) (Alper, 2014). Nina's way of thinking about Iris was somewhere between these two: she largely favored the social model as a political perspective, but as the person responsible for Iris's care she also felt connected to the medical community. Melanie Yergeau (2018) writes that some forms of "autism awareness [are] better termed perilous than . . . positive or gainful" (p. 5).

[62] Tawfiq Ammari, Meredith Ringel Morris, and Sarita Yardi Schoenebeck (2014) discuss how parents of children with SEN use social networks, finding that they use them both for diagnosis-specific and geography-specific information, and also that they struggle to strike the right balance between complaining about children and appearing too triumphal if a child is doing well. They found that overall, parents of children with SEN found online spaces to be less judgmental than offline spaces.

After her viral post Nina reflected on how she didn't want to be just "another *autism mum*," but rather, that she should "just facilitate Iris to speak for herself rather than speaking for her." For Nina and others, parent blogging also raised the ethically troublesome dilemma of *who* has the right to speak—insofar as it was the parent speaking on behalf of herself, the child remaining unheard.[63] For Nina, sharenting involved ethical compromises she struggled with, since in sharing her own experiences as a mother she necessarily also laid bare Iris's experiences. Although many psychological understandings of identity emphasize its social and relational nature,[64] in everyday judgments, identity is understood in individualist terms. For example, could Nina really express herself separately from her connection with Iris? Or, more generally, can a parent express him- or herself as a person without acknowledging his or her identity as a parent? This dilemma was intensified in the face of Nina's daughter's vulnerability since Nina, as the parent, was precisely the person primarily responsible for protecting her child's privacy.[65] Yet it was these dilemmas, of course, that made her story more impactful, being an often-untold story that needed to be told and shared within the wider community.

Significantly, Nina criticized herself (and felt herself held to account by an imagined future Iris) for speaking on her daughter's behalf when seeking to represent her own identity as a parent. She discussed with us how a lot of children including "nonverbal autistic kids with technology are now speaking for themselves. . . . I think that a level of understanding will go up because people can now advocate for themselves." The idea that Iris would be able to use technology to express herself was so important to Nina that she imagined her future as a time when Iris

> has the ability to record her feelings. She can petition, she can go to forums. All that isolation is gone, all the misunderstandings that she's the only one like [this]. She's a minority but she's a significant minority.

Putting her vision into action, Nina helped Iris set up a blog, which, at the time of our visit, had one entry—Iris's perspective on being an "Aspie"—and she had helped Iris write an article about her experiences at school that appeared in a national newspaper.

---

[63] L. K. Lopez (2009); Pedersen & Lupton (2018).
[64] Burkitt (2008); K. J. Gergen (2009).
[65] Blum-Ross & Livingstone (2017), Livingstone, Blum- Ross, & Zhang (2018).

Rhetoric and disability studies scholar Cynthia Lewiecki-Wilson describes "mediated rhetoricity" as the process whereby a parent or caregiver "co-constructs" language with a child with disabilities—especially those who are nonverbal or otherwise noncommunicative, so that the child might speak on his or her own behalf.[66] Iris was certainly capable of language and self-expression, but Nina used her cultural and social capital, including her knowledge of digital media, to amplify Iris's voice in the national press. This echoes Alper's work on how parents of disabled children support and intervene in their children's communication, it not being the technologies per se that create the conditions for "voice," but rather how they are embedded within social contexts that are themselves patterned by unequal resources. As Alper explains, some parents, under some conditions, can use these tools to "selectively amplify voices within and across various publics and audiences, but their existence does not automatically call the status quo of structural inequality . . . into question."[67] Moreover, Nina felt she had to tread carefully—not wanting to be another stereotypical autism "hero" or "warrior mom" (as discussed on the autism parenting blogs), and especially not wanting to violate Iris's privacy or her ability to speak on her own behalf.[68]

It was ironic that when we revisited Nina's blog while writing this chapter, we found only the plaintive (viral) post left standing. The loss of the more mundane, funny, self-deprecating, and very relatable posts that Nina had previously posted seemed to amplify the very effect she was trying to resist.[69] Previously there had been posts about trips to the library, playing in mud, things that had made the two happy and were unrelated to Iris's autism. Now there was only Nina's voice, asking (reluctantly, we had learned in the interview) for support, alongwith signposting to sources of support for

---

[66] Lewiecki-Wilson (2003, p. 8).

[67] Alper (2017, p. 2).

[68] Jack (2014); Sousa (2011). There have been a couple of major pushbacks on some recent "autism mom" memoirs lately from the autism self-advocate community. For example, a book called *To Siri with Love* (Newman, 2017), written by a neurotypical mother of a teenage autistic son, shares how Apple's Siri has helped her son navigate the world and was met with considerable backlash from the autistic community for assumptions the author makes about those with autism being unfit to parent (Sparrow, 2017). Other critical responses to popular autism books such as Jenny McCarthy's *Mother Warriors* (2008) include Kehler (2015) and Robison (2017).

[69] Melanie Yergeau (2018), a digital studies, rhetoric, and disability studies scholar (and self-described autistic activist), asks, is there space to listen to both the parent and the child, the person with autism and the person without? Certainly Nina's dilemma about how much she could or should share about Iris online while also seeking a lifeline for herself was one shared by many parents active on social media—especially for those for whom social media sustained connections for a parent who could not leave the house or participate in the daily face-to-face parenting rituals like music classes or greetings at the school gates.

readers (and she had left intact the nearly 700 comments that the viral post had received).

Ryan and Amy Campbell had a similar level of privilege, but less of an expectation that Kyle would "voice" his experience. They were less concerned to challenge the dominant narratives about disability or express their own experience of parenting. But they did want to ensure that Kyle's opinions, preferences, and needs became known to those who could help him realize his interests. The hours they spent taking pictures of window displays in shopping malls or the files they filled of his drawings and computer designs to show his teachers at school were their way of facilitating his voice.[70] Ryan put the problem starkly: "Those who don't speak, people think they don't exist." It was his mission to remedy this, to speak for and with his son when he could. Sandra and Jonno Stubbs had few economic resources, but they similarly were determined to find a way to support if not Lucas's "voice" then at least his passions, which they clung to as a positive vision of his future.

Conclusions

Throughout this book we have considered how particular hopes and fears about the future, fanned by popular media, policymakers' pronouncements, and commercial and peer pressures, fuel parents' imaginations and worries. In considering the experience of parents of children with special educational needs and disabilities—especially those with autism—we have seen how these hopes and fears intersect with parents' understanding of the affordances of digital technologies and their child's own interests and aptitudes. While the notion of "elective affinities" between autism and technological affordances marks out a positive path that parents try to pursue, this analysis has revealed the inequalities that limit what opportunities can ensue and for whom.

Parents of children with special educational needs and disabilities, like all parents, are struggling to balance the great promise of digital technologies

---

[70] Ryan and Amy's plan to inform the school about Kyle's interests can be read as showing faith in the school to listen, and it's worth noting that we did also hear positive stories of schools recognizing parental and out-of-school efforts. For instance, Alice (family 1), mother of Sophia, aged 15, who has Down syndrome, told us how Sophia's head of media studies at school had requested that Sophia enroll because of what she had been doing at LYA, saying that "she's really an inspiration."

with the challenges they present—both in the here and now and imagined into the future. In so doing, they constantly look back, often re-evaluating long-held values, resources, and expectations, as well as looking sideways to consider those of their peers and their children's peers. Miles Taylor,[71] whom we met in Chapter 2, explained:

> You have this preconceived notion of how your life would be with your child and you, kind of, try to aspire to that. When you're told that they won't be able to do this and they won't be able to do that . . . at first you try and challenge those ideas because you don't want to see it or believe it but then as things become more and more apparent, it can be disheartening.

Parents of children with special educational needs and disabilities conveyed a strong sense of being out of step with parents of "typically developing" others (this sometimes included contrasts to how they themselves parented a typically developing sibling), a difference experienced with pride and sometimes with sadness. As Nina Robbins put it:

> We can dream all we like about how the future's going to be, but it, you know, it's not going to be that textbook scenario. You have to emotionally let go of all of those things that everyone told you expect, then you've got to rebuild it.

We have also documented how providing digital pathways for their children not only facilitated opportunity but also added to the individualized burden parents bore, thus perpetuating multiple forms of inequality. Many of the families discussed in this chapter accessed some form of state services, but these services were generally inadequate to the task of supporting particularly vulnerable families. As Miles told us, "I've been close to losing my mind" in fighting for state support for Jamie. Moreover, the withdrawal of crucial forms of state support when a child becomes an adult casts a long backward shadow, making it painful for many parents to contemplate the future at all.

Thus, it was largely the relatively privileged parents who imagined futures that led them to create workarounds and new solutions in the present—whether home-schooling with *Minecraft* or providing teaching aides or

---

[71] Family 5.

investing their hopes in digital technology as offering a compensatory mechanism in the present (social connections, confidence, expression) or future (employment, independence).[72] Part of Nina's rebuilding effort was to embrace technology wholeheartedly: she described herself and her husband as "cautiously, hysterically excited" about what the future might hold for Iris. But it must be recognized that her knowledge, enthusiasm, and privilege made her vision of Iris's future more plausible, and more positive, than that for many less privileged children. Sandra and Jonno Stubbs had fewer economic resources but shared Nina's embrace and indeed some of her cultural capital, so they hoped that with great effort and plenty of support Lucas too might find his place in the world. Laura Andrews expressed no such aspirations for Zachary; she was pleased with the help and pleasure technology gave them both in the present, but her horizon did not extend beyond this and the family's prospects were highly uncertain.

Our focus on parents with children with special educational needs and disabilities reminds us that "balance" is highly individual, varying from one family to the next. The benefits that these parents held dear—social connections, pride, warmth, respite, and calm—along with their struggles over time spent online, appropriate content and behavior, or translating digital interests into future benefits had much in common with those of other families we interviewed. So, rather than bracketing these families as exceptions to the rule, we contend that understanding the experiences of these families and the work that these parents did to balance technology given their child's particular vulnerabilities exemplifies the often-hidden work that all parents do to calibrate their family media use.

Similarly, these families remind us that while children with special educational needs and disabilities have particular needs, they also enjoy the pleasures of digital technologies and test their parents in similar ways to their typically developing peers. Yet these children have vulnerabilities that may be particularly exacerbated by the use of technology (both individual and societal)—think of Lucas's inability to resist social pressure, Jake's hours spent online to his father's consternation, or Sana's difficulty separating fact from fiction.

As for other parents in this book, parents of children with special educational needs and disabilities moved between embracing, balancing, and

---

[72] Parents of children with SEN are less likely to say they are doing a good job as a parent, report less support from friends and family, and are less satisfied with their lives, according to the Parenting for a Digital Future survey (Zhang & Livingstone, 2019).

resisting technology—according to their own experiences, skills, and values and the needs and desires of their children. Embracing technology may mean the difference between a hopeful vision of the future and a terrifying one, a present defined by connections and support or not. Resistance to technology may be necessary to support a vulnerable child, or to reduce family conflict.

Following from this, we can see how an "asset based" approach to these families might provide us with insights relevant to all families.[73] The parents discussed in this chapter were pursuing, often instinctively, what might be thought of as a form of "personalized learning," focusing strongly on their child as an individual with particular interests, strengths, and potential trajectory and determinedly finding the right tools (technological and otherwise) to support them.[74]

In conclusion, families with children with special educational needs and disabilities destabilize the notion that there is a single approach to "digital parenting." Put more generally, as argued by media and communications scholars like Elisabeth Ellcessor and Gerard Goggin, among others, by drawing on disability studies and media studies together, we should destabilize the idea that there is a single way of interpreting or understanding digital media "users"—including the so-called (and implicitly able-bodied) digital natives—or that there is any such thing as "normal."[75] We might even suggest that having a child who is not "typical" actually allows for greater freedom in making parenting decisions—for these parents can see opportunities and respond in a less "standard" way, eschewing normative pressures based on what everyone else seems to do since these clearly don't apply. Our point here is not to construct a false envy of parents of children with special educational needs and disabilities, but rather to point to the pressure to fit in that, often unnoticed, constrains most other parents, this in turn perpetuating the norm that serves to exclude those who don't fit. More positively, the experiences of parents here point to the scope for better opportunities for support and engagement for parents, from educators, and for inclusive or child rights–friendly technological design. This could benefit both families with children with special educational needs and disabilities and potentially all families.[76] We explore some of these issues in the next chapter.

[73] Alper et al. (2016).
[74] Grant & Basye (2014).
[75] Ellcessor (2016); Goggin & Newell (2003).
[76] Clarkson et al. (2003); Inger (2011); Newell (2003).

6

Parents and Digital Learning

Local parent and volunteer Beth Hale had scoured the supply cupboards at Bluebell Primary School to find a beaten-up old hard drive. When we visited the school computer room, Beth and two year 4 boys (eight and nine years old) were busily unscrewing the sides of the boxy hard drive. Beth jokingly asked, "Who controls your family?" to introduce them to the idea of the "motherboard" as the nerve center of the computer. Beth had been midway through her PhD in computer science when she joined a "Women in STEM" network. Through the network she'd heard about a national non-profit organization that taught kids to code offering a curriculum for teacher- or volunteer-run after-school clubs to teach basic "computational thinking."[1]

Beth wanted to give the students at Bluebell, a significantly underresourced school, "some kind of fundamental understanding of how you code," as well as "making and tinkering" activities like pulling apart the hard drive, to help the "concepts get really embedded." Reflecting the school's intake, the club was attended by a mix of students from African, Afro-Caribbean, Asian, and some Latin American backgrounds; two thirds of them were boys. The curriculum used Scratch, a coding language for kids developed at the Massachusetts Institute of Technology (MIT) so that young people could "share and remix" ideas while learning "important mathematical and computational concepts, as well as how to think creatively, reason systematically, and work collaboratively: all essential skills for the 21st century."[2]

Observing at the club, Alicia recorded

a palpable sense of excitement when different tasks are completed, shouting out to me or to Beth, "Miss! Miss! Come see! Come and look!" when they

---

[1] Wing (2008).

[2] Resnick et al. (2009, p. 60). Along with these other more broad outcomes, coding has been promoted as a learning goal in its own right—evident in the rollout of the computing curriculum in the United Kingdom in 2013 (Department for Education, 2013).

Parenting for a Digital Future. Sonia Livingstone and Alicia Blum-Ross, Oxford University Press (2020). © Oxford University Press.
DOI: 10.1093/oso/9780190874698.001.0001

have successfully gotten the rocket to get to the moon or made the sun turn into crazy colors.

While the inventors of Scratch have designed social dimensions to their program—for example through the social features on their website—in practice Bluebell students worked individually, since, for reasons of privacy and child protection, the school blocked access to the social network functionality of the Scratch website. In the club, students sat at their workstations and rarely asked their neighbors for advice, being more likely to turn to Beth, her covolunteer Eliza (or even Alicia), when they got into trouble, perhaps because turning to a teacher mirrored the expectations of the school day.

Though Beth didn't know it, one of the students taking apart the computer, nine-year-old Braydon Datong,[3] was strongly supported in his interests by his mother, Samantha, and father, Olu. Samantha (whom we met in Chapter 2, sharing the family's love of video games) was hopeful that Braydon's participation in code club might help lead to a career path, given that Olu worked in information technology (IT) support at a nearby hospital. She explained:

> Braydon has always said that he wants a job working with computers. So I said, well, maybe this might help you. You know, I said, you're going to secondary school soon. . . . It would be helpful if you knew exactly how computers worked—just for his own knowledge really.

Samantha had never actually seen any of Braydon's Scratch designs, since the school did not permit the students to use the public-facing galleries on the Scratch website. Nor could she learn much from Braydon, since he never went "into detail" about the class—although Samantha could tell that he was "having fun." Feeling excluded left her with plenty of anxieties, however, since her previous work in child protection meant she had a detailed vision of digital risks. Braydon talked more deeply with Olu; Samantha described them "talking about binary. . . . He shows Braydon what he does or when he works on call and he has to do it from home." Samantha laughed that Olu was "almost grooming him to be another IT guy."

Braydon's interest was not entirely lost on Beth, for he was an active participant in the club. When Beth brought out a Makey Makey (physical computing) device, it was Braydon who immediately grasped the principle

---

[3] Family 13.

of circuitry, saying, "You make a circle and then it goes into your blood!"[4] However, there was little opportunity for Beth to learn what Braydon had been doing or talking about at home, or for her to build on it in the sessions. There was equally little opportunity for Samantha and Olu to support Braydon's coding by building on what was happening in the classroom. Yet Braydon's parents had a better grasp than most parents of this under-resourced school's ambition to set its students on the path to "digital" jobs. Typically, students in the free club had signed themselves up, their parents being little aware of what they were doing. Though generally positive, most parents (unlike Samantha and Olu) were mystified by the idea of coding.

In this chapter we examine the connections and disconnections between parents and educators. Informed by educational research and public policy on "the home–school link"[5] as well as the theory of connected learning, we explore how families' values, practices, and beliefs about digital technologies influence children's learning opportunities outside the home.[6] As we will show, Samantha and Olu were far from the only parents guided by a vision of a "digital future" although, to keep this in perspective, our survey showed that while two thirds of children had participated in some kind of extracurricular (after school or outside nursery/school/college) groups or lessons in the past year, most of these did not involve digital technology.[7]

How is the role of parents envisaged and enacted in digital learning initiatives? Drawing on observations and interviews with educators in extracurricular digital learning sites, we ask, why is parental investment and commitment so little recognized or valued?[8] And we consider what changes could be made.

---

[4] Makey Makey is an electronic invention kit that shows users how everyday artifacts connect to computer programs (Makey Makey, 2018). Beth had petitioned the school to buy the Makey Makey kit, which they used to hook up objects like a fork or banana to trigger coded commands within the Scratch interface.

[5] Hallgarten (2000).

[6] As explained in Chapters 1 and 4, the theory of connected learning holds that learning is best enabled when it is interest led, peer supported, collaborative, and production oriented. For these conditions to be met, young people's learning should encompass and connect their activities across different sites, possibly in ways that are digitally mediated (Ito et al., 2013, 2020).

[7] These activities included 41% in a sports club or team, 24% in creative or performing arts (e.g., music, dance, drama, art, crafts), 14% in scouts/guides/young cadets, 12% in science or maths club, 9% in academic tutoring, 7% in religious instruction, 7% in computing or coding clubs (e.g., Code.org, CoderDojo, or Scratch), and 6% in some other technology-related club (e.g., video games, Lego Mindstorms, video editing, music technology).

[8] Livingstone & Sefton-Green (2016); Sefton-Green (2013a); Sefton-Green & Erstad (2016, 2019).

Anticipating the role of parents

With an array of public and private institutions and funders, London, like other major cities, has long been home to a particularly wide and stimulating array of digital youth initiatives, makerspaces, creative arts centers, and extracurricular activities. In recent years there has been an explosion in initiatives for children to learn coding, app and game development, music and film production, web design, and more, as well as a growing market targeted at informal digital learning opportunities at home. In 2013, then-education secretary Michael Gove called on schools to prepare "students to work at the very forefront of technological change."[9] This call was widely supported by technology advocates who underlined the need for the United Kingdom, an increasingly postindustrial nation, to prepare children for the "digital jobs" of the future, centering on teaching coding in schools[10] rather than the much-criticized "IT" lessons preoccupied with what have come to be considered rote computing skills like the Microsoft Office package. At Bluebell the coding club was not part of the formal curriculum, but the IT teacher and senior leadership in the school greeted Beth's proposal to run an afterschool club enthusiastically, believing that coding would be useful for the students and help the school meet its own institutional targets, since it was, at the time, under close scrutiny by the school's regulator, Ofsted, having previously received a poor inspection.[11]

While there are many kinds of learning site, we focus on those that, by contrast with the more constrained formal curriculum, prioritize the ways that digital technologies can motivate, diversify, and enhance children's learning.[12] In this chapter we compare three learning sites: Bluebell (an underresourced primary school where we visited the after-school code club and related school activities), London Youth Arts (LYA, a free, low-cost, cross-arts venue where we visited after-school, weekend, and school-holiday classes in digital animation and music production as well as the weekly digital technology classes for children with

---

[9] Gove (2012).

[10] Curtarelli et al. (2017); UK Digital Skills Taskforce (2014). Huw Davies and Rebecca Eynon (2018, pp. 3976, 3974) critique the tech-utopian discourse of today's enthusiasm for coding. They observe that young people in a coding program in Wales were asked "to believe their ability to code will transcend the structural conditions of the job market." This proved implausible, inviting both a competitive individualism and generating disillusion given that both mainstream and niche interests were unlikely to translate into "the pipeline to prosperity."

[11] Introduced in 2013, the computing curriculum is becoming embedded in schools. It contrasts with some of the more creative digital learning opportunities we describe elsewhere in this chapter. Further, although announced with some fanfare, the rollout has been "fragile" and often reliant on underprepared teachers rather than more ambitious, creative, or critical forms of digital engagement (Royal Society, 2017). Ofsted is the United Kingdom's official educational standards inspectorate.

[12] Sefton-Green & Erstad (2019).

special educational needs and disabilities (SEN) that we detailed in the previous chapter), and DigiCamp (an expensive summer camp offering classes ranging from digital making to advanced coding using software like Python). All three tended to attract parents or children (depending on who instigated the sign-up) who had in some sense *voted with their feet* to embrace an imagined digital future. Yet they varied considerably, mirroring the three groupings we discussed in Chapter 3: those living below the poverty line (often from ethnic minorities), those living creatively (often educated but with constrained finances), and elite families (privileged and competitive across multiple dimensions). In this chapter we focus on families for whom our observational and interview evidence includes the perspectives of parent, child, and educator.

For parents from all walks of life, their approach to digital learning opportunities is framed by what have been described as "folk" or "lay" theories of learning, often centered on the idea of technologies being *educational* or *creative* as well as highly motivating for children.[13] As previous chapters have explored, it is by imagining the potential of digital technology for learning that parents justify their often-considerable investment in both digital resources at home and their child's educational activities outside the home. The larger promise is that digital technologies can "scaffold" young people's spontaneous interests toward academic achievement, career progression, or civic participation.

Oddly little attention has been paid to where and how children's interests in digital technology originate, notwithstanding discussions about children "finding" their "spark" or "passion." Nor is it always acknowledged that parents, given that they know their children throughout their lives and not just at a particular moment in time, are better positioned than educators to sustain children's interests over the long term. Yet research on childhood socialization shows the profound and long-lasting influence of the culture and practices of the home on children's development and life chances.[14] Educationalists Suzanne Hidi and Ann Renninger propose a model of *interest development*, finding that a learner's interest is strongly situationally grounded, being stimulated and sustained substantially within the family.[15] Parents generally know this intuitively, experimenting with possible interests by trying out multiple extracurricular and informal learning opportunities with their child, positioning themselves as their child's "champion" in relation

---

[13] Drummond & Stipek (2004); Sefton-Green (2013b); Swartz & Crowley (2004).

[14] James (2013); Ribbens McCarthy & Edwards (2011).

[15] Ben-Eliyahu, Rhodes, & Scales (2014); Csikszentmithalyi, Rathunde, & Whalen (1993); Hidi & Renninger (2006); Peppler (2013); Renninger & Hidi (2011).

to school and keen to pass on their own particular interests and passions or encourage their child to develop an interest they feel themselves to have been denied. In our fieldwork, parents described offering their child as enticing a range of options as they could to see what caught their fancy or sparked an interest. This is a resource-intensive process undertaken over years in the face of repeated hope and disappointment, until the parent reaches the point of summing up, sometimes with a regretful glance back at the paths not taken, that "my child likes to do this or that, and therefore this is who he or she is."

How does this work in relation to digital learning? Developmental psychologist Brigid Barron and her colleagues studied how parents act as children's "learning partners" in privileged Silicon Valley, identifying seven "scaffolding" roles for parents: "teaching, collaborating on projects with, providing nontechnical support to, brokering learning opportunities for, providing learning resources for, learning from, and employing children to assist with technical projects."[16] They showed, further, that a parent might occupy and move between several roles, depending on their values and circumstances.[17] Given the privileged nature of their sample, we wondered whether parents of more diverse means can convert family interests and activities into external achievements (see our discussion in Chapter 3).

In contrast, communications scholar Melissa Brough and her colleagues interviewed the parents of exceptionally engaged, low-income "connected learners," revealing a spectrum of "hands on" and "hands off" ways that these parents found to encourage their children toward technical interests.[18] Parental supports could be as simple as "encouraging touchpoints" to stimulate conversation—for example, when children saw their parents taking digital photographs. In such families, parents supported children to develop a high degree of autonomy over their digital lives. Other studies have found that such a democratic approach to using digital technology is common in immigrant families, for example when children use media (digital and nondigital) to help their parents negotiate in an unfamiliar language or context.[19] Vikki Katz and Victoria Rideout found that low-income Latinx families in the

---

[16] Barron et al. (2009, p. 71).

[17] In this way, parents could ensure their children "took advantage of school-offered electives, joined clubs, attended camps, found online tutorials and examples, participated in affinity groups, read books and magazines, and engaged nonparent mentors in learning partnerships" (Barron et al., 2009, p. 60). See also Gutiérrez, Izquierdo, & Kremer-Sadlik (2010); Hoover-Dempsey & Sandler (1997).

[18] "Connected learning" is inspired by the tradition of "critical pedagogy," in which an adult acts not as a "teacher" in the traditional model of disseminating information but rather as a "facilitator" who supports young participants to determine their own forms of knowledge creation (Friere, 1973).

[19] V. S. Katz (2014).

US were much more likely to engage together with their children in watching or playing with technology or using it to support learning and achievement, including as it related to school.[20]

These and other studies suggest that for many families, digital technologies provide "anchors" for children's interests and cognitive and social development. For example, in Chapter 2 we saw how religious families used apps and online media to support their religious practice, while other immigrant parents used satellite radio or internet content to bolster their children's ability to speak parents' native languages while growing up in an English-dominant culture.[21] "Joint media engagement," as researchers term it, is particularly valuable in scaffolding a range of specific learning outcomes and also for digital media literacy.[22] Concerned that society has "too narrow a picture of how people are using media together and what and how they are learning while doing so," learning scientists Lori Takeuchi and Reed Stevens argue:

> What children learn and do with media depends a lot on the content of the media, but they depend perhaps as much on the context in which they are used or viewed, and with whom they are used or viewed.[23]

Acknowledging the potential benefits of "connected learning" or "joint media engagement" takes us in a far more promising direction than the medical model of "screen time" we critiqued in Chapter 2, opening up more roles for parents than limiting and policing children's time spent with technology.[24] But for all the work parents do to support children's digital interests at home, they must connect to and be recognized by others outside the home if such interests are to translate into lasting forms of success.[25] Whether it is through recognition by teachers, other educators, or online or offline peers, digital interests and values at home need to be bolstered elsewhere to be transformative in young people's lives. Such preparations for a digital future, we contend, involve more than providing learning opportunities of instrumental value, for as we will show, both parents and educators seek to shape

[20] Rideout & Katz (2016).

[21] For example, families 16, 24, 25, and 35.

[22] For example, Gutiérrez, Zitlali Morales, & Martinez (2009); Nathanson (2015); Reiser, Williamson, & Suzuki (1988).

[23] Takeuchi & Stevens (2011, p. 71).

[24] Blum-Ross & Livingstone (2018).

[25] Brough, Cho, & Mustain (forthcoming).

the learner as a *person*—in Stanton Wortham's terms, to mold the child's "learning identity."[26]

For all families, as we saw most intensely with the "geeky" families (Chapter 4) and some of those whose children had special educational needs and disabilities (Chapter 5), family investment in digital learning committed not only money and time but also children's identities, family practices at home, and parental hopes for the future in ways that remained highly uncertain of delivering future benefit. But as we explored in Chapter 3, some parents were better resourced to seek out and identify opportunities for their children to engage in learning what they had already embraced,[27] while other parents found themselves with a litany of barriers and missed opportunities. Whatever their circumstance many parents stand ready (or not) to support children. However, as the chapters thus far have illustrated, the "success" of a parents investment in digital learning relies not only on their own abilities but also those of other adults who play a part in children's lives. So in addition to talking to parents, we also consider "connected learning" from the perspective of educators, asking what they know or think of the efforts parents make.

Bluebell—inclusive efforts

Before Beth established the code club at Bluebell, she had run it at a better-resourced local state school. But there she had found the students unmotivated and their behavior challenging; since they had many other after-school clubs, coding had seemed like "too much work." However, at Bluebell, a school able to offer few other after-school opportunities and serving twice the national proportion of students receiving free school meals (an index of deprivation), the club was oversubscribed.[28] Bluebell's affable IT teacher, Sean, who was responsible for implementing the computing curriculum and running the "digital leaders" scheme,[29] was tasked with teaching not only

---

[26] By learning identity, Wortham (2006) points to the combination of personal, social, academic, and cultural influences that combine to create a sense of oneself as a learner at any particular moment. See also Erstad et al. (2016); Livingstone & Sefton-Green (2016); Sefton-Green & Erstad (2016).

[27] See Rafalow (forthcoming) on the high-income parents of Sheldon who sought out the fancy private school for their children and then acted "on" the school to ensure the school's digital curriculum fit with their digital values at home.

[28] Extracurricular activities were something the leadership team was actively working on, since they'd been designated as "needs improvement" in the previous government report (by Ofsted), and so they were thrilled when Beth offered the club as an option.

[29] The digital leaders were an ad hoc group of older students that Sean recruited based on their interest in technology and that could be called in to other classrooms to help teachers troubleshoot computers or technology like interactive whiteboards. Many of the digital leaders had been in Beth's first cohort in code club.

the students but also the other teachers about technology, despite being only employed part-time. Additionally, he was the school's "eSafety champion," again training both students and teachers as required by the government inspectorate (Ofsted).[30] One day after school Alicia observed him lead visibly exhausted teachers through a professional development session on online safety at the end of a long day. Unsurprisingly, no mention was made of positive uses of technology in teaching; the focus was entirely on risks. When the discussion turned to parents, teachers were keen that "parents are educated about grooming" and they lamented that "parents are handing down their smartphones," resulting in some students being cyberbullied "on the bus, on their way home." The sense was that parents were clueless, leaving the teachers feeling responsible for educating not only the children but also the caregivers.[31]

It was in this context that Beth sought to integrate the code club into the school and to involve the parents. She described the teachers as "really adaptable . . . they just go out and look for resources everywhere," but lamented that they were "too busy" to come to the club. The parents, also, were usually harried and rushed at pickup, meeting their children in the downstairs entrance and not invited up to the computer room. Several spoke limited English, so while friendly toward Beth, they could not ask much about what had gone on in the sessions, had they wanted to.

Cecilia Apau[32] (whom we met in Chapters 2 and 3) was aware that her son Eugene was doing code club but said, "I don't know what he is doing really. He tries to explain but I don't really understand what he's trying to tell me." Cecilia didn't ask Beth, perhaps because there was little opportunity, perhaps because she'd found her previous attempts to interact with the school unsatisfying. When we visited the family at home, we tried to prompt Eugene to describe to Cecilia what he had done at code club, but he couldn't articulate the "coding" part, focusing instead on the game play. Possibly he did not grasp the nature or potential of coding from participating in the club, for after a while he quit, describing it as "boring," while his mother wondered if this was "because he can't practice it at home." Even for those more motivated to

---

[30] Ofsted (2018).

[31] As part of our agreement with the school, Alicia was asked to give an "eSafety" talk to parents. A handful of parents turned up, some with a long list of questions about appropriate games or websites, many with concerns about tech "addiction" or predators or bullying online. In her warm-up activity, Alicia invited parents to free-associate about "technology." One or two mentioned Skyping with relatives; most said variations of "time wasting."

[32] Family 34.

continue, there was no option to do so. The club was oversubscribed, so no one was allowed to continue for more than a term, to make way for others.

In short, much of the learning in code club was opaque to parents. Meanwhile, there were more familiar ways that parents engaged with school. For example, Bethany Carson,[33] a low-income single mother, knew little of what nine-year-old Dixon did in code club beyond the fact that "he's really interested and he's really focused, which is good to hear, because he doesn't keep focus long." Yet being out of touch with his activities at school was the exception rather than the norm. As she noted ruefully, Dixon's teacher at Bluebell was in touch with her daily because Dixon apparently talked incessantly in class, was often cheeky, and was falling behind in his work. So Bethany was called in for face-to-face meetings, but to resolve problems rather than for more positive purposes. When we described how we'd seen Dixon engaging in code club and working with his neighbor, Bethany was visibly pleased—to her, coding was an abstract good which benefitted Dixon not simply by learning the technology but also by getting him to engage, listen, and focus.

Bluebell was also beginning to use digital technologies to connect with parents, usually via text messages in a unidirectional manner, to send messages home rather than invite parental input. Such messages largely served the school's administrative needs—such as sending reminders about bringing PE uniforms from a number the parents could not respond to, though Cecilia Apau had been told by her older daughter's teacher about an app to help with preparation for the country-wide standardized exams. During our fieldwork, the school was rolling out a new "digital homework" platform called Education City.[34] Attending the information session, we watched as IT teacher Sean heroically tried to get parents and children set up with passwords on the school's iPads—although half did not have the required Flash software, so the demonstrations did not work. Further, only a handful of parents attended, so problems with passwords and lending out the iPads stretched over weeks. Education City was composed of a series of "drill and skill" literacy and numeracy apps—a far cry from the more creative activities that Beth was trying to build into the code club.[35]

---

[33] Family 14.

[34] Education City (2015).

[35] While the system was awkward, some parents managed it. Ariam Parkes (family 11, see Chapter 2), whose daughter Elen was a digital leader, described how Elen "loves going on the computer. . . . [The digital homework] is a chance for her to be doing something to do with her learning. . . . Her maths skills have improved 100%." Elen, who had previously been in code club, told us how she'd since developed her interest, explaining: "I really like using Scratch and I've got an account at home. I've made lots of projects."

In the sessions we observed we saw that Bluebell managed to reach mostly the parents who themselves sought out the school, often those higher in cultural capital (and to an extent economic capital, for although none were wealthy, they were better off than the many families at Bluebell living below the poverty line). The school's contact with other parents was either unsuccessful or defined more by problems than opportunities—as we saw with both Cecilia Apau and Samantha Winston, earlier. Ironically, the informality of the code club as an extracurricular activity might have aided better home–school connections, given that children were often enthusiastic about technology both at home and at school. But parents were nonetheless still impeded by the seeming opacity of what their children were doing. In our survey too, we found that only around half of parents—usually those with younger children rather than teenagers—thought they were well informed about what their child learned at nursery, school, or college.

Our experiences at Bluebell highlighted both problems and possibilities. Cecilia, Samantha, and Bethany were all interested in what their children were learning, but they didn't have access to it or an invitation to take part. Of the three, Samantha and her husband, Olu, were the most active in supporting their son's interests. Not coincidentally, both Bethany and Cecilia were single mothers, and so while they may have had some willingness, they had limited time and neither had Olu's digital skills (by which we don't mean to imply that mothers cannot or do not have these skills—for example, Beth Hale was also a mother at the school). We were left wondering how these parents—mothers especially—could have been invited into the experiences at the school, given the limitations of a volunteer-run after-school club and the parents' own pressures. We couldn't help but notice the contrast between the code club experience and Bluebell's efforts to connect with parents when children were in trouble, to instruct them about eSafety or offer them instrumental digital activities such as test prep or "drill and skill" homework apps.[36] For anything more creative or open-ended where, as we discussed in Chapter 4, the rewards could be significant but often nebulous, parents were largely on their own.

[36] J. Anderson (2015); Barseghian (2013); Marsh et al. (2015).

DigiCamp—the leading edge

The rapid prototyping class at DigiCamp met at a Central London "makerspace" filled with bits and pieces of "making" kits, from wearables to rolls of vinyl to copper fabric for conducting electricity. We observed lively collaborative learning as students were initiated into prototyping (a fast-paced class in which the students learned how to design, make, and iterate physical objects). All were wearing T-shirts with the slogan "Make the future." The students were mostly boys and mostly White, although there was a substantial minority of Asian students. There was confident talk about this being a "world-class center" and about the students already being "good at" technology ("you're a maker," "you're an expert"). A telling metaphor was reinforced to the students on the first day: "Everyone is working on an airplane and you are the pilot; we want to make sure you take off by the end of this week." In this messaging the educators were the "control tower" ready to help the students "launch."

Tech entrepreneur and DigiCamp founder Suzanna Rogers' vision was of a thoroughly professional enterprise: "I didn't want to base my thing on volunteers, because I wanted to be able to tell people to what standard I want it to be done and how I want them to act." She'd purposefully decided to hold her classes in institutions that would convey the prestige of her camps and hopefully inspire the students to future pathways—renting rooms at and collaborating with the makerspace at an elite London university. Although demanding of the staff, she was more flexible with the students "as long as the kids have something that is finished by the end of the week." She explained:

> They can have it be beautiful or they can have it be complicated or, you know, they can have spelling errors. We don't put the brakes on any of that stuff. What we do is hold them to staying focused and on task.

In addition to prototyping, DigiCamp ran a range of classes from learning how to code (using more complex coding languages like Python and Java) to creating video games to designing wearable technology. The model was one of self-paced, independent learning through problem solving and tinkering (either with physical objects or with code), supported by both peer and expert guidance as needed. Staffed by young educators keen to tell us that they were makers, coders, designers, and gamers in their spare time as well as at university or work, DigiCamp classes provided only minimal instructions, the ethos being to let the students make creative decisions and then live with their mistakes or redouble their efforts. This "geeky" ethos celebrated digital expertise while paying little attention to the social side of the camp. For instance, Marc Thiebault,[37] so confident at home (Chapter 3), was a loner in the Python II class, learning intently but sitting on his own at break times, seemingly in a world of his own. In this he was fairly typical, with the lack of either organized or spontaneous social interaction arguably contributing to the geeky identity of the students and the camp.

In a web design class, we observed the students work in comfortable, well-behaved silence with periodic chatter and a bit of helping among neighbors. It was fiddly work getting the code right and the students were given little creative flexibility, having to copy instructions from the whiteboard and meticulously hunt down any rogue errors to recreate an already-completed site.

Twelve-year-old Oliver[38] was a small, bespectacled boy who worked cheerfully if not very effectively. He had invited his school friend Jasper[39] (whom we met in Chapter 4) to join him at DigiCamp. The boys enjoyed the classes, working hard but also listening to music on YouTube and sharing a laugh. DigiCamp's policy was for students to bring in their own laptops—and the boys were keen to show us their specialized games machines, with lots of RAM and impressive video and sound cards. Those who brought their own laptops could leave with copies of the software installed under the DigiCamp license, meaning those with more privilege had an easier time continuing with the work at home, a sharp contrast to Bluebell, given that none of the children from Bluebell could or did carry on with their work outside of the club, and most parents did not have the means to check it.

While Jasper's mother struggled to appreciate or support his geekiness, Oliver got more support from his mother, Kylie, a high-flying business-woman unusual among our wealthy families for not having been to university. Her motivation for Oliver was twofold. First, she sought to compensate for what she saw as the failings of his private school, which restricted use of information technology outside class time, and which concentrated on

[37] Family 57.
[38] Family 52.
[39] Family 61.

the useful but hardly creative Microsoft Office software suite. As she put it: "That's just housekeeping. IT is understanding programming, web design, mobile device design." She added:

> We have a digitally savvy generation of kids and I don't think schools, even the private schools that are supposed to be really well equipped, are doing nearly enough about it.[40]

Second, she believed a different approach was needed for Oliver, who, she explained, was a visual learner, into design but inexperienced in coding and likely to find "deep coding . . . too boring"—hence he was registered in the web design course, not, say, Python.[41] Watching him play *Minecraft* "made me think he might be good at coding and had sort of an engineering mind because he was just building these amazing things all the time." Thus, Kylie described the classic "interest-driven," peer-supported process of learning, saying that "he goes and looks for stuff on forums and stuff and gets help from older kids, you know, suggestions and stuff. . . . Whatever he wants to find, he'll find." She explicitly disavowed pushing Oliver to achieve. After an interview that ranged across technology, sporting, musical, and other activities, Kylie summed up by saying:

> I want to introduce him to lots of things but then he'll just take up what he takes up. It's a bit frustrating because he often likes things but doesn't pursue them.

We heard from many parents about this mix of trying things out to see what got taken up, and while it may appear as concerted cultivation, it was also the means through which the parents supported an interest-driven learning and a self-motivated learning identity.

While Kylie focused on providing learning activities outside the home to compensate for what she perceived as the limitations of Oliver's school,

---

[40] Indeed, despite considerable privilege, Kylie felt considerable disconnection between home, school, and informal learning. Talking of Oliver's DigiCamp learning, she complained to us: "I haven't mentioned it to the school . . . it's a separate world. . . . I'm beginning to learn that schools, especially private schools, just do what they do and they pretend they're interested in what parents think. . . . What you have to do is look at other things that they're not doing that you can help sort of fill in, expose them to what the school aren't doing, basically."

[41] The notion of learning styles—as in "visual learner"—has long been popular with both teachers and parents, though a mounting body of research debunks the idea that the use of such styles is effective (Husmann & O'Loughlin, 2018).

12-year-old Esme's[42] parents saw greater complementarity between home, school, and extracurricular learning. Esme appeared to us to be one of the most self-directed students in the rapid prototyping class. We observed her designing a desert island to be cut by the laser cutter. While most students were trying to copy ideas they found online, Esme's project was ambitious and original. She was also persistent, redoing her project over and over again as she learned how to do "intersections" and "unions" using the software Inkscape, so that her pieces would fit together once created.

Esme talked about coding being "the future," a route to successful employment, and so was keen to make DigiCamp complement her learning of Scratch and Python at school and at home. For example, anticipating the transition from her state (public) primary school to her new, private secondary school, where she knew they'd be using Scratch, Esme told us:

> I experimented, because before I went to my new school I didn't really know much about coding with Scratch or anything like that. So I just experimented with it, looked up stuff, and then when I came back to school, put in the stuff that I'd practiced.[43]

Here we see the language of connected learning: interest driven, trial-and-error based, peer supported (one of her best friends loves coding too), and academically recognized.[44]

Notably, Esme had opportunities to pursue her interests at home, at school, after school, and at DigiCamp, resulting in a virtuous circle of support. This was partly anchored by a positive relation between home and school. Her mother, Anne, told us, "I think these things are generally to be embraced and I think your child has to navigate life, full stop." Both Esme's parents were professionally successful, and her father was especially keen to support her media literacy (Chapter 2) and digital making by providing specialist resources at home (Chapter 4). Esme was excited about the Makey Makey her parents gave her for Christmas (adding to the Raspberry Pi and littleBits robotics kit she already had). She and her father, Dave—a computer

---

[42] Family 53.

[43] When asked about her future ambitions, Esme told us: "I would like to become a coder, something to do with coding, like technology, like designing, like coding phones or something like that."

[44] Ito et al. (2013, 2020).

early adopter who told us he'd been "proudly online" since 1983—were figuring it out together.[45]

Anne and Dave were more enthusiastic than anxious, loving technology and, in the course of our interview, enjoying comparing social media platforms and discussing Gamergate, the potential of 3D printing, and the internet of things. They were also positive about DigiCamp—Dave went to the showcase, Anne displayed the palm trees Esme made in her office, and both parents talked to Esme about what she was learning. Although Dave was critical that the educators did not explain enough about the importance of failure in prototyping, how it's part of the process, nonetheless Esme learned critical independence from her teachers and Dave stayed involved in her learning.

While clearly her parents drew on their considerable skills, interests, and resources to support Esme, few others in our fieldwork could harness the opportunities available to them to such good effect. Two theories of learning were in play in this family: the tinkering narrative of geek culture (discussed in Chapter 4) and a more common narrative of the delicate balance required to sustain and scaffold sometimes-wayward adolescent interests without seeming to push. As Dave explained, it was not that "she'll be a software developer; this is about confidence."

DigiCamp founder Suzanna was more explicitly ambitious, telling us, "The kids are very entrepreneurial, and we want to start running some start-up, boot camp kind of stuff," since the students were constantly asking questions about "monetization and distribution."[46] Suzanna took pains to include students from a range of backgrounds—seeking out corporate sponsorship to support scholarships for low-income children like Lucas Stubbs[47] (discussed in Chapter 5). But although Anne and Dave seemed to prioritize present interests over future gains for Esme, the cultural and economic capital that we saw in abundance among DigiCamp parents suggests that they implicitly understood the possible pathways opened up by DigiCamp. By

---

[45] Raspberry Pi is an affordable minicomputer that users can use to learn programming (Raspberry Pi, 2018). LittleBits is a startup that provides easy-to-use electronic building blocks that snap together so that children can create and invent various toys and artifacts (littleBits, 2018). Illustrating the power of parents who embrace children's digital interests and parents with high cultural capital and professional privilege, Dave recounted the time that a younger and more innocent Esme had foolishly given a friend her password to the game *Moshi Monsters*. When the friend shared the password and Esme's lovingly tended pets were destroyed, Dave heroically worked his professional connections on the site LinkedIn to get them reinstated.

[46] Blum-Ross & Livingstone (2016b).

[47] Family 62.

contrast, although Samantha and Olu had a similar narrative about Eugene at Bluebell, and educator Beth was working to create contexts for creativity, the scope was much more limited, the vision less expansive, and the results less ambitious.

London Youth Arts—creative reshaping

LYA started from a child-centered vision of learning very different from Suzanna's entrepreneurship. By mixing digital media arts with other kinds of creative activities (music, drama, dance), the aim was to foster a range of expressive and "soft skills";[48] or, as SEN educator Gus put it, "It's all about fun and the arts and using the arts as a way of communicating." Explaining its social justice mission, Gus added that the "mixed ability teaching environment at LYA where everyone is on an even keel doesn't exist at school. And doesn't exist much elsewhere." Although LYA eschewed the more individualized, competitive ethos of DigiCamp, it was not immune to the potent public discourse of an individualized and competitive digital future.[49] For example, Diana, LYA's enthusiastic, no-nonsense animation teacher, discussed with her class how

> computer games are now taking over as the sort of highest-grossing industry at the moment, and . . . Britain actually is one of the leaders in recruiting people in the gaming industry, but they are really desperately short of people.[50]

Over a series of classes, Diana had the students make a comic strip about "my future life," beginning with a storyboard in Word, editing photos found from a Google search in Photoshop, and then animating the whole thing using Flash.

At LYA we watched 12-year-old Lee Styles[51] patiently spend hours carefully removing the copyright logo from his chosen images using Photoshop, while Diana encouraged the class by telling them that they could make £40,000 to

---

[48] Jenkins (2006).

[49] Blum-Ross & Livingstone (2016b); Selwyn (2014); B. Williamson et al. (2018).

[50] Diana often mixed skills teaching with a critical discussion of the aesthetic and semiotic world of the game and the wider political economy of the gaming industry, establishing a link for her students between present pleasures and future employment possibilities.

[51] Family 45.

£50,000 per year in the future by editing celebrity images of Beyoncé and the like. Lee's older brother Evan (age 17) participated in the class and worked as an assistant for Diana. He told us:

> I am making essentially a game, and I know someone who made the same thing that I'm doing, as a sort of portfolio to get a job, and they got a job.

Lee too believed this was "something I could do and learn to do well." Lee and Evan's father, Peter, was entirely supportive, believing that both the development of specific skills *and* a learning identity were required if young people were to fit themselves for a changing world. Reflecting on his own experience of being made unexpectedly redundant, Peter argued:

> Jobs for life are long gone, to be honest. . . . I think what gets you on, if you're flexible, and you will try your hand at different stuff, and you're not, "oh I can't do that." . . . [So] if you can show people your added value you will do okay.

From LYA parents we heard plenty of talk about the importance of finding one's passion or talent and nurturing it—indeed, many parents were themselves doing just that, as artists, teachers, or designers (and several had attended LYA themselves as children). Theories about digital learning were plentiful at LYA, possibly because it deliberately constructed a counternarrative of its organizational "identity" as not-school.[52] The primary theory centered on confidence: especially for children lacking confidence at school, digital technology was seen as enabling an appealing and engaging route to creative expression within an inclusive, empowering, and respectful community. Hence, LYA emphasized self-paced, interest-driven learning, with educators giving individual attention and prompt feedback as needed and older students mentoring younger ones. As we heard educators say to students on several occasions, "You're in charge." Nonetheless, the educators were torn about whether to let the kids have fun or get them to achieve and perform—their pedagogy pushed them toward the former, but a sense of expectations from funders and parents, and perhaps even their own pride, pushed for the latter.

---

[52] Sefton-Green (2013a).

We saw over and over again how, although technology appeals and sometimes empowers, it brings its own problems. At times, it seemed that educators spent more time troubleshooting than teaching. For instance, students interrupted animation teacher Diana with endless, minor technical questions: Where is it saved? What's the password? Why won't it start? Meanwhile, the students quietly ignored the puzzling questions constantly asked of them by the software: Do you want to save your password? Do you want to update the software? Beyond the in-class difficulties, there were particular problems using software to learn across sites. Often the software used in class differed from anything available at home, so children could not continue their work at home and their parents could not see their child's work or support its development (in contrast to the more privileged students at DigiCamp, who left the sessions with the software installed on their own laptops). Like Kyle in Chapter 5, we often saw children use exciting new software for the period of a free offer, without funds to continue.

Owen[53] (age 14) and Giovanna[54] (age 13), the only girl in the class, ended up sitting side by side at LYA despite very different starting points. Owen's mother, Rebecca Cox, had hunted out the free or cheap cultural activities of London for her children, believing that "education doesn't just stop at school." Although she was broadly positive about school—"I feel that they have picked up on where his strengths are and they want to push him because they believe in him and can see some sort of talent in him. . . . I'm thankful to them for that"—she captured what many parents told us about LYA as a complement to school:

> I think it gives him the freedom. He can go and express himself and be who he wants to be and doing what he wants to do with a different set of people. He can just develop the skills in the areas that he's interested in. So I feel it's good for his confidence, his self-esteem.

In Diana's class, Owen had taken the prompt of "my future life" to design a comic strip and spent a lot of time hunting online for very specific types of images to fit his chosen aesthetic.[55] He was confident in his work, perhaps because, as he told us, his dad (who was separated from his mother) was really good at Photoshop and they sometimes made parody images to "make

[53] Family 47.
[54] Family 15.
[55] Rideout & Katz (2016).

fun of each other." Despite his strengths, Owen needed close management by Diana. He worked with music on his headphones, interrupting the class by singing aloud periodically and adding lively political commentary (on gender, environmentalism) during the class discussions.

Giovanna also kept her headphones on during class but worked quietly, seemingly little interested in the assigned task or the others in the room. We observed her working with single images in Photoshop rather than trying to tell a story, cutting around a picture of a professional footballer and hoping to make the football break into pieces when kicked; she showed Sonia the YouTube animation that inspired her. Although Diana thought Giovanna's digital animation meant she had "found a sort of niche," Giovanna gained more confidence in the next class, where she took up her role as assistant director of video production (with Owen as the star actor).

As was the case so often, meeting these teenagers outside class, along with their parents, deepened our understanding—in this case of seemingly quiet Giovanna and naughty Owen.[56] Meeting Giovanna's mother, Luisa Trevisi, was something of a surprise, as Luisa told us how she had left her wealthy home and husband in Italy for a tiny flat in London to give Giovanna and her older sister a better life. Luisa said she "lives for her daughters," having sacrificed much to ensure that they became "part of the movement, part of the fiber. Be ahead of times, if they can," but was open to any direction they chose to take: "I gave them a taste of everything, so they will decide what they want to do." We noted too her signal lack of knowledge or interest in technology, framing it as a means to an end only (albeit a means "to live better"), especially as she also wanted her daughters to enjoy "those lazy Sunday mornings," to read (paper) novels (which they did), and to enjoy their childhood. Despite putting huge effort into ensuring that her daughters passed the entrance exam to a highly academic state school, Luisa was not much interested in talking about the girls' school or its relation to LYA, assuming blithely that they would complement each other. Her focus was on brokering learning opportunities for her daughters wherever they appeared.

Giovanna told us she liked to take photos at home on her phone, using iPhone apps to edit them, and she came to LYA because she didn't have Photoshop at home and because the teaching on offer was at a much higher

---

[56] We interviewed Giovanna and her mother in separate interviews in a quiet room between classes at LYA, and we visited Owen at home to interview him and his mother, Rebecca, again separately. See Gutiérrez et al. (2009); Nathanson (2015); Reiser et al. (1988).

level than at school (as she explained by eloquently rolling her eyes). Though she was quiet in digital animation, outside the class she had found like-minded peers, saying of her friends, "They're into photography like me and editing pictures." Although only 13, this mix of friends, parental support, and five years' experience at LYA seemed to have given her the confidence to map out her future:

> I want to do something with films. I like directing and I also like acting, but it's quite a hard industry to get into, and Photoshop, I think it's more like a hobby, but I would like to go into the film process industry.

Where Luisa was distinctive in greatly reshaping her life in order to push her daughters, irrespective of their chosen direction, Rebecca faced the challenge of trying to keep up with her son, Owen. He described himself with some bluster as a "computer genius" who planned a successful computer games business career and demonstrated considerable awareness of what it takes to achieve this, telling us:

> The first time I heard about the government saying they want people to learn to code I was already into it. I truly believe that coding and all that stuff is the future, so getting into it now will open opportunities that aren't even there now.

Both mothers sought strongly to support their children, and both were in-clined to theorize their parenting philosophy (Luisa talked more of the imperative to face competition; Rebecca described herself, by contrast, as "quite bohemian"). Both too felt they faced an uphill task to transcend their modest incomes and lone-parent responsibilities to ensure their children could get ahead. So while Rebecca hoped for a future of "interesting work" and fulfil-ment for her children, her philosophy being that "we never stop learning" and "anything is possible," she also felt that she herself "can't really just go off and follow a dream." Thus, she told Owen to "focus all of your energy on something that you are interested in doing and happy doing." Regarding technology, Rebecca's vision was more dystopian than Luisa's: she saw the future as a world of automatons, worrying that as the world becomes more technological, "the human touch is what's missing from a lot of these things." These ambivalences—utopian/dystopian views of a digital future and competitive/humanistic philosophies of learning—were echoed also in our interviews with educators. While sharing many of the same preoccupations as parents, educators tended to be more positive than parents about the digital future but less positive about the parents themselves.

Connecting learning—where parents fit in?

In institutional and individual efforts to connect children's sites of learning, children are inevitably the focus, for they move among the different sites routinely, while for parents such movement is generally impeded, deliberately or not. This leaves parents guessing about how their child's experiences all fit together, and about their own responsibilities. It is no wonder that they are full of often unsubstantiated theories about what, where, and how their child learns and what may benefit their child. As we have seen, parents' knowledge about what actually happens at school or in digital learning classes is limited, since neither educators nor, often, children are very forthcoming. Ironically, parents' theories can further disconnect them by creating a conflict of expectations with educators. Educators—insofar as they hear from parents at all—tend to experience parents as more problematic than insightful.

Perhaps surprisingly, the home–school disconnection was as obvious at DigiCamp, the privileged learning site, as it was at Bluebell, the under-resourced school—albeit for different reasons. Notwithstanding what we learned of Esme's and Oliver's highly supportive home circumstances, as well as the struggles faced by Jasper and some other children to gain similar support, we heard some of the educators say that they saw the parents as "demanding," expecting the course to deliver results for their own "special snowflakes."

DigiCamp positioned parents as customers expecting a high-class service,[57] striving to meet—or appease—parent demand while setting clear boundaries to maintain control over process and quality. Each class was self-contained, neither assuming that children knew much already nor mentioning how projects could be continued at home or prove useful in school. Little was said during the classes about how parents might contribute to children's learning, though founder Suzanna was aware that some parents had high-tech expertise of their own. Similarly, though she knew some parents had bought technologies such as Raspberry Pi, she assumed

---

[57] Blum-Ross (2016).

these were gathering dust at home. A carefully staged show-and-tell was provided for parents at the end of each week's camp, with students performing in the Friday afternoon session and parents clapping. The tensions this generated were visible in the clamor from parents as each sought to gain a few precious minutes' attention from Suzanna or one of the other educators.

The frustrations were reversed at Bluebell, where the educators struggled to catch the parents at drop-off or to get them to turn up to school-sponsored showcases and events. There, the teachers assumed little knowledge or interest on the part of the parents, missing opportunities for connection with families of children like Braydon Datong, whose parents actively engaged with his interests at home. This was largely a problem of resources: overextended teachers tended to reach out only when there were problems; overstretched parents attended events only when they seemed vital, and volunteer Beth Hale, who ran the code club, had little time available to corral either teachers or parents. What would it take to arrange designated moments in which parents, educators, and indeed children themselves could come together to make these connections?

At LYA, parents were invited to showcases at the end of term (or, for holiday classes, at the end of the week) and had an outreach officer for the students with special educational needs and disabilities (Mia) who telephoned parents regularly, and a newly formed parent group had begun to fundraise for LYA. But none of this was proving easy to sustain or make inclusive. Mia really hoped that technology could help in the relationship with parents. As she put it:

> I have all the information I require from them, but I don't have an ongoing dialogue. I don't know how they are at home or how they're getting on at school, which could really inform what we do at work. . . . I had an idea of having, like, each young person having a USB that we can keep all their work on, so they can take it home. . . . I think, with any parent, they want to see some of the progress they're making. Hopefully that's impacting on their home life and their school life.

Although Mia was actively looking to find means of supporting these connections, as hinted at by her choice of the word "hopefully," she was far from sure that participation at LYA was benefiting the children at home or school.

In interviews with educators, we would often start with an open question about how the site worked, who used it, and what the approach to learning was, and then we would listen for spontaneous mention of parents. Often there would be none, as if children arrived from and left for nowhere, or nowhere interesting. We then invited educators to imagine the parents' response when the child brought home his or her new knowledge or showed anticipation of the next class. While wanting to know more about the LYA children's lives at home, SEN educator Gus conveyed his frustration that parents were unable to keep up with learning and progress made in class during their time at home. At Bluebell the perception was that parents were mostly partners in children's discipline, including in relation to their "screen time"—but not especially in relation to their digital learning.

But more common than a pejorative view of parents was no view at all. This is puzzling insofar as the educators were often enthusiastic and reflexive about their teaching and nuanced in their treatment of individual students. This led us to wonder whether there is a structural problem in making parents visible within learning? Learning sites provide few opportunities for parental engagement. Drop-off and pickup are often busy and a bit chaotic. Performative show-and-tell moments favor one-way demonstrations to parents of what children have learned. Newsletters, emails, intranets, and other digital communications are, equally, unidirectional,[58] with dialogue reserved for troubleshooting a child's problems.

Yet in the digital age there are experiments underway to connect learning at school, home, and elsewhere. Such connections could support learning across and, therefore, within sites.[59] But they risk introducing inequalities— with more time-limited or less digitally skilled parents less confident in using the services; with nonstandard forms of knowledge gained at home unwelcome, or perceived to be so at school; and with educators reluctant in practice to "open the floodgates" of parental problems, including the demands of middle-class parents, into their carefully managed and externally accountable learning sites.[60]

[58] Bazalgette (2010); Buckingham (2007).
[59] The Connected Learning Research Network has explored how nonformal learning initiatives experiment with digital technologies precisely because they afford flexible and creative ways to connect, learn, and participate. Drawing on these insights, it has sought ways to redesign educational institutions so that the unique properties of digital technologies can be used to "scaffold" young people's interests into academic achievement, career progression, or civic participation. See Ito et al. (2013); Sefton-Green & Erstad (2016); Ito et al (2018); Ito et al. (2020).
[60] Buckingham (2007). It might be said that DigiCamp found ways to supplement its instrumental teaching with some learner-led and mentor-supported practices, while at LYA, which explicitly avowed a social justice discourse, funding pressures resulted in a degree of instrumentality (Blum-Ross & Livingstone, 2016b).

Conclusions

Though children move between home and outside learning sites, the adults in their lives do not, and so each is sometimes left with frustration. Educators lament that parents are "hard to reach" or in some cases "pushy." Parents feel frustrated with what their children are (or are not) learning but are often too busy—or in some cases too disenfranchised—to overcome this. In our research, parents' and educators' theories of learning embraced both digital technologies and the affective and identity-led ways in which children gain skills such as focusing, communicating, perseverance, and, indeed, creativity. Both parents and educators saw themselves as responsible for fostering these qualities, but each seemed to be doing so in isolation. In our survey, around half of parents thought their child's teachers valued what they learned at home, fewer thought their child's teachers valued what they learned in extracurricular activities, and just one in three thought what their child learned at nursery/school/college connected with their family activities at home. The survey also showed that parents were working hard to enable opportunities online while addressing risks, although they tended to lack support for dealing with digital dilemmas or recommendations about which opportunities might lead to actual benefits.[61]

Even when parents are addressed by educators, rather than there being a readiness to learn from parents' and children's interests and expertise, "parents are seen essentially as agents in ensuring the conformity of childhood to . . . state agendas," educationalist Berry Mayall comments acidly.[62] For sure, educational organizations may keep parents at arm's length because they fear that listening to and including parents would be disruptive. But as we have found, it is problematic for parents that schools find it challenging to respond to their conceptions of their role and its possibilities. Consequently, for all their talk of "parental involvement," schools tend to miss a host of educational and cultural practices that are already happening in children's homes.[63]

---

[61] Livingstone, Blum-Ross, Pavlick, & Ólafsson (2018). For instance, more than 4 in 10 UK parents used the internet to support their child's learning or schoolwork (48%) or watched a video (e.g., on YouTube) to help them or their child learn something new (44%).

[62] Mayall (2015, p. 319).

[63] Livingstone & Sefton-Green (2016); Silander et al. (2018). For example, Brooker (2015) showed how Muslim children had, with considerable effort, memorized verses of the Qur'an, only to see this less acknowledged at school than the English nursery rhymes learned by their peers. Lisa Guernsey and Michael Levine (2017) formalize what's needed from community organizations to structure this support, calling for attention to inclusion, responsiveness to community needs, evidence of impact, training for parent mentors, and harnessing of the potential of online connectivity.

This disconnect—born of institutional conservatism, predispositions, lack of time and imagination, and sometimes exacerbated by the very technology meant to help ameliorate these problems—means that the promise of new learning pathways is often undermined by missed opportunities and iniquitous outcomes. The more it becomes convenient or taken for granted to assert a deficit rather than an enabling theory of parents and parenting,[64] the more frustrations result for parents and, also, for educators, who feel they must *make up for* the limitations of the home.[65] The result, of course, is a negative spiral in which positive connections across learning sites become ever more elusive, further burdening the child to do the work of "connecting" his or her own learning and learning identity.

To answer policymakers and educators who are serious about promoting children's digital skills and competencies: our time in digital learning sites suggests that increased efforts to enlist parents and connect with children's learning lives at home could pay dividends. Possibly, well resourced learning sites can show the way, since they often do better at including or connecting with parents, and since parents with more cultural capital are better able to build continuities home, school and other learning sites. This is no surprise, of course, but we hope that by examining how this works we have provided food for thought for policymakers who could, given the political will, provide resources (money, equipment, training) for less advantaged children. Such resources, if made available, would stretch further if parents – many of whom are willing to participate – could be included in the very design of the learning site: welcomed, informed, listened to, respected for their own skills and interests, perhaps tasked with ways to extend their child's learning at home. Although this remains a proposal more than a reality, and notwithstanding the risk that policymakers' and educators' efforts might serve further to burden parents and "curricularize" the home,[66] our fieldwork suggests that, creatively managed, the gain could be on all sides. The current enthusiasm for digital learning on the part of parents, children, and educators could provide fertile ground for such experimentation.

---

[64] Ito et al. (2013); Ramaekers & Suissa (2012).

[65] Extracurricular educators felt they had to compensate for the deficiencies not only of home but also for school. We heard their sometimes-justified critiques of school, with its exhausted or overburdened teachers, tied to the dictates of the national curriculum or lacking capacity for excitement or innovation.

[66] Buckingham (2000).

7

Imagining the Future

Looking back, to look forward

Although only eight, Mia Ealy[1] was already a "digital leader" and excited about learning something "special" at Bluebell Primary School's code club. Her mothers, Rachel and Erin, were determined that Mia's gender would not channel her "down this bystander route rather than the person who is instigating the action, the maker, the doer." Rachel worked part time as an artist and gardener, a creative if hardly lucrative combination that allowed her time to volunteer at the school and keep a close eye on Mia's "portfolio" of opportunities. Like many parents we interviewed for this book, Rachel saw digital technologies as promising her daughter a path to self-realization that she too embraced in forging new practices of family, class, and gender.[2] And importantly, opportunities that she had not experienced herself, having been prohibited, as a girl, from pursuing her youthful interest in woodworking.

Yet Rachel had little specific to say *about* these digital opportunities—here too she was typical of parents we interviewed. Digital technologies were focal in visions of the future—for good and for ill—but parents struggled to make sense of what, in practice, this might mean for their children. In looking back to understand the present and imagine the future, Rachel focused on her specific experience of being limited by her gender as a point of comparison, while others had different experiences to compare. Not all parents were as sanguine as Rachel that they could take steps to ensure that digital technologies could benefit their children. But whether motivated by a nostalgic vision of a lost "golden age" of childhood or, instead, keen to improve on memories of "the bad old days," the past is at least tangible. Many parents described to us a childhood of too many rules, parents who were "old school" or "traditional," fathers who were too strict or absent. Such vivid memories motivated them to parent differently, as befits the more democratic family. By contrast,

---

[1] Family 20.
[2] Averett (2016).

Parenting for a Digital Future. Sonia Livingstone and Alicia Blum-Ross, Oxford University Press (2020). © Oxford University Press.
DOI: 10.1093/oso/9780190874698.001.0001

and necessarily, the future remains an abstraction—far away and hard to predict, and thus for parents a source of uncertainty. Web designer dad Henry Stoddard[3] reflected:

> If we are going to live in a society that is hugely affected by technology in every single way . . . then kids have got to learn a different way of thinking, learn a different way of doing things. I don't know if it's necessarily bad or what?

Middle-class "mum blogger" Melissa Bell[4] (Chapter 4) fretted:

> I really can't predict. Things have changed so much even in the last 10 years; it's unrecognizable from 10 years ago. I've got no idea what will be around in 15 years' time.

Meanwhile, Daya Thakur,[5] a low-income single mother of four (Chapter 2), echoed the vague yet hopeful views of many: "I don't know. I imagine them to . . . I just want them to be happy and independent . . . and successful." Daya imagined her children's future unfolding in more challenging circumstances than she remembered from her own childhood, having grown up in a tight-knit Bengali community all of whom lived nearby. Today, she said, "it's society, the fear. When I was growing up everybody knew each other and now nobody hardly knows each other. . . . They've got closed lives now." This loss of social support was felt acutely by parents with children with special educational needs, for whom the future was almost unthinkable. Ali Kader, father of Sana[6] (a 16-year-old on the autism spectrum; Chapter 5), said: "I don't think much, really, for the future. Because otherwise I get mad. So I better just take it step by step." And Alice Sheldon,[7] a single mother with little social or financial support for herself or her daughter, Sophia, who has Down syndrome, simply said, when asked about Sophia's future, "I hope that I outlive her."

As we discussed in Chapter 1, parents' sense of being left "to their own devices" in coping with a challenging present and an uncertain future is not

---

[3] Family 32.
[4] Family 38.
[5] Family 10.
[6] Family 9.
[7] Family 1.

so much a result of individual actions. Rather, it is a product of the long-term trends in individualization and neo-liberalism that, together, divide parents from each other and "responsibilise" them for the effects of societal transformations. These trends are manifest in the changing and often difficult social and economic conditions that shape families' lives. As we have shown in this book, society tells parents that they should support their children's development and build their future by engaging with, and managing, digital technologies. But, it seems, society then prefers to criticize parents for their digital practices more than to enable or support them.[8] This raises the critical question: what societal structures and forms of solidarity are needed, given that traditional forms of representation and support are waning?

In this chapter, at the conclusion of our journey through the homes and lives of a diverse group of families in London, we argue, on the one hand, that how parents imagine the digital future shapes the present lives of families and, on the other, that many present actions regarding digital technologies are likely to have future consequences. We then examine whether and how it matters that these daily negotiations that stitch together past, present and future often take place on the terrain of the digital. For, as we further argue, the digital is far from neutral, and it brings its own opportunities and risks. In relation to these, as in other matters, parents are too often spoken for or about, rather than really listened to. Hence we end with their voices, paraphrased as recommendations to those with the power to improve families' lives by developing and promoting new forms of engagement and inclusion.

Future talk

Imagining the future seems simultaneously necessary and impossible for parents. It is necessary because the most mundane activities of parent and child are constantly weighed for their potential to realize parents' hopes and fears for their child, decades hence. If "part of the experience of being a parent is to want one's child to be and do certain things," then being able to imagine those "things" and to realize them in practice is crucial.[9] It is impossible not only because parents know the future cannot be predicted, but also because the clamor of future predictions in the public sphere (from politicians,

---

[8] As Elizabeth Gee and colleagues observe, the messages parents receive can leave them "fearful and hopeful, and oftentimes just plain confused" (Gee, Takeuchi, & Wartella, 2017, p. 2).

[9] Ramaekers & Suissa (2012, p. 74).

experts, media gurus, marketers, and science fiction writers) is contradictory and contested, with multiple competing interests at stake.[10]

Using the term "future talk," Alper analyzes the dialogic process through which societal and political discussions of "the future" and of technology are drawn on to construct personal, intimate narratives within families.[11] For instance, Lena Houben's (Chapter 1) "future talk" centered on the expectation that "we are heading towards a kind of virtual and robotic cyborg future," shaping her present parenting in distinctly resistant ways.[12] She launched into an impassioned account of teaching her children cooking and where their food came from. Her concern was less with producing a meal than with encouraging "the handling of physical things as much as possible [to] prepare them for the virtual world, making sure they had a concrete world before." Yet Lena's resistance went only so far, for she sought balance too, enabling her daughter Miriam to share her poetry on a blog.

Such balancing is linked to a considerable ambivalence over the meaning of *now*—the present moment between the parents' remembered childhood and their anticipation of their child's adulthood. Like many, blogger Melissa Bell was torn between looking backward ("I want my children to have a *Famous Five* upbringing, you know, running around in the garden") and forward ("technology is the way forward, and jobs-wise, you know, it'll give them a head start, and I just think it'll become the norm").[13] Such parents were nostalgic for the past: that childhood of fresh air, creative play, and muddy knees, which offers so evocative a counterpoint to a sanitized, dystopian science fiction future. But they were also pragmatic: if technology is the future, let's get on with it.

Our survey suggested that hopes for technology are widely felt across society: nearly all parents (88%) believed "It's important for my child's future that they understand how to use technology." The associated anxieties were also largely unrelated to socio-economic status: half of the parents surveyed said that society *should* worry about technological change, with little difference by income. This is not an easy balancing act: Lena's, Melissa's, and Rachel's accounts of their parenting sustained an ambivalent mix of

---

[10] Education researchers Bill Penuel and Kevin O'Connor (2018) "call attention to the need for more explicit attention to where images of the future come from—so that we can be appropriately critical of them" (p. 68).

[11] Alper (2019).

[12] Family 6.

[13] *The Famous Five* is a widely popular collection of children's adventure–mystery novels written by Enid Blyton.

embracing and resistance not only to technology but also to the competitive culture of individualism which commonly promotes its value.

We heard these ruminations most explicitly (although not only) from middle-class mothers who seemed to bear the personal responsibility of juggling competing values and desires within the family and in relation to society's normative expectations.[14] Perhaps it was also easier for them to feel the proximity of that aspirational (if rosy) vision of the past—for Melissa Bell did have a leafy garden just outside her suburban terraced house—unlike Daya Thakur, who lived in a high-rise council flat. However, it is too easy to vilify the anxieties of middle-class mothers—think of recent books about "helicopter parenting," "tiger mothers," and "paranoid," "free-range," or "sacred" parenting.[15] Parents were generally reflexive about the rising anxiety they felt—and they tried (not always successfully) to resist it. Kylie Jackson,[16] high-income mother of 12-year-old Oliver and 8-year-old twin daughters, described how

> I've lived with nothing but fear from the moment they were born. Yes, because it's so important and they're so vulnerable and things can go wrong. . . . [But] you can't be overprotective—that's going to have an adverse effect on the child. . . . I can't spend my entire time nagging him, badgering him, to do things that he ought to be doing that are good for him because it would just make everybody's life a misery.

Grappling with "the fear" and trying, somehow, to move past it was far from specific to parents' struggles with technology. As Amber Boon, mother of Maggie (age five) told us, facing an "amazing amount of choice is quite anxiety-making [since] we live in an extremely competitive world."[17] As we argue below, the uncertainties of the digital, along with the competitive pressures from society, intensify these anxieties and distinctively disempower many parents.

Yet it is a mark of how influential this image of anxious parents is that we were sometimes surprised to find ourselves visiting calm and cheerful families. Across class backgrounds, as this book has revealed, we met some parents

---

[14] Oster (2019); Warner (2006).

[15] Faircloth & Murray (2014); Furedi (2008); Hartas et al. (2014); Kohn (2016); Littler (2013). See also Douglas and Michaels (2005), who state: "Intensive mothering is the ultimate female Olympics" (p. 6).

[16] Family 52.

[17] Family 19.

at ease with their children's digital activities, seemingly able to strike an easy match between present pleasures and future aspirations. Sometimes this reflected parents' confidence in their particular "parenting philosophy,"[18] implicit or explicit. Sometimes, parents were confident in their ability to parent in the face of social change because, to use Diana Baumrind's influential term, they adopted an "authoritative" parenting style, characterized by open and warm communication yet also maintained clear boundaries.[19] For some more high-tech parents (e.g., Dani,[20] in Chapter 4), this confidence was born of having advanced digital literacy—accompanied by curiosity about their children's "geeky" interests. This allowed them to bridge the gap between present and future by meaningfully engaging with their children through technology, providing resources, setting them challenges and spurring on their interests.

Even for parents with few digital skills, an open-mindedness about digital technology, or an empathetic identification with the experience of being a child, allowed them to support their children by asking questions and finding new resources. Daya Thakur had no particular digital skills but could enjoy her daughter's growing prowess at doing hair, learned from YouTube. Rachel Ealy was not particularly digitally skilled either, but she could see (and knew to ask about) the elements of creativity and learning in Mia's activities as a "digital leader," which included coding, game play, and robotics. Other parents valued digital opportunities to maintain contact with distant family and friends or to connect with religious and cultural practices and values. As we discussed in Chapter 3, we heard the most reflexive accounts of parenting that eschewed society's (over)critical judgement from lower-income but well educated parents who created parenting philosophies alternative or resistant to the seemingly accepted norm of "concerted cultivation" or "intensive parenting." In other words, the balance they achieved in relation to digital parenting was grounded in their alternative parenting values more generally.

But whether their circumstances were fortunate or difficult, and whether expectations ambitious or modest, many parents nonetheless seemed to us

---

[18] Clark (2013).

[19] Baumrind's (1971) landmark studies found "parenting styles" differed in the degree to which parents exerted authority over their children and the degree to which they showed their children warmth and affection. She differentiated "authoritarian" (high control, low warmth), "authoritative" (high control, high warmth) and "permissive" (low control, high warmth) parents. Developmental psychology has shown the disadvantages of "authoritarian" compared with the optimal style of "authoritative" parenting. Similar findings hold in the parental mediation literature (Clark, 2013; Livingstone et al., 2017; Nikken & Schols, 2015).

[20] Family 56.

confident, even optimistic—as confirmed also by our survey findings, where three-quarters of UK parents said they were fairly confident or very confident of their child's future.[21] Migrant filmmaker Wembe Kazadi said rather romantically of his daughter Mani's shy interest in fashion and son Bintu's growing interest in mechanics, "I would like to see them having their dream happening." Such optimism contrasts not only with media panics about technology but also with the critical social science literature, full of pessimistic predictions about the rise of neo-liberalism in which flexibility is configured as precarity, technology as a driver of inequality, and solidarity is doomed.[22]

We heard from parents familiar with portentous predictions but who created positive visions anyway, to retain a hopeful vision of the future. Peter Styles,[23] whom we saw in Chapter 6 encouraging his sons to gain digital media skills, drew on the dystopian predictions of labor market crises prevalent in the financial press to explain to us that "jobs for life went a long time ago." He nonetheless felt hopeful about their future when contrasted to his own "lousy childhood" dominated by "rules, rules, rules" and parents who "didn't really spend any time with me." A middle-income information technology (IT) worker, Peter had experienced precarity the hard way when he was unexpectedly made redundant. Now he urged his sons to try to be flexible and open to whatever the future may demand of them.

Watching and listening as parents embraced, balanced, and resisted— sometimes with acute anxiety and sometimes without—we came to an understanding of how future talk shapes the present. Next we explore how the future itself is made, however intangibly or indirectly, through the activities of the present. Our focus is on inequality, given our findings about how economic and cultural capital helps middle-class parents face their problems, leaving the poorer families, and the parents of children with special education needs and disabilities, to bear a more acute individual burden. Recall Leila Mohammed,[24] from Chapter 3, who spent much of her income on extra classes and technology for her girls, or the parents of Lucas Stubbs[25]

---

[21] In the Parenting for a Digital Future survey, compared with their own childhood, 70% of parents said their child had more opportunities, although two thirds also thought they faced greater pressures. Relatedly, The Children's Society's (2019) *The Good Childhood Report 2019* shows that UK children are broadly happy, though recent years show a slight decline.

[22] We develop these ideas in Livingstone and Blum-Ross (2019); see also Ito et al. (2013, 2020); Jenkins, Shresthova, et al. (2016).

[23] Family 45.

[24] Family 35.

[25] Family 62.

in Chapter 5, who were elated to win the scholarship at DigiCamp.[26] These parents' investment in technology can be so hopeful and yet it is less recognized, often leaving them without support to help their children achieve what their parents may imagine.

Future consequences

Are parents right to believe that, by encouraging in digital media learning at home, school or through extracurricular activities, they can increase the chance of their child keeping up or even getting ahead? This and similar questions about parental investment are all the more urgent now that young people are, for the first time in decades, forecast to be less prosperous than their own parents.[27]

In the postwar period in the United Kingdom, United States, and other wealthy countries, jobs were plentiful, education offered a reliable route to a good standard of living, the middle class was expanding, and inequality was falling. Sociologist John Goldthorpe documents how, in effect, for today's grandparents:

> The rise of the salariat—creating ever more "room at the top"—and the corresponding decline of the working class . . . created, in the middle decades of the last century, what has been aptly called the "Golden Age" of social mobility, when social ascent clearly predominated over social descent.[28]

But in recent decades, inequality has risen,[29] unionization has fallen, wealth has become more concentrated among the elite, education (itself

---

[26] Marianne Cooper (2014) observes that she heard seemingly disproportionate worries about risk and security from families who were objectively better off.

[27] As John Goldthorpe (2016, p.96) states, "Younger generations of men and women now face less favourable mobility prospects than did their parents—or their grandparents: that is, are less likely to experience upward mobility and more likely to experience downward mobility."

[28] Goldthorpe (2016, p. 93). Although claims about social mobility through the 20th century remain hotly contested among sociologists and economists (Savage, 2015b), young Britons are pessimistic about their prospects for social mobility (Social Mobility Commission, 2018). See also Exley (2019). The mass media reinforce this pessimism, with headlines such as "More Than Two Thirds of Millennials Believe Their Generation Will Be 'Worse Off' Than Their Parents" (*The Telegraph*, July 8, 2019). Interestingly, technologically experienced parents are particularly optimistic that they can prepare their children for a digital future (TechUK, 2019).

[29] Long-term trends suggest that, since the late 1970s, around when today's parents were born, income inequality has increased. But since the economic crisis of 2008, UK government efforts to reduce inequality through benefits and taxation have proved effective (Corlett, 2017; Cribb et al., 2013; Goldthorpe, 2016; Office for National Statistics, 2017a).

increasingly stratified) no longer produces secure dividends, and social mobility has declined. Like Lareau and others (discussed in Chapter 3), Goldthorpe predicts that middle-class parents will, henceforth, make ever greater efforts to give their children advantages, to forestall downward mobility even if they cannot guarantee upward mobility. One response is to hope that digital technologies can provide the magical ingredient needed to secure children's prospects. For others, "wasting time" on digital media and technologies symbolizes the potential for a child to fall behind.

As we have shown, these hopes and fears are compelling not just for the middle classes but, for a range of reasons, for parents across the socioeconomic scale. According to The Social Mobility Commission, families in London have more cause for optimism than those living elsewhere in Britain. They report that "The capital provides more opportunities for its residents—including its poorest ones—to progress than elsewhere."[30] Some of these opportunities are specifically in the digital and creative sectors. Savage adds that elite occupations in the field of information technology "may be more open to talent drawn from wider pools," supporting parental hopes that the digital revolution may enable greater social mobility.[31]

Supporting these employment prospects is the critical mass of educational and cultural resources that a capital city can provide, something that many parents we interviewed were very aware of. Of course it matters whether or not parents positively enable their child to take up such opportunities: a long history of social science research shows the importance of early parental investment in shaping children's life chances.[32] But will this make the

---

[30] Social Mobility Commission (2017, p. iv). Specifically, London has "by far the highest development outcomes for disadvantaged children" as well as "the smallest attainment gap between disadvantaged children and their peers" (p. 25). It adds: "Good outcomes in London are likely to be due ... to a mix of demographic factors, parenting styles, social capital and the breadth of opportunities on offer in London (e.g., parent and baby classes, museums, libraries, art galleries etc.)" (p. 25). Improved school results over the past decade also play a role (Balestra & Tonkin, 2018; Selby-Boothroyd, 2018). But living in London brings other problems. While the Social Mobility Commission (2018, p. 5) found that Londoners were more optimistic than the rest of the country about their opportunities, they were also more likely "to feel worse off than their parents in terms of overall living standards, job security, and housing," with the cost of housing playing a large part in this.

[31] Savage (2015b, p. 197). It is not our argument that all parents hope for future employment for their children in the digital sector, though they are aware that most jobs will involve use of technology in some form. But parents do recognize that digital activities attract children, stimulate motivation, build confidence, afford diverse choices, make visible learning pathways, and promise plausible outcomes. In short, they afford a practical, yet often risky, means to actualize the values parents live by—for their children and also for themselves. This was most clearly articulated by the parent bloggers we interviewed (Blum-Ross & Livingstone, 2017).

[32] J. S. Coleman et al. (1966); Feinstein & Sabates (2006); L. L. Putnam & Fairhurst (2015). "Successful progression" to adulthood or work depends on the role of parents and, especially for

difference? Social mobility is stable overall, but among today's parent generation, around one third have stayed in the same social class as their parents, one third have moved up, and one third have moved down. If this pattern continues, there will be an equal chance of a child doing better or worse than the parent—accounting for the high hopes and the anxious fears. As our fieldwork and survey found, parents are generally more optimistic than pessimistic, with almost half thinking their children's future chances for stability will be better than their own, whether or not this is merited.[33]

The factors that underpin social mobility (or its absence) have been heavily researched. But they cannot provide a definitive prediction for an individual child, for the many influences on children's life chances are difficult to disentangle.[34] Studies that follow up on ethnographies of teenagers some years or even decades on tend to conclude that powerful forces of social reproduction mean that, as a generality, children's life chances often, but not always, turn out to be similar to those of their parents.[35] We had the chance to explore how this works in our present study, since some of the families we visited at age 18 had been visited a few years before, when 14, as part of a previous book, *The Class*.[36] Even after this fairly short interval of years, families' class positions did not straightforwardly predict children's outcomes. For example, Abby Adams,[37] from a low-income home, had overcome a history of significant personal problems, including learning to cope with haters and bullies online, and been accepted to a good university to study business. She credited her interest in business to a childhood helping out on her father's market stall. As an older father, Jonathan saw the digital world as "a foreign territory, because we've not been used to it," but his confidence

---

marginalized or minority youth, on informal local networks (S. Henderson et al., 2012; Sefton-Green, Watkins, & Kirshner, 2020).

[33] In the Parenting for a Digital Future survey, when asked about their vision of their children's future financial and professional stability, 44% of parents thought their child's chances were greater than that which they had enjoyed, while 36% thought them about the same and 20% thought them worse.

[34] In *The Class*, Livingstone and Sefton-Green (2016) identify a host of seemingly minor but potentially consequential factors that shape children's prospects. Relatedly, Sefton-Green and Erstad (2016, p. 4) explore "the changing place of the meaning of education and institutional pedagogies across all the nooks and crannies of everyday life," worried by what they call the growing "pedagogicization" of everyday life (see also Bernstein, 1990; Erstad et al., 2016).

[35] S. Henderson et al. (2012); Lareau (2011); McClelland & Karen (2009); Thomson (2011).

[36] Of the 28 children (from diverse ethnic and socioeconomic backgrounds) who originally took part in *The Class* when they were then aged 13 or 14, eight agreed to be reinterviewed four years later, at age 18. Revisiting those families helped us understand how things had developed during those crucial years. Of those eight who could be recontacted, two were from low-income, three from middle-income, and three from high-income homes.

[37] Family 66.

came from his personal and professional experience as a Christian and an ex-youth worker, respectively, helping him to both scaffold Abby's learning and rebuild her self-esteem. He told us with pleasure that at last "she has a future in front of her."

For those from wealthier homes, the outcomes four years on were also mixed. Alice Cantrell[38] had plans to go to a good university to study psychology, seemingly following in her mother's footsteps. Her professional parents, Maria and Theo, had always been confident she would do well, though they had had a prolonged struggle with the school over its failure to address Alice's dyslexia.[39] However, Sebastian Cooper,[40] from an upper-middle-class professional family, had eschewed the traditional university entry process and had turned his love of drama, long shared with his mother, into an ambition for a career in film. He had had a psychological crisis a year before our follow-up interview due, his mother suggested, his sense of academic pressure and anxiety about his future. With significant family support, he was working as a technician in the school's media department while trying for film school. His future seemed, therefore, "digital"—and also very uncertain.

As far as we could tell, what made the most difference were parents' own interests and expertise, and the culture and resources of the family and school, along with a mix of unplanned biographical events. Throughout our fieldwork, parents talked to us of the digital as a source of both hopes and fears, but with the possible exception of the geeky families discussed in Chapter 4, it is hard to know whether parental investment specifically in digital opportunities brings benefits over and above other opportunities. Education scholars Richard Arum and Kylie Larson[41] report a positive association between children's participation in digital media learning sites such as we have discussed here (see Chapter 6) and their educational engagement and persistence with learning at school and outside it. Thus although technological resources and expertise are unequally distributed, as are forms of social and cultural capital that enable the reproduction of social advantage,[42]

---

[38] Family 68.
[39] Alice herself marked her growing maturity through her learning to manage digital communication—no longer getting embroiled in fraught exchanges with strangers online. We had a similar exchange with Megan (family 71), who was determined to rebut the negative claims about "the younger generation" (that they have no sense of privacy and are addicted to technology, rude, and without values) and crossly asserted that such talk, in and of itself, is harmful to young people. This is made poignant by hearing just such negative views anxiously reiterated by her mother.
[40] Family 73.
[41] Arum & Larson (forthcoming).
[42] For instance, middle-class families discuss the pathways in much more concrete terms—aware of the steps to be taken, naming universities to apply to, recounting the statistics for the professions,

we cannot rule out the possibility that those parents and children who made efforts to harness the "geeky" opportunities of the digital age (Chapter 4) may yet see some success flow from their investment, of identity and resource.

Why is the digital so salient?

While we have been researching this book, innovations in connected devices, algorithms, virtual and augmented reality, robotics, artificial intelligence, and smart everything from homes to cities have been much in the news. Science fiction is blurring with public policy predictions and commercial business models, all pitched not only in the distant future but just a few years hence. Both experts and the general public are trying to grasp and manage changes that are highly complex, fast-paced, and all-encompassing, with potentially wide-reaching implications for work, leisure, learning, and public and private life.

Although societal change is, as social scientists repeatedly point out, evolutionary, not revolutionary, popular talk of "the digital" (as in "digital parenting" or "digital natives" or, indeed, the "digital future") favors a compelling narrative of dramatic transformation unfolding from a set of technological innovations—the invention of the internet, the launch of the smartphone, the internet of things.[43] Meanwhile, the future is viewed with a mix of utopian, futuristic, science fiction imagery and dystopian, doom-laden policy predictions (the end of "jobs for life," the demographic "time bomb," the bankruptcy of the welfare state, health crisis, periodic pandemics, and more).[44]

No wonder that mention of digital technologies seems to catalyze hopes and fears for children now and in the future. For the present generation of parents—whose own childhoods were more technologically simple than their children's—the narrative of transformation seems to have particular appeal as an organizing principle. Nine-year-old Elen Parkes,[45] also a "digital

---

reading thought leaders whose ideas have influenced them, ready to tackle their child's school if they judge more could be done. Josephine and Michel Thiebault, from one of our wealthiest families, discussed in Chapter 3, mentioned Schumpeter's economics, the theory of disruptive capitalism, neural networks, and the future of digital identity in our interview with them.

[43] Helsper & Eynon (2010); Livingstone (2018); Mansell (2012); Prensky (2010); Twenge (2017).
[44] For example: "By 2030, populations' needs and resources will be orchestrated by self-learning, digital technologies.... Digital natives will lead the charge ... [but the benefits] will be limited to the digitally literate" (Institute for the Future for Dell Technologies, 2017, p. 10).
[45] Family 11.

leader" at Bluebell, hoped for a job working with technology. She got lots of support from her mother, Ariam, whose explanation illustrates several of our findings:

> I do recognize how important technology is now more than ever. I believe in human progress and how far we've come. I came here [from Eritrea] for a better life, and I'm absolutely intent to take advantage of [it]. I think life has changed for the best. I think there's a lot of negative stuff about technology, but I think the positive outweigh the negatives.

Like many parents, Ariam believed that technology is changing society in important ways, contributing to "human progress." Also like many—as confirmed by our survey findings[46]—she believed she could balance the positives against the negatives. Further, like other migrant families we interviewed, Ariam Parkes came to the United Kingdom "for a better life," which, she envisaged, includes benefitting from digital technology—for herself and for her daughters. The challenges of such a move must have been (and will surely continue to be) considerable.

So while for most parents, the digital marks the distance between their own childhood and the experience of their child, for migrant families it is also symbolic of the difference between the life they left behind and the life they can now provide for their family. Other parents had yet other reasons for anchoring their hopes for the future in their child's digital activities—whether because of the "elective affinity" between technology and a child's special educational needs and disabilities (Chapter 5); because digital opportunities could potentially overcome poverty or disadvantage (Chapter 3); or because a "geeky" identity affords an alternative route out of personal difficulties (Chapter 4). Our point, here, is that the digital is salient because, whatever the deep-seated problems facing families, it seems to offer a viable future path—for some parents the only such path they can foresee.

Compounding parents' various reasons for focusing on the digital, we have also argued that they cannot avoid the acute interest evinced by the

---

[46] Our survey found that parents weighed the benefits a little higher than the harms, seeing the value of technology for supporting school learning, pursuing hobbies and interests, being creative and expressive, and preparing for future work. They were more doubtful, but still not negative overall, about benefits to their child's relationships with family or friends (Livingstone, Blum-Ross, Pavlick, & Ólafsson, 2018).

wider society in all things digital.[47] It has taken just a few years for the global technology companies to displace those from the domains of manufacture or natural resources as the world's largest and most profitable—and it is precisely their business to fill our time and imaginations.[48] With a host of predictions about the implications of technology for work, education, social mobility, health, and more, as well as continuous headlines warning of digital risks, parents find themselves bringing up their children in a cultural climate of intense speculation about the digital future. Parents wanted to discuss with us not just their personal dilemmas but also the societal implications of technological innovation—its ethics, its creative potential, the consequences for education, a host of online risks of harm, the future of crime, datafication and the end of privacy, and more. The question was not just "What kind of future will my child have?" but also "What kind of world will they live in?"

This wider culture of speculation explicitly hails parents, calling on them to avail their child of opportunities to learn yet simultaneously to limit their screen time, to contact their child's teacher electronically but to stop staring at a screen or sharing images of their child, and to keep up with the latest developments but to regulate their child's digital activities and their own. To meet these expectations, parents are inevitably drawn further into monitoring the media landscape for news of the latest opportunity or problem or for available advice, heightening their awareness of their digital responsibilities. Since the rise of parenting culture (discussed in Chapter 1) has coincided with the digital age, one result is an explosion of official and unofficial advice on "digital parenting"—along with a fast-growing market in expert seminars, self-help books, apps, and technical tools. Probably some of these help, but they come with considerable baggage, motivated by a range of (largely tacit) official, commercial or ideological interests that may or, crucially, may not put parents' interests first. Certainly they are hard to ignore.

Notwithstanding these often burdensome expectations, for many parents, the digital is associated with agency—not only for their child, but also for themselves. Parents are keen to bring up their children in their own way, endorsing an ethos of individualization that means they wish neither to follow in their own parents' footsteps nor necessarily to obey the diktats of

---

[47] Arguably the media self-interestedly hypes its own importance, deploying considerable resources to promote the latest technology innovation or disaster and invest it with utopian or dystopian predictions about the future (Cassell & Cramer, 2008; Critcher, 2003; Kamenetz, 2018; Nature Canada, 2018; Nelson, 2010).

[48] Livingstone & Blum-Ross (2019); Wooldridge (2016).

official advice. Their primary strategy is to facilitate learning opportunities, whether at home, at school, or elsewhere. Parents are not unaware of social science findings showing that education is the best investment parents can make in their child's future. And the digital is promoted as offering exactly this opportunity.

Of course, the digital is also salient because of the mundane practicalities of living with what Lena Houben called the "tsunami" of digital stuff entering the home (Chapter 1)—the screens that parents trip over literally and met-aphorically. These demand a never-ending series of seemingly mundane yet somehow fateful decisions about expenditure, use of time and space, and needed expertise and, more subtly, about relationships, values, and identity. Some of these decisions concern risks of harm unfamiliar from the parent's own childhood, this very unfamiliarity adding to parents' anxieties, though some manage to take the risks in their stride.[49] In relation to questions of risk as for other challenges of the digital environment, parents cannot draw on the parenting they received themselves. Nor can they turn to their own parents for digital advice, as they can for advice on other matters, as our survey showed.[50] Digital decisions also challenge parents' expertise or re-sources, including by comparison with their children's sometimes-greater knowledge.

For all these reasons and more, the digital can be exciting or worrying, resulting in considerable domestic negotiation, and sometimes conflict. But although seemingly familiar, digital technologies are in many ways strange and challenging, transforming family life as much (or more) as they are finding their place within it, as we examine next.

What difference does the digital make?

In this book, we first answered this question in terms of parental imaginaries, examining whether it matters that contemporary parenting culture is pre-occupied by the digital. Reflecting on how keen parents were to talk about how they managed technology at home, we have argued that the digital offers

---

[49] As the EU Kids Online project has long argued, the risks keep changing as the socio-technological environment changes, while the harms to children are more familiar. The point of dis-tinguishing risk (the probability of harm) from actual harm is to recognize that parenting, childhood vulnerability or resilience, media literacy, social context, education and a host of other factors me-diate the highly-contingent relation between risk and harm (Livingstone, 2013).

[50] Livingstone, Blum-Ross, Pavlick, J., & Ólafsson (2018).

a "safe" way of expressing anxieties and seeking support about parenting decisions, certainly by comparison with difficult conversations about the other challenges they face—such as inequality, relationship conflict, values, migration, poverty, sexuality, or racism. The emotion that often accompanied our interviews led us to suspect that, although discussing digital-related experiences, parents were *really* telling us about their struggles—to make ends meet, to envisage a future for a child with learning difficulties, to stay in contact with their country of origin, or even to feel "in control" of their child and relationships. Perhaps it is easier to talk *in relation to* the digital, as this is a terrain in which, regardless of special circumstances, *everyone* is interested, allowing more unequally distributed concerns can be addressed while remaining tacit.

But at the same time, talking about the digital may be displacing or, more problematically, obscuring other concerns. Many of the structural problems facing parents are due to circumstances not of their own making, and are difficult if not impossible for them to resolve. But parents *do* feel personally responsible for the influx of digital media into their children's lives. Thus, they feel doubly burdened—responsible for introducing such risky technology into the home yet still hopeful that they can realize the promise of cherished learning resources, creative opportunities, and valuable workplace skills. Hence the frustration many parents told us about, on seeing a child lost in his or her phone, staring at a screen, or upstairs immersed in a game and deaf to calling: these everyday experiences of seeming unreachability make visible to parents their limited power to manage not only their child's digital activities but also, and more profoundly, their present and future.

Whether or not it is effective, at least digital parenting guidance offers practical steps (buy a computer, enroll in a coding club, download educational apps, install a filter, or limit screen time). This leads parents to feel they can—and should—control their family's digital life. This contrasts strongly with other dimensions of family life where practical steps are often lacking. For instance, it is not easy for parents to secure the future for their disabled child, or resolve their marginal status as a migrant family, or cope with poverty or family breakdown. Indeed the wider struggles around power in the democratic family (see Chapter 1) offer no handy guide, for cultivating a culture of mutual authority is hardly as simple as buying a piece of tech.

But the digital is hardly neutral in its consequences for family life. So we also ask, what difference does the digital make by examining the nature of the digital itself. Several digital affordances are of particular importance.[51] Technology is complex and fast-changing (and thus challenging for people to mold to their advantage). It is largely proprietary (operating in the interests of global business). It brings new audiences with whom to share experiences but also radical uncertainty as to who is listening, or how to control one's privacy. Scalable platforms enable ready access to a huge breadth of available information but provide no easy way to select what is *good* for one's child. Any of these *may* be beneficial, provided one has the digital literacy and social position to manage them. Further, technologies afford new practices—for example, enabling parents to work from home, to find new kinds of social support (Chapter 2), and to redesign the timetable and spaces of domestic life to scaffold and connect children's learning in creative ways (Chapter 6).[52] What enthuses many parents is how the digital affords new ways of "doing family." As one young blogger mum, Beth,[53] from a professional family, cozily described:

> Sometimes, like at the weekend, they will come up to our bed, we will all have toast in bed, we might put the telly on, they might want to play on the iPad, that's more a kind of, oh, we can stay in bed for just half an hour more.

The family curled up in bed together, sometimes watching a show together and sometimes pursuing individual preferences and interests—in sleep or in apps on the iPad—demonstrates, first, the ways in which the digital affords egalitarian and entertaining activities which suit the ethos of the late modern democratic family (Chapter 2). The way in which the digital enables both communal and individual preferences while also symbolizing tensions between these was, in one way or another, evident in most families. However, new opportunities give rise to new inequalities, and we found a host of ways in which opportunities are missed, tensions arise, or barriers are erected, especially for families living in poverty (Chapter 3) or facing problems because of their child's special educational needs and disabilities (Chapter 5). Thus the effects of the digital interplay with other circumstances, of gender,

---

[51] Digital devices, services, and networks have been characterized by danah boyd (2011) as being distinctively characterized by the affordances of persistence, replicability, scalability, and searchability.

[52] The Connected Learning Research Network (Ito et al., 2020) seeks not only to conduct research but also to guide the design of digital media learning initiatives so that they foster young people's own interests; mentor affinity-based activities; build accessible links from youth activities to systems of opportunity; support collaborative production; provide pathways for participation, coordination, and brokering across settings; and ensure mechanisms for progress and achievement.

[53] Family 7.

race and ethnicity, the presence or absence of family or social supports, and the context of parental relationships, necessitating an intersectional approach.

Society's deployment of the digital intensifies future uncertainties by promising greater opportunities but worse risks than traditional pathways—and here too we see inequalities based on parental influence and social capital. The very nature of this promise questions received knowledge—suggesting, for instance, that it might be playing computer games rather than good grades that leads to a career in the creative industry. But whether these promises will be realized is necessarily uncertain, since it is difficult for research to predict future outcomes, certainly by comparison with the decades of longitudinal research examining which benefits flow from choices about education or neighborhood or "good parenting." Thus, there are few grounds on which parents can judge these digital promises or rein in their excesses. They are, in short, stuck in the middle of an experiment in digital parenting which they and their child cannot evade. The resulting anxieties not only compound pre-existing tensions but also send parents in search of expert guidance that may or may not answer their questions or serve their interests. Yet some families—particularly the geeky families who embrace a digital lifestyle, but also some of the poorer or more marginalized families in our study—may succeed in harnessing the alternative potential of the digital to sidestep or find a workaround for traditional forms of socioeconomic exclusion.

Despite their frustrations with control in the here-and-now, in some ways parents are prepared to live with future uncertainty, for seeking total control over their children's lives does not fit the contemporary parenting ethos. Rachel Ealy resisted the idea that

> I am determining to an extent what she would do when she is 35 and 40 and 50. Now that seems crazy to me because I imagine the world being full of choices.

Indeed, many parents told us that, as Luisa Trevisi[54] (mother of Giovanna, Chapter 4) put it, their guiding principle was to give their child "a taste of everything, so they will decide what they want to do." In other words, modern

---

[54] Family 15.

parents choose to give their child the opportunity to *choose for themselves.* Their efforts are often less designed to foster a particular route than to ensure the child will have choices. This may explain their vagueness about the future, for they may not have, or even expect, to imagine a particular future for their child. Food blogger Andrea[55] told us:

> I just want them to be able to make good decisions. I want them to be able to be comfortable and confident with who they are. I don't want them to be sheep, to just follow the crowd.

Critical scholars may judge that parents mistake their own best interests in endorsing this seemingly neo-liberal philosophy. But there's no doubt that many expressed it, and that it dovetails with the sense of rapid change and future uncertainty of the digital age, providing parents with a narrative to live by.

Listening to parents—what did we learn?

We invited parents to reflect on family life in the digital age. They told us how digital technologies make life harder, because they are attention grabbing, high maintenance, often divisive or controversial in their immediate effects, and uncertain in their long-term consequences. But they also make life easier, they added, because they pacify, they are individually rewarding, and they enable shared pleasures, learning and future possibilities. But over and above telling us how they embraced, balanced, or resisted digital technologies in navigating a path between what was practical and what they hoped was "best," parents also revealed their deeper values and beliefs. It is these that we have tried to listen to in writing this book.

What has been the value of foregrounding parents' voices and experiences? First, we have challenged outdated notions still circulating in policy and public domains of parents as "digital immigrants" who understand little about technology or obsess only about policing their children. We have also challenged ill-conceived assumptions of working-class parents being neglectful or uninvested in their children and middle-class parents being hyperanxious and pressurizing. On the contrary, we have shown that many

---

[55] Family 64.

are confident, and many try to do a good job by continuing to learn, as a life-long process, using the affordances of the digital age.[56]

We have also challenged the narrative that family troubles are centered primarily on digital devices, recognizing the profound—if less headline-grabbing—difficulties that parents face associated with financial insecurity, migration, disability, or family reconstruction. This has allowed us to challenge the popular temptation to homogenize parents or to judge their actions out of context, by instead revealing the diverse circumstances of family lives. Nonetheless, we have heard that, although the digital is often not the main problem, technologies loom large in parents' minds and families' problems are mediated by the digital in ways that are far from neutral, often serving to reconfigure or complicate or intensify prior problems in new ways.

Although parents' narratives shared many similarities, in effect seeming to bind "separate biographies" into a kind of "collective experience," this appeared to generate little solidarity among parents.[57] Parents conveyed little sense of collective agency, but also, over and over again, they told us how they felt unsupported by their own parents, their peers, their child's school, and professionals whose task it is precisely to advise them or develop policy and practice for families. They were also relatively unsupported by the digital environment, which addressed them largely as irrelevant to their child's online experience, although occasionally giving them opportunities to police or cheerlead.

Just as parents negotiate their family's past, present, and future in part through a focus on the digital, policymakers concerned with family health, childhood, and early years of education are also focused on parenting in the digital age, often fixating on screen time as the telling indicator of good or bad parenting. In response to official screen time advice, we heard parents castigate themselves as "lazy" or "crap" because of their child's screen time, or they sought to prove their good parenting by telling us about nondigital family activities. Having found that this advice both erased families' diverse and often reasonable motivations for engaging with technology and occasioned intergenerational conflict, we now welcome signs that the two-by-two screen time mantra (see Chapter 2) is being rethought.[58]

---

[56] Our survey found, for instance, that many parents agreed, with little variation by socioeconomic status, ethnicity, or child's age, that "I feel I am doing a good job as a parent" (29% strongly agreed and a further 55% agreed).

[57] Beck & Beck-Gernsheim (2002, pp. xxiii–xxiv).

[58] See Stiglic & Viner (2019) for a rethinking, and see the World Health Organization report (2019) for a more conservative view. New advice is also being developed by the American Academy of Pediatrics.

But the landscape is broader than just screen time. Digital affordances should be understood as material, social, and institutional in their origins and consequences. The actions and values of designers, marketers, policymakers, and users all combine to give meaning and consequence to the digital, as has been long argued by social studies of technology against any simple form of technological determinism.[59] By the same token, therefore, those actions and values could be rethought or redesigned in ways that alter what the digital affords families now and in the future.

Having listened to parents' hopes and fears, researched the considerable diversity of their circumstances, and reflected on their lack of collective voice, we end this book by highlighting six recommendations that could support parents as they take steps as towards realizing their visions for their children's future in a digital age.

1. *Provide support for parents that encompasses the digital environment.*
   Many of the professionals tasked with guiding and supporting families (health visitors, social workers, educators, local government, librarians, general practitioners, consumer protection, even law enforcement, etc.) struggle to keep up with the latest developments, research and advice regarding the digital environment. Mechanisms are needed to inform them in their work with parents, whether by state, public, or third-sector organizations, to provide independent sources in addition to the fast-growing market in commercial products targeted at parents. Creative approaches are also needed to reach beyond middle-class urban parents, including support for other caregivers, including grandparents, as well as for parents of children with special educational needs and disabilities. This might harness public interest in the digital but should also go further, since digital problems are rarely experienced in isolation from other kinds of difficulty. Outreach for families should not only emphasize children's safety online but also help parents and other caregivers recognize quality experiences and helpful learning environments. Prioritizing safety without opportunities will only exacerbate digital inequalities.
2. *Offer parents a realistic vision in public and media discourses.*
   For journalists and policymakers tempted by hyperbole: don't play to parents' greatest hopes and worst fears, and avoid polarizing and extreme formulations of problems, whether in relation to parents, children

---

[59] Hartmann (2008); Mansell & Silverstone (1996).

or technology. Instead, recognize and reflect parents' lived realities and offer positive directions, informed guidance, and balanced solutions. In discussing childhood, education, or family life, a child-centered approach should be integrated with a parent-respecting approach, avoiding the temptation to pit children and parents as opponents in a battle or a zero-sum game. While digital innovations provoke legitimate speculation about their potential impacts, ensure that coverage is evidence-based and does not obscure needed critical attention to the other problems that families face. Industry providers should avoid promoting fearful messages and products that treat parents as ignorant, encourage placing children under surveillance (above all without their knowledge), or oversell technological "solutions" for deep-seated problems.

3. *Recognize the contribution of parents in educational settings.*
   Educational institutions, especially but not only schools, should recognize that parents are instrumental in enabling children to access educational resources and need to be offered information, understanding, expression, and routes for possible complaint. Anticipate that parents will try to foster their child's learning across sites, including at home, and design convenient and sustained opportunities for parents to engage with and support their child before, during, and after their participation in learning sites—including designing opportunities for parents themselves to learn from the educational context or directly from their child. While media and digital literacy within the population is rising, so too is the complexity of the digital environment. Public and industry initiatives to support media literacy must be expanded, both for children and also to reach parents from all walks of life. The burden for parents (and teachers) of understanding, evaluating, and using technologies effectively should be eased by better technology design, and resources of genuine educational value—independently assessed to the extent possible—that can be widely shared and used.

4. *Increase attention to the design and governance of the digital environment.*
   There is a lively debate in many countries about the desired balance between empowering the public through education versus regulating the digital environment. Any resolution is likely to unfold over time, with campaigners calling for child protection, speech rights (including for children), ethical design, privacy and data protection regulation, regulatory oversight of businesses, technological innovation in the interests

of children and families, and more. In this often-clamorous contestation, parents' voices should be included in ways that respect their efforts to empower their children and secure their future in deeply unequal and uncertain times. Practically, this has implications for both policymakers and industry. Each should create and disseminate easy-to-use resources—such as an accessible "one-stop shop" for informing parents and responding effectively to their concerns. The industry especially should harness its capacity to reach parents, providing parent-friendly resources and guidance tailored to the needs of diverse groups, and there should be a robust public discussion—including parents, industry, policymakers and research—about whether these resources are having the desired impact. This should include deliberation about which design features can promote opportunities and which impede or detract from them, undermining parents and potentially harming children. It is also time to implement, and ensure compliance, for child-appropriate and family-friendly design of services used by children.

5. *Make room for parents' voices in policymaking.*

For those responsible for developing legislation, regulation and policy that impact on families, children and the digital environment, don't exclude parents as "hard to reach" or speak for parents when they can speak for themselves. Do not assume parents to be unaware of the contours of the digital world or simply interested in policing or spying on children's media use, nor imagine them to be a homogenous group facing equivalent challenges. Avoid symbolically erasing parents as people and citizens in official talk of "the home" or "the family" and actively consider the mediating role of parents in children's access to resources. Identify and support groups who speak for parents collectively, and make efforts to represent the diversity of parents and their circumstances in the development of policy, services, and practice that affects them. Research parents' actual concerns and existing practices, as well as the conditions that shape them. Recognize their collective and individual agency and interests, to anticipate and meet their needs as well as enable their participation in educational and other relevant institutions.

6. *Ensure that policy, and the design of technology, is based on evidence.*

There is a robust literature on parenting, including on parental mediation of digital technologies, and on family dynamics, but little of this is heard within policy debates nor in relation to the design of digital services. Policymakers, educators, and industry should develop advice, tools and resources for parents that are grounded in evidence not media panics, and that address both short and long term concerns. For parents to choose apps or digital resources with educational merit, knowing that they have been designed and evaluated to ensure there is evidence for claimed learning benefits is vital. This can include independent evaluations, collaboration with experts or mechanisms for iterative design and testing that incorporates feedback from parents, children, educators and research. Parents, and society, want to know whether current and emerging forms of digital commercialization genuinely limit or prejudice children's choices and life chances. It is time that robust evidence was generated to resolve the heated debate over technology use and children's health and well-being outcomes. The evidence needed to address these and a host of further issues must be mindful of intersectional issues like gender, class, race, (dis)ability, and more. And evidence is needed to inform societal as well as individual dilemmas of digital parenting—for example, regarding the growing culture of parent shaming, or changing norms of parental monitoring at the cost of children's privacy, or adults' undermining of civility online in ways that impact harshly on children and families.

Final words

Too often, society looks through or past parents to their child without properly considering the identity commitments and resources invested by parents. Recalling Beck and Beck-Gernsheim's observation that the West has framed the child as its "last hope of enchantment," this book has conceived of parenting as a particularly intense "project of the self" (to use Giddens' term). Giddens' notion of the project of the self has proven particularly resonant for the culture of late modernity, and we have also found his notion of the democratic family helpful. Yet it is striking that Giddens (and Beck) says little about family life, especially that lived between parents and dependent children. It is thus easier for him than for us to align the project of the self with the historical trend towards individualization (and even with the ideology of individualism). We have instead highlighted the shared nature and responsibilities of family life, encompassing both the extended family (and, for some, community) and the family stretching across generations into the past and future. Hence the idea of 'the project of the family' captures the imaginative investment in oneself and one's family over and above the practical demands of raising a child. In the digital age, parents' imaginations are intensely mobilized by their hopes and fears about technology. These hopes and fears are fanned by a society that takes little responsibility for the realities of families' digital lives or the opportunities open to them, preferring to pass the responsibility to the parents it then judges for their "failures" or ignores as muddle-headed or "hard to reach."

We have argued that parents are caught in a pincer movement in late modernity, simultaneously more burdened with responsibilities under neo-liberalism and yet less able to exert control, given that the ethos of the democratic family means they must respect the agency of their child, and that the unfolding risk society leaves them less supported by traditional structures. This leaves much to negotiate—both by society and within the family. We have further argued that, to a significant degree, the negotiation of authority, values, and relationships now takes place in relation to digital technologies, not least because these are now highly focal, appealing and yet frequently disconcerting. Among those parents who, often because of their specific circumstances, particularly embrace *or* resist technology, the heightened public attention to all things digital intensifies their uncertainties. Even though most parents, most of the time, seek a balance between these contrasting approaches, their everyday struggles may be compounded by their family's immersion in the digital world, with its own novel and complex affordances.

Our inclination is to judge parents' effort to balance as wise, given the uncertain benefits of both embrace and resist. But we have also sought to demonstrate how different families balance in different ways, according to their inclination, resources, and imagination. Balancing is, precisely, a constant and necessary *effort* to weigh the practical options and negotiate these both within and beyond the family. Significantly, our fieldwork has revealed a considerable diversity in parenting practices, values, beliefs, and imagination, to the point where alternative lifestyles become ordinary and what is supposedly typical proves relatively elusive, with "normal" itself perhaps a parenting imaginary. Yet, we have also found many commonalities in parents' experiences, in their efforts to respond to the demands and judgments of society, capitalize on the resources available, cope (or not) with the challenges they face, and strive for meaningful family and cultural narratives across the generations.

The digital means parenting on a larger canvas of possibilities than ever before, but in conditions often not of parents' own making. Through their construction of parenting philosophies that vest effort and values in ordinary tasks, and through their adoption of embracing, managing, and resisting practices, parents aim to enact an everyday calculus of what is worth doing, why, and what the costs might be. Thus they show themselves to be inventive in navigating the uncertain path between past, present and future. Yet this path is strewn with difficulties, misunderstandings and missed opportunities. It is now for society—policymakers, educators, journalists, designers, industry, and more—to hear parents' voices, value their efforts, address the inequalities that divide them, all to better support them as they strive to make sense of, and prepare for, the digital future.

Research Methods

Our approach

This book is informed by several disciplinary traditions within the social sciences. By training, Sonia is a social psychologist and Alicia a sociocultural anthropologist. The research was conducted in a department of media and communications, and was largely funded by the MacArthur Foundation–funded Connected Learning Research Network. The network draws researchers from sociology, anthropology, psychology, education studies, learning sciences, disability studies, informatics, human–computer interactions, science and technology studies, and beyond. This multidisciplinary mix led us to frame an in-depth qualitative study, supplemented by a quantitative national survey of UK parents.

The Connected Learning Research Network grew out of an intensive study of young people's digital and creative practices, which explored the emerging "genres of participation" for engaging with digital media and technology.[1] In its founding statement of 2013, the network defined connected learning as

> socially embedded, interest-driven, and oriented toward educational, economic, or political opportunity. Connected learning is realized when a young person is able to pursue a personal interest or passion with the support of friends and caring adults, and is in turn able to link this learning and interest to academic achievement, career success or civic engagement.[2]

In recent years, the network has examined the diverse efforts underway to construct supportive learning pathways that enable children to transition into adulthood, including into the world of work (whether creative or not), so as to identify when and why digital technology can facilitate these pathways in a fair and inclusive way. Among a series of intersecting projects, the network funded Sonia's previous research, with Julian Sefton-Green, which resulted in the book, *The Class: Living and Learning in the Digital Age*,[3] a study of a year in the lives of a single class of 13- and 14-year-olds in London, some of whom were revisited for this study. There, we drew on the idea of "connected learning" to explore what happens in the different "sites" of young people's lives (home, school, extracurricular or interest-driven learning spaces, with peers) and how these sites are connected or disconnected.[4]

In the present research, we were guided by three core principles that integrated theoretical and methodological considerations.

---

[1] Ito (2003); Ito et al. (2010, p. 15); Livingstone & Lunt (2013).
[2] Ito et al. (2013); see also Ito et al. (2018, 2020); Jenkins, Shresthova, et al. (2016); Watkins (2019).
[3] Livingstone & Sefton-Green (2016).
[4] Ito et al. (2020); MacArthur Foundation (2014); Reich & Ito (2017).

First, we invited parents to share their "stories of the self," including their efforts to grasp how "the apparently haphazard contacts of everyday life may still constitute some kind of structure holding the individual to one biography."[5] Inspired by the tradition of narrative research, we see parents' stories as "strategically constructed and voiced narratives" so that they are both personal and constituted by wider social and cultural processes.[6] We attended to the ways in which parents respond to what is undoubtedly a lively public conversation about digital technologies, parenting, and the task of "parenting" digital technology in the present and future, without attempting to ascertain the "truth" or "fiction" of these narratives.

Second, we looked for "future talk" within these narratives, fitting with our interest not only in present practices but also in how these shape and are shaped by future fantasies, worries, and imaginaries. Though we were interested in conceptions of the future, parents often found it easier to discuss the future in relation to the present or the past. Thus, we listened for explicit or implicit future orientations within our interviews, acting in what Ruth Levitas calls an "archaeological mode" to excavate "shards and fragments" to assemble into a cohesive delineation of a desired future.[7]

Third, we chose to research parents in their own right and to reflect on their own experiences, hopes, and fears, including but also going beyond what they wished for their children. In our main field of media and communications, parents are primarily researched as a conduit to understanding the lives of children. In youth culture studies, we found plenty of research on young people's engagement with digital technologies, but their parents were often shadowy figures or entirely absent. By prioritizing the voices and experiences of parents and by recognizing not only their commonalities but also their diversity, we hope to counter instances where parents are spoken for in their absence and to recognize their experiences within academic and policy debates about the family or children and digital technologies.

Selecting the families

We took two complementary approaches to organizing our selection of families. On the one hand, we sought out diversity, recruiting parents across the spectrum of age, social groups, and life circumstances. The 73 families whose lives with technology we discuss in this book included the rich and the poor and those in the middle, from different walks of life and of different ethnicities. We interviewed parents who were straight and gay; lone parents and couples; parents sharing care with ex-partners, grandparents, and paid caregivers; parents of all religions and none; parents who were happy and sad and worried.

On the other hand, we purposefully sought out those who might have something particular or even exceptional to say about the role of digital media and technology in their own or their children's lives.[8] We elected to search for families who would give us insight into practices connected to emergent or changing technologies, environments, and social

---

[5] Burkitt (2008); Goffman (1963, p. 92).

[6] T. Miller (2005, p. 8), Giddens (1991); Goffman (1963); Gubrium & Holstein (2009); L. A. Jackson et al. (2009); Lieblich, Tuval-Mashiach, & Zilber (1998); Polkinghome (2007); Gillies (2011); Duggan et al. (2015); Andrews (2014).

[7] Levitas (2013). See also Alper (2019).

[8] Palys (2008); Roy et al. (2015).

debates and/or issues and groups we felt were underexplored in the current literature.[9] We chose to prioritize the following:

- Parents of children and young people who were engaging in digital learning experiences in code clubs, apps development, digital design, new media production, and more. We found a curious absence of information in the research and practitioner literatures about where young people's digital interests come from or the role of parents in sustaining or undermining them. Thus, we were interested in families who had in some sense "voted with their feet" by signing up for digital opportunities, whether instigated by the young person or the parent.
- Parents who blogged about their family lives and participated heavily in social media as part of their parenting.[10] In this case we wanted to understand the practices of highly digitally skilled parents to explore the popular stereotype of parents as "digital immigrants"[11] (a stereotype this book refutes) and to understand the intersection between children's and parents' identities online. This allowed us to explore the interplay between parents' experiences and skills with digital technologies in their own lives and how they conceived of the digital world for their children.
- Parents of children with special educational needs (SEN) and disabilities. The ways in which parents of and children with SEN relate to, through, and around digital media are often rendered invisible in studies that focus only on able-bodied families.[12] Yet, as we found, parents and children with SEN often invest significant emotional and financial resources in digital technologies and associated learning opportunities, resulting in particular barriers and risk but also new workarounds and pathways.
- Parents who could reflect on how "the future" had played out or was playing out in the lives of their children. To do this, we took the opportunity to do longitudinal follow-up interviews with children and parents who had been previously interviewed as part of *The Class*. Recontacting families four years later permitted a unique insight into how family engagement with digital technologies changes over time.

Some families fell into more than one category. Not all families fell into one. We kept an eye on diversity, so some families who were recruited based on their participation in digital learning sites ended up being interesting because of the presence (or absence) of resources, or because they were parents whose children had disabilities who also blogged about their experiences.

Siting our research in London brought strengths and limitations. Our participants were characteristic of those living in global and super-diverse cities, with high levels of income inequality and considerable diversity in culture and ethnicity. London is a center both of migration and of the creative industries—we found that we had higher-than-average numbers of parents who were migrants and/or were either securely or marginally employed in digital or creative fields.[13] Although we made proactive efforts to find families

---

[9] Sometimes called a "systematic nonprobabilistic" sample, the aim is to "identify specific groups of people who either possess characteristics or live in circumstances relevant to the social phenomenon being studied" (Mays & Pope, 1995, p. 110).

[10] Lenhart & Fox (2006).

[11] Prensky (2010).

[12] Alper (2014); Cranmer (2017); de Wolfe (2014); Rutkin (2016).

[13] The Creative Industries Federation quotes the UK government definition as "those industries which have their origin in individual creativity, skill and talent and which have a potential for wealth

in digital learning sites who were from low-income backgrounds, we struggled to find families who could be described as "White working class." This is most likely because low-income London families are disproportionately from migrant or minority ethnic groups and many of the low-income White families we interviewed lived with considerable disparity between their high cultural capital and relatively low economic capital, reflecting our efforts to recruit creative and digital families.

Given that our interviews were conducted over the course of a year, by the time we held our final interviews with families, we were already well into our analysis. At that point we realized that we had found the limits of what we could grasp and write about, with "data saturation" meaning that newer interviews tended to produce further evidence for themes and codes already identified, rather than radically new topics.[14]

Recruitment

We recruited families by a variety of means. Initially we approached several learning sites, conducting single or multiple initial gatekeeper interviews in which we detailed our research, presenting the head teacher, program manager, or other relevant authority with written information about our research. We explained that we wanted to approach families for in-home interviews ideally but might also interview parents on their premises if they and the parents agreed and so wished. These sites included (all names are pseudonyms):

- **Bluebell Primary School**, a multiethnic (majority Afro-Caribbean, African, and Black British) primary school in South London serving a high-deprivation community with above-average numbers of students learning English as an additional language, and two thirds of students eligible for the "pupil premium"—a criterion that gives a sense of the high levels of poverty, some of them officially in the care of ("looked after" by) the local authority.[15] We conducted six visits of two to three hours each to the after-school coding club, also interviewing the parent volunteer who ran the club. We recruited parents during parents' evenings and by approaching parents at school and at code club pickup, facilitated by members of the parents' committee or teachers. We observed an eSafety training for Bluebell staff and met parents during information events for the school's new "digital homework" platform. We visited the affiliated "Children's Centre," which ran various sessions for parents, including a morning drop-in frequented largely by Muslim women.[16] In exchange, we were asked to give a talk to Bluebell parents on eSafety, and did so.
- **London Youth Arts** (LYA), a youth and community-oriented venue funded mainly through public and some third-sector grants. LYA offers free or very low-cost classes

and job creation through the generation and exploitation of intellectual property." According to its statistics, the creative industries generate 5.5% of the UK economy and employ more than two million people, a figure that has risen by 30% since 2011. See https://www.creativeindustriesfederation.com/statistics.

[14] On data saturation see Bowen (2008); Fusch & Lawrence (2015).

[15] "Looked-after children" is the UK government (Children Act 1989) designation for children for whom a court has granted a care order, including children who are fostered or living in local, authority-run care homes ("Children in care, Looked after children," 2007; UK Government, 2017).

[16] Children's centers can be attached to primary schools as part of government policy to provide additional support for low-income families.

in a range of performance and media-based art forms for children and young people aged 5 to 26. The families attending LYA are highly mixed; the venue is in an affluent area but draws families from across North London, with a preponderance of high-cultural-capital parents, some of whom attended LYA themselves as children or, lacking significant economic resources, were keen to take advantage of the low-cost activities. We visited the Saturday morning classes in music production and digital animation as well as a class in digital media production for young people with SEN that met weekly for several months. We were invited to evening showcase events for parents. We approached parents, with the introduction of staff, during Saturday and evening sessions while parents waited for their children or as they dropped them off or picked them up. Separately and together we visited LYA approximately 16 times over several months, also interviewing several of the educators formally and informally. At the conclusion of our research we were invited to prepare an informal report for the staff of the SEN group, and we visited them to give our feedback directly—also recording this session for our research, with their permission.

- **DigiCamp,** a fee-paying summer camp emphasizing "high tech" digital opportunities for young people aged 9 to 17, which took place both at a makerspace and at an elite university in Central London. The camp largely attracted families who could afford the significant (by London camp standards) fees, but also offered scholarships to students who could not otherwise afford to attend, although this comprised only a small overall percentage of attendees. We visited the camp over several weeks in summer sessions, visiting separately seven times while observing classes on rapid prototyping and coding with Python (an advanced coding language). We interviewed the camp founder and spoke with some of the educators. We approached parents directly during drop-off or pickup as they waited for their children, and the camp founder facilitated introductions by including a description of our research in the camp newsletter and emailing introductions to a handful of families directly at our request—including parents who were involved in the running of the camp and those whose child had received a scholarship.

To include some less digitally focused families, we supplemented our recruitment efforts using convenience and snowball sampling. First, we included four families previously recruited via a pilot European study on the digital literacy activities of families with young children.[17] We also revisited a number of families from *The Class*, as noted earlier. In a few cases, parents we had interviewed recommended friends to speak with, whose participation we pursued, although with not more than one such "snowball" referral per family; this helped with the inclusion of families who were not specifically interested in digital technologies.[18] Last, to reach parent bloggers, we contacted the editor of the Mumsnet Blogging Network, a network of (then) 8,000 blogs about parenting and associated issues that are registered on Mumsnet, one of the most popular online fora for parents.[19] We explained the project and asked the editor if she would be willing to pass details about our project on to London-based bloggers, who we then contacted directly. To supplement

---

[17] This research was part of a seven-country European study (Chaudron, 2015). It was funded and coordinated by the Digital Citizen Security Unit Institute for the Protection and Security of the Citizen, European Commission. See also Livingstone et al. (2014). The sampling for this study involved contacting schools selected as "ordinary" and inviting parents to volunteer for the research project. They were included here to help balance the more digitally focused forms of recruitment.

[18] D. L. Morgan (2008).

[19] N. Henderson (2011); Mumsnet (2016); Pedersen (2016).

the blogger parents, we combined snowball sampling, searching online for "London mum/dad blog," and interviewing "dad bloggers" attending a national parent blogging conference.

Not all parents that we identified via these means were interested in participating, of course. Once we had made initial contact with parents, we followed up with an email, text, or phone call—making sometimes more than one but not more than two to three attempts to contact them. Of those we spoke with briefly, about a third to half gave us their details for us to follow up, and of those about half to two thirds actually resulted in interviews. Approaches to "captive" audiences—namely the parents hanging around at LYA while waiting for their child to finish a class—yielded slightly higher numbers.

There were strengths and weaknesses to our approach to recruitment. The first is that even though we took pains to approach a wide variety of families, our participants skew toward those who felt they had something to say about parenting and/or children and technology, were knowledgeable about research or interested in our topic, felt some social obligation to the person who had introduced us to them, or were interested in receiving the voucher we offered. We had stretched our budget to include these vouchers, even though this is not necessarily standard practice in ethnographic research, thinking (as our interviews bore out) that this might help us gain access to parents who might otherwise not see a research interview as being "for them."

Fieldwork

Before beginning the project, we sought and obtained approval from the London School of Economics' Research Ethics Committee, and we each obtained official criminal record checks. Interviews took place between April 2015 and October 2016. Although we did not conduct "traditional" long-term ethnography, we conducted participant observation in learning sites. Our primary research corpus consisted of "ethnographic interviews"[20] in sites familiar to our participants, building rapport by adopting a flexible and informal interview style and listening to parents' concerns even when they didn't correspond to our research questions—indeed, often *particularly* when they didn't. After all, we were not "hypothesis testing," although we had a sense of some of the areas we would investigate from the outset, informed by our review of the literature and our previous research.[21]

Our interview protocol was semistructured, allowing us to be responsive to the topics raised by parents in discussion.[22] Often we deviated from the guide if the parent raised a particularly interesting line of discussion. In later interviews we sometimes took the opportunity to ask about or reflect on some themes emerging in our analysis, cross-checking our insights with parents. Participant observation took place in learning sites either intensively over a period of few weeks or sporadically over the course of a few months (as earlier).[23] We took intensive field notes in these sites, joining classes—sometimes observing from the sidelines, sometimes joining in the activities and discussion.

---

[20] Skinner (2012); Spradley (1979).
[21] Agar (2008); Ito et al. (2013); Livingstone (2009); Livingstone, Hasebrink, & Görzig (2012); Livingstone & Helsper (2008).
[22] Doucet & Mauthner (2008); Patton (1990).
[23] Participant observation is when the observer participates in ongoing activities and notes their observations (P. Atkinson & Hammersley, 1994).

For some parents we held interviews on site at the learning sites while they waited for their children, finding a quiet corner or going to a nearby café. Other families specifically requested that we meet at another location, for convenience or perhaps out of a desire not to reveal their homes to us. However, the majority (two thirds) of interviews were held in family homes. Sometimes we visited during the day while children were at school or while a stay-at-home parent tended to a baby or toddler. Sometimes we visited in the evening while the children were in bed or watching TV or playing games in the next room. Sometimes we visited over the weekend while the whole family was around. Interviews were scheduled opportunistically, as it was clear that family time was precious and that most of the families we interviewed (across social class) led very full lives—visiting family and friends, engaging in religious activities, shuttling from one class to the next, or making time for swimming, bike riding, movie nights, and more.

Visiting families at home allowed us to see for ourselves the influx of digital devices in family life—sometimes neatly stacked away and awaiting permission to be used, other times casually present underfoot or easily within reach. Some parents had tidied up for our visits, apologizing as we arrived, pushing aside evidence of "too many" consumer and media goods, just as perhaps they tidy up for other guests, the self-judging inner voice ever present in their minds. Some saw no need to tidy, or to apologize—perhaps confident in their approach or unconcerned about impressing us—while others seemed to live permanently tidy lives. It is easy to assume that there were things the former were not telling us, limiting what we could learn. But in practice we found their apologies engaging, almost inviting the gentle inquiry that would uncover the messy complexities that lie behind the public face.

In scheduling the interviews, we responded flexibly to the circumstances of each family. Sometimes we conducted interviews with the whole family together if the parent preferred. Sometimes we interviewed parents with young children underfoot, and so our transcripts include interjections about puzzle pieces or comments on TV shows. Perhaps ironically, for those with young children present, the parent often set the child up with a show or game on the TV or tablet while we spoke, occupying them so as to minimize interruptions. Again, it was telling that the parent often explained to us how "unusual" this practice was, necessitated by our visit. In most families we interviewed one parent, although in 11 cases we were able to include the perspective of both parents. Seventeen families were headed by a single parent; of these, three were fathers.

Although the parents were the focal point of our research, we sought the perspectives of children wherever possible. Older children were interviewed directly (either with or without their parents present, as they preferred, in an open area or bedroom with door open). For younger children, we incorporated a participatory card game[24] based around pictures of media devices, along with activities that helped us gain insight into their favorite pastimes and to get them talking. In some cases, when we knew in advance that children would be present, we visited in a research team of two—one of whom would interview the parent(s) and the other of whom would separately interview the child(ren). We (Sonia and Alicia) conducted all of the parent interviews ourselves. In the case of seven families one or the other of us was accompanied by a research assistant (Svenja Ottovordemgentshenfelde), who interviewed the children present using the participatory

---

[24] Chaudron (2015); Mallan, Singh, & Giardina (2010).

card game to invite children to select and talk about their favorite (technological and non) activities. Usually during or after interviews we asked either the parents or the children to give us a tour of the home, show us their devices, and tell us where and how they spent time together as a family or apart.

Some families we came to know quite well, having observed the children in their digital media and learning sites over several weeks or months. This also meant that we sometimes encountered their parents several times, in a few cases interviewing them more than once and more often talking with them informally during our field visits and including observations from these sessions in our field notes. For over half (45 out of 73) of the families, we were able to include interviews with or observations of the children alongside those of their parents, and observations and conversations with other children, parents, and educators fed into our fieldwork along the way.

Once our interviews were to begin, usually over a cup of tea, we explained our research and our research ethics procedures. At the start of each interview we obtained informed consent from all those interviewed, reminding them that they could withdraw at any time and that all information would be kept confidential from other participants and stored only in anonymized and secure form, with no identifying information shared beyond the research team. Interviewees, including children, had the choice to opt in to audio recording and give their consent for our taking photographs (mainly used as an aide-mémoire during the analysis and for project presentations). We gave shop vouchers for £40 in exchange for these interviews. Some parents accepted these directly; others gave them to their child(ren). We also gave parents the option to donate the voucher to the learning site where we had met them, where relevant—an option that a handful took up. In one case a parent wanted to be interviewed but not audio-recorded, so we took extensive notes during the interview.

We also interviewed the educators in our three field sites about their work with children and their relationships with parents (see Chapter 6). For interviews with educators, we used the same ethical procedures as those we followed with parents—explaining our project, giving them information about it, and asking them to sign a consent form. For the educators, we did not offer vouchers but, rather, a kind of research–practice partnership, discussing mutual interests during the fieldwork and sharing insights we had discovered at the end.[25]

Our shortest interviews (on site at LYA) were around 30 minutes; our longest visits, to some families who asked us to stay for lunch, play with children, or talk with partners, lasted several hours. The majority of interviews and home visits lasted about an hour and a half to two hours. After each interview, we immediately wrote one or more pages of field notes to complement the interview transcript, including our visual impressions of the home and family and our initial reactions to what had been interesting or gone well (and not well) in the interview.

We were initially surprised by the depth of emotion in many of our interviews. Our questions revealed how parents' hopes and fears can be very near to the surface. Moreover, some parents had few opportunities to talk about their experiences raising children. A handful of parents told us as the interview ended, or over email later, that the visit had been "like therapy." Although all qualitative research has the potential to elicit emotions, we found that for many parents the sensitive nature of talking about their parenting

[25] Coburn & Penuel (2016). This was done most formally at LYA, which was particularly invested in our research; we prepared a report that the organization could present to its own funder.

required particular forms of "emotion work" from us as researchers, eliciting and indeed requiring our empathy toward the parents we interviewed. That we are both mothers ourselves influenced the ways in which we were able to build rapport in the interviews, for example, in commiserating about a particular dilemma or sometimes sharing a bit about our own lives and children (Alicia's twins were then toddlers; Sonia's children were in their mid-20s).[26]

Although we had not conceived of our research as discussing especially "sensitive" or "difficult" topics, we were mindful of our ethical responsibilities. There were a number of interviews in which parents cried, and occasionally we did as well, reminding us that intersubjectivity and vulnerability are part of the ethnographic encounter. Sometimes this meant pausing the discussion and the recording so that the interviewee could collect him- or herself, redirecting the conversation if a mostly unrelated but difficult topic had come up (e.g., family illness), or revisiting a topic later in the interview or from a different angle if it felt appropriate.[27] Often we reflected on how the same line of questioning might be perceived by parents very differently, depending on their values and experiences. For instance, when we asked the same questions about rules for technology use, some parents assumed that we were judging them for being too lax, others for being too harsh.

Parents were inevitably influenced by salient aspects of our identities—we are both White women who are easily identified by our profession, clothing, and ways of talking as being middle class; Sonia is from southern England and Alicia is from California. Our accents, our ages, and the ages of our children influenced, for some, how parents interacted with us and us with them. Some parents were deeply embedded in the turbulent task of raising teenagers, which Sonia had already passed through; this meant that some asked her for reflections and advice. Alicia was often asked questions about screen time and what she did and did not allow for her own young children. We were both often asked for our expertise on what families should or should not do. Not wishing to put words into people's mouths, we tried to defer answering, although many parents pushed us toward the end of an interview, for example:

ALICIA: I'm going to let you go in a minute, but I just wanted to ask you to do one more practical thing if that's okay [asks some details about the demographic questionnaire].

HABIBA: Yes. I want you to advise me as well, would you advise me now, on this age, 10 years under, 10 years old, how you deal with iPad and iPhone, how am I going to deal with them?

The depth of emotions in the interviews and the pleas from parents for advice highlighted to us just how few avenues parents have when they need either support to deal with a difficult dilemma or a recommendation for where to find positive opportunities. This led us to explore where parents turned for support when faced with digital or nondigital parenting dilemmas.[28]

In this book, we focus in detail on the families that we came to know better, about whom we are more confident of what we learned from them, and those who exemplified

[26] Dickson-Swift et al. (2009); Duncombe & Jessop (2012).
[27] Behar (1996); Demarrais (2002).
[28] Livingstone, Blum-Ross, Pavlick, & Ólafsson (2018).

the debates at hand. There were some hard decisions, though, as for reasons of space we had to leave out some families who illustrated points already made. Families interviewed more briefly are drawn on more for a telling instance or insofar as they support, qualify, or contradict the direction of our argument. At the conclusion of each interview we asked the parent to fill in a brief demographic questionnaire about the family's ethnicity, income, parents' occupations, whether the children had SEN, and approximately how many devices they had and how much time they spent online doing different activities. In our accounts of families, we have left out some identifying details to preserve privacy. We have settled on a style of quoting parents that is close to the original transcript but that is lightly edited for readability (e.g., removing interstitial phrases like "you know" and occasionally condensing phrasing rather than using brackets).

The survey

We conducted a nationally representative survey of British parents in late 2017, to check our qualitative conclusions against a wider account of parents' experiences of digital technologies in their and their children's lives, in the context of parenting pressures and expectations. Its design was informed by other recent surveys on digital device use by parents and children,[29] adding new themes and questions derived from our qualitative research. Particularly, instead of just focusing on parents' accounts of their *children's* digital technology use, as is common in parental mediation surveys, we prioritized questions to parents about their own digital skills, practices, and values.

We commissioned a specialist market research company to administer the survey we had written for parents with children from babies to 17-year-olds, resulting in a sample of 2,032 parents, representative by region across the United Kingdom and by ethnic background, socioeconomic status (SES), gender, and inclusion of parents with low or no internet use. The data were collected between October 3 and 23, 2017. For reasons of efficiency and cost-effectiveness, we used an online panel of adults ("main sample"). The obvious limitation of using an online panel was that by its nature it would not reach parents who did not use the internet. Therefore, we chose to include a supplementary sample of low- or non-internet-using respondents, recruited and interviewed face to face.[30]

Participants in the main sample were given information about the study, informed that their responses were anonymous, and asked to give informed consent before participating. All panel recruitment, research ethics, and consent procedures were conducted in accordance with ESOMAR guidelines.[31] The online panel provider gives incentives for people's participation in their research after a survey is completed. In the case of our 12-minute survey, this ranged from a cash amount to loyalty points within sign-up reward programs. We collected postcode information from respondents to generate an overall

[29] Livingstone, Hasebrink, & Görzig (2012); Ofcom (2017); Wartella et al. (2013).

[30] This task was complicated insofar as we could not find, even after consulting with relevant experts, reliable up-to-date information on the frequency of internet use among UK parents. We estimated that a sample of 100 parents (5% of overall sample) would represent parents who were low or non–internet users (based on data from the Office for National Statistics, 2017b, and Eurostat Press Office, 2016).

[31] ESOMAR (2016).

index of deprivation. Respondents in the supplementary sample were given an incentive of £10 in vouchers for general high street stores. The online panel completed quotas using demographics and behavioral and attitudinal profiling, randomizing email invitations to reduce bias. Representative quotas were generated, and responses in excess of the quota criteria were discounted.[32]

Analysis

Once our qualitative fieldwork interviews were completed, all interview recordings were transcribed and then transcripts and field notes were anonymized and uploaded by a research assistant into a qualitative analysis software database (NVivo). A thematic coding framework was then developed iteratively, combining inductive and theory-led themes. Early in the fieldwork process, we invited three colleagues to read two full transcripts before meeting and discussing these *inductively* as the basis for developing themes and questions to guide the analysis. We created a draft codebook, designing it to allow for inclusive coding by including fewer but more encompassing and potentially overlapping categories. We then double- and then triple-coded another transcript, now using the draft codebook for reference.[33] The codebook was then refined and, to organize the many resulting codes, we identified six meta-codes for the parent interviews:

- *Family*—the family's access to resources, daily habits, and relationships
- *Parents*—parents' identities, values, pressures, or parenting philosophy
- *Children*—children's development, interests, learning, and identity
- *Digital technology*—digital interests, skills and practices, parental mediation, and hopes and fears
- *Future*—the future of society, the future of parenting (including comparisons to the parent's own childhood), and the digital future
- *Miscellaneous*—reflections on methods, emergent themes and family characteristics, and "great quotes"

We and our research assistants then coded the interviews and transcripts. Double coding was done at the outset and again when a new research assistant was hired, to ensure shared interpretations of codes. However, for reasons of time, and knowing that we would return to the interviews holistically later, we did not double code all of our material. Once all of the interview transcripts and the field notes for a single family had been coded, whoever had done the coding then wrote a one-page "pen portrait" of the family—briefly describing them and raising the most salient issues so they could be revisited later. Research assistants were all postgraduate (master's or PhD students) hired from within the Department of Media and Communications at the London School of Economics and Political Science, and so had undertaken methods and research ethics training as part of their studies, including ethnographic research, discourse analysis and content analysis.

When it came time to analyze the material, we returned to the codes in NVivo and the original transcripts. So, for example, when we began writing Chapter 3, on social and economic capital, we searched by nodes including "Family/Capital," "Family/Resources,"

---

[32] For further details on the survey methodology, see Livingstone & Blum-Ross (2018).
[33] Bauer & Gaskell (2000); Saldaña (2009).

"Parents/Pressures," and others. This helped identify some salient issues and families that were important to focus on, but we complemented this node search by rereading whole transcripts and field notes to ensure we had not missed important context. Thus, our interpretative process continually demanded a return to close readings of the original transcripts, in an "intense conversation" between researcher and data.[34]

In this book, each time we tell you about a particular parent's experience, we have asked ourselves how to frame it. Is their experience widely shared or interestingly distinct? Does it fit within a larger group of experiences or contradict any tempting mapping onto demographics? Our questions received different answers depending on parents' circumstances, values, and experiences and the particular needs of a particular child. All of this underlines that there is no simple way to characterize "normal" family life, no single voice of parents, even within the same family. Further, unlike some important studies in our field that have focused on families with similar demographics,[35] or where researchers have spent more time with fewer families, we have tried hard to balance depth and breadth.

Undoubtedly there are limitations to our data; in interpreting our findings, we have therefore referred to multiple sources in an effort to consider the extent to which they are supported by or contrast with the findings of others working in this field. We also analyzed the survey findings during the writing of this book.[36] This enabled us to check, as we interpreted the qualitative findings, on our tacit assumptions or explicit claims about what was common or unusual across families and what was similar or different by demographic groupings. The analysis and the writing of this book were done iteratively; we outlined the chapters together and then each author would write an initial draft before the chapters were passed back and forth—in most cases through upwards of eight rounds of revisions, including feedback from a copy editor. The book is therefore a true reflection of our joint analysis.

Demographic classifications

Household income

We asked parents to indicate their household's approximate annual gross income by choosing from £15,000 or less; £15,000–£25,000; £25,000–£40,000; £40,000–£60,000; £60,000+. Realizing that this last category included some very wealthy families, we retrospectively identified those earning more than £100,000/year based on average salaries for their field of employment. Notwithstanding the many nuances within and across these categories, we classified families loosely as follows.

- "Low income" families earned a household income of less than £25,000/year.
- "Middle income" families earned between £25,000 and £100,000/year.
- "High income" families earned more than £100,000/year.

---

[34] Ely et al. (1991, p. 87).

[35] In contrast, we're thinking here of previous studies of middle-class Silicon Valley families, working-class Latinx families, or single-parent families. Many studies have focused on middle-class families (Barron et al., 2009); however, corrective efforts have been made by several scholars including Domoff et al. (2017); Hays (1998); Katz, Moran, & Gonzalez (2018); Lareau (2011); Rideout & Katz (2016).

[36] Livingstone, Blum-Ross, Pavlick, & Ólafsson (2018); Livingstone & Ólafsson (2018); Livingstone, Blum-Ross, & Zhang (2018); Zhang & Livingstone (2019).

Note that national statistics for 2016 (the period of our fieldwork) show that the UK median household disposable income was £26,300, with the poverty level in 2016 defined as households earning below 60% of the median gross household income.[37]

Ethnicity

Recognizing that London is distinctive in the proportion and diversity of its several generations of migrants,[38] we asked parents to categorize their child using the categories of the most recent (2011) UK census.[39] That census showed that, of London's population of 8,173,941 people, 59.8% were White, 18.5% were Asian/Asian British, 13.3% were Black/African/Caribbean/Black British, 5% were from mixed/multiple ethnic groups, and 3.4% were from other ethnic groups.

For simplicity, we use the terms "White," "Black," "Asian," and "Mixed/multiple ethnic groups," in accordance with the UK census categories (and capitalization conventions), adding further context as needed. Unless otherwise specified, parents and children were born in the United Kingdom. Household income and ethnicity were interrelated across the 73 families, as shown in the following table. This in part reflects the relationship between these factors in the London population, though it also reflects the focus and limitations of our recruitment.

Families (identified by number, see family descriptions below)	Low income	Middle income	High income
White	1, 2, 15, 19, 28, 30, 36, 40, 44, 49	3, 4, 6, 7, 20, 27, 31, 32, 33, 37, 38, 48, 51, 56, 60, 61, 63, 64, 65, 67, 70	21, 39, 42, 45, 52, 53, 55, 57, 59, 68, 71, 73
Black	12, 14, 25, 29, 34, 35, 69	13, 22, 24, 26	
Asian/Mixed/multiple/other ethnic groups	5, 10, 16, 46, 62, 66	8, 9, 11, 17, 18, 23, 41, 43, 47, 50, 58, 72	54

[37] The Child Poverty Action Group (2018) excludes housing costs (so they set the poverty line at £20,852 for a couple with two children, or £15,444 for a single parent with two children). Critics of the Office for National Statistics' (ONS) approach to measuring inequality note that it focuses on income rather than wealth, though wealth is a key source of inequality (Corlett, 2017).

[38] The ONS data show that a markedly higher proportion of the population in London are migrants, compared to the United Kingdom (for total population, 23% versus 9%; for live births, 58% versus 27%) (Office for National Statistics, 2016).

[39] Office for National Statistics (2011).

Special educational needs

The category of "special educational needs" is broad and can range from young people with profound and multiple disabilities through to those with mild learning difficulties, physical disabilities, or communication support needs. UK government statistics in 2017 showed that one in seven children (14.4% of school pupils) had SEN, and 2.8% had a "statement" or Education, Health, and Care (EHC) plan, which specified the extra help or provision they should receive according to a formal assessment. Among this latter group, autistic spectrum disorder was the most common type of need for a statement or EHC plan.[40]

Employment status

Given our particular interest in parents who seek digital interests and related creative opportunities, and recognizing that many of those we interviewed were primary (often stay-at-home) caregivers, we classified parents as follows:

- *Caregiver*: Unpaid caregiving work, for example, stay-at-home parents (usually, although not exclusively, mothers)
- *Health care*: Health-related professions including doctors, nurses, dentists, home health care assistants, and paramedics
- *Creative*: Employment (steady or not) in the media and creative industries, including artists, designers, craft/artisans, and filmmakers
- *Small business*: Small business owners or self-employed people
- *Professional*: Professions requiring an advanced degree, including high-level administration, law, finance, and government
- *Administration*: Administrative positions including secretaries and low-level information technology (IT) or sales roles, not requiring an advanced degree
- *Education*: Employment (full or part time) in formal and nonformal education including teachers, administrators, academics, nursery workers, and childminders
- *Precarious*: Hourly wage work in temporary or insecure jobs (without set schedules/anticipatable income), for example, in retail, driving mini-cabs/taxis, or as security officers

Family descriptions

Here we provide basic demographic information on each of the 73 families interviewed for this book. We have also sketched a little detail that captures something memorable about each family, and the chapters in which the families are discussed. Not every family is discussed by name in the book, and so therefore not all have chapter listings, but all have been considered and informed our analysis.

Family 1: Low income, caregiver, White
Alice Sheldon, from Scotland, lives with her daughter Sophia (15). Son Dennis (27) does not live at home. Alice is currently a stay-at-home mother; she used to own a café/

---

[40] Department for Education (2017).

bakery. Sophia's dad is not in contact. Sophia attends LYA, loves dancing, and has moderate SEN (Down syndrome).

Family 2: Low income, caregiver, White

Jen Pearson lives with her daughters Tegan (14) and Charlotte (11). Jen is separated from the girls' father, who sees them regularly. She has an art degree and is a full-time caregiver home-schooling her daughters. Charlotte attends LYA and has mild to moderate SEN (multiple learning difficulties). *Chapters 4, 5.*

Family 3: Middle income, small business/caregiver, White

Robert and Elaine Kostas have sons Jake (15) and Dominic (12). Robert is a small business owner; Elaine is a full-time caregiver. Jake and Dominic play video games together. Jake attends LYA and has mild to moderate SEN (autism). *Chapters 2, 5.*

Family 4: Middle income, creative/health care, White

Ryan and Amy Campbell have son Kyle (13). Daughter Pia (20) is at university but frequently visits home. Ryan is from the United States and is a filmmaker; Amy is from Peru and practices alternative medicine. Kyle loves graphic design, attends LYA, and has severe SEN (autism). *Chapter 5.*

Family 5: Low income, caregiver, Mixed/multiple ethnic groups

Miles Taylor is a single father to son Jamie (13). Miles is a full-time caregiver. Jamie, who attends LYA, is boisterous, makes friends easily, attends special school, and has moderate to severe SEN (autism, physical disabilities/medical problems). *Chapters 2, 7.*

Family 6: Middle income, education/creative, White

Lena Houben and Avery Dahl have daughter Miriam (12) and son Marko (8). Lena is from the Netherlands and a former academic, now tutor, writer, and blogger; Avery is from Australia and works in media. Miriam and Avery disagree about how much technology Miriam and Marko should have access to. *Chapters 1, 7.*

Family 7: Middle income, small business/professional, White

Beth and Tom Watson have children Wyatt (4) and Hazel (2). Beth runs a small business and is a blogger; Tom works in finance. The family enjoys YouTube dance parties in the kitchen. *Chapter 7.*

Family 8: Middle income, professional, Mixed/multiple ethnic groups

Sweta and Bill Fletcher are raising sons Nikhil (4) and Sanjay (1). Sweta has recently returned to work in higher education and runs a blog; Bill is also a professional. Sweta is concerned about how much time she spends on her own phone. *Chapter 2.*

Family 9: Middle income, creative/caregiver, Other/Arab

Ali and Khadija Kader, originally from Iraq, have daughter Sana (16) and son Ahmed (age 12). Ali works as an architect; Khadija is a caregiver and sometime artisan. Sana loves the *Twilight* saga, attends LYA, and has moderate to severe SEN (autism and other learning difficulties). *Chapters 5, 7.*

Family 10: Low income, caregiver, Asian

Daya Thakur is a single mother raising Kaval (14), Zefira (12), Kiya (10), and Kashi (7). Daya is currently trying to retrain to work in education. The children have contact with their father but do not live with him, though the parents try to agree on screen time rules for the children. Kiya loves hair tutorials on YouTube. *Chapters 2, 3.*

Family 11: Middle income, caregiver/professional, Mixed/multiple ethnic groups

Ariam and Patrick Parkes have daughters Elen (9), Hanna (8), and Sarah (2). Ariam is from Eritrea, a stay-at-home mother, and school governor retraining to work in human resources; Patrick works in media. Elen attends Bluebell Primary School and is a "digital leader" at her school. *Chapters 2, 6.*

Family 12: Low income, creative, Black

Wembe Kazadi is raising his son Bintu (10) and daughter Mani (5), who attend Bluebell Primary School. Wembe is an asylum seeker from the Democratic Republic of Congo and is studying and working as a filmmaker. The children's mother still lives in their home country; they communicate with her via video chat and text. *Chapters 2, 6.*

Family 13: Middle income, small business/administration, Black

Samantha Winston and Olu Datong have son Braydon (9) and daughter Jade (2). Olu is from Nigeria and works as an IT support worker; Samantha works as a cleaner and is trying to start a small cleaning business. The family love to go to movies and play on their game consoles. Braydon is in code club at Bluebell Primary School. *Chapters 2, 6.*

Family 14: Low income, caregiver, Black

Bethany Carson is a single mother to two sons, Dixon (9) and Daniel (5). The boys have contact with their father but do not live with him; they love *Ben 10,* and Dixon attends code club at Bluebell Primary School. *Chapter 6.*

Family 15: Low income, caregiver, White

Luisa Trevisi is raising her daughters Lorena (15) and Giovanna (13). Luisa moved from Italy (the girls' father is still there) as she saw opportunities for her daughters in London. Giovanna attends LYA and is one of the only girls in her animation class. *Chapters 4, 6.*

Family 16: Low income, precarious/health care, Mixed/multiple ethnic groups

Claudia and Felipe Ferreira, originally from Portugal and Brazil, are raising Mariana (9) and Xavier (9 months). Mariana attends Bluebell Primary School. Felipe is a cleaner at a hospital; Claudia works as a physician's assistant. Mother and daughter are learning to knit from YouTube and listen to Portuguese radio. *Chapter 3.*

Family 17: Middle income, health care, Mixed/multiple ethnic groups

Janet Daly and Eamon O'Shane are raising son Ryan (8), who attends Bluebell Primary School. Daughter Katie (15) lives with her mother elsewhere. Janet and Eamon are both nurses; Eamon is from Ireland. The family likes to ride bikes together on the weekend. *Chapter 2.*

Family 18: Middle income, education/creative, Mixed/multiple ethnic groups

Stephen and Mary Aronson have three children, Lillian (11), James (7), and Vivi (4). All three children attend LYA, as did Stephen as a child. Stephen teaches primary school; Mary (born in Kenya) makes crafts and is the main caregiver; both are strongly embedded in their neighborhood. *Chapter 3.*

Family 19: Low income, creative, White

Amber and Francis Boon have daughter Maggie (5). Francis is a musician and Amber a writer. Maggie attends LYA drama classes. Parents specifically try to avoid screen time for fear of commercialism, stereotyping, privacy, and loss of communication. *Chapter 7.*

Family 20: Middle income, creative/education, White
Rachel Ealy and Erin Reynolds have daughter Mia (8), who attends Bluebell Primary School. Erin is a teacher; Rachel is a part-time gardener, artist, and the main caregiver. Mia is a "digital leader" at her school, and Rachel has high hopes for her future digital career. *Chapter 7.*

Family 21: High income, caregiver/professional, White
Jess and Lawrence Reid have sons Alex (15) and Richard (13). Daughter Olivia (20) does not live at home but visits often. Jess is a trained solicitor but is taking time off to help Alex with school; Lawrence is also a solicitor. Alex attends LYA and a football club and loves going to the gym. He has moderate SEN (Down syndrome). *Chapter 2.*

Family 22: Middle income, administration, Black
Anna Michaels, a single mother, lives with son Derrick (13) and daughter Dionne (10). Dionne attends Bluebell Primary School. The children's father has regular contact but not custody. The family lives in a council flat and Anna has recently started working in sales. Derrick is a tinkerer and attends a military club. *Chapters 1, 2.*

Family 23: Middle income, education/small business, Mixed/multiple ethnic groups
Holly and Kalden Zangpo have daughter Dolma (8) and son Metok (5), both of whom attend Bluebell Primary School. Kalden is from Tibet and works for a small business, and Holly is a childminder. Dolma and Metok begged for tablets, which Holly keeps tight control over. Children move fluidly between *Minecraft* and Lego. *Chapter 2.*

Family 24: Middle income, precarious, Black
Afua Osei and Kwame Tuffuor are from Ghana and have sons Nigel (11) and Adrien (6) and daughter Samata (8). Afua is a part-time assistant at the Bluebell Children's Centre and Kwame drives a mini-cab. Religion plays a strong role in family life, including the use of a Jehovah's Witness app. *Chapter 3.*

Family 25: Low income, education/precarious, Black
Habiba Bekele and Stephen Augustine have sons Feli (10) and Dejen (4) and daughters Dawit (9) and Dilla (6). Habiba is from Ethiopia and Stephen from St. Lucia. They are observant Muslims and use digital media for religious instruction and to keep in touch with family. Habiba is a childminder and Stephen a security guard. Feli loves to cook, Dawit to draw. Habiba attends a drop-in session at Bluebell Children's Centre. *Chapters 2, 3.*

Family 26: Middle income, professional, Black
Jay and Karla Paulson have daughter Eve (12) and sons Felix (8) and Eric (6). Jay is a solicitor and Karla works in tech. Eric attends classes at LYA, as did his father. Felix, who has moderate to severe SEN (Down syndrome), uses assistive technology to help him at home and school. *Chapter 7.*

Family 27: Middle income, professional, White
Zoe Andrews is raising twins Elsa and Reuben (11). Zoe is a professional and values the "creative outlet" that LYA offers her children. Both are doing dance and music technology classes. Elsa is learning to play the saxophone and Reuben the guitar. Zoe does not especially encourage these activities at home.

Family 28: Low income, creative, White

Lucy Cyan is a single mother to Chris (12). Lucy is an artist and caregiver, and Chris is an enthusiastic actor, taking classes at LYA. Their creativity and shared identity as artists are important to mother and son, but technology is a source of conflict, as Lucy feels Chris is too invested in it.

Family 29: Low income, creative, Black

Michael Harris is a DJ living with son Kurt (9), who attends LYA, as did Michael as a child. Kurt watches *Minecraft* videos on YouTube and is taking drama classes. Michael has taught himself the technology he needs for work and finds it "irritating," while Kurt takes to it naturally.

Family 30: Low income, health care/caregiver, White

Jacob and Daisy Bardem have sons Matthew (8), Declan (6), and Nico (3). Jacob was a photographer and is now a paramedic; Daisy is from Wales, trained as a jewelry designer and is now a stay-at-home mother. Declan has learned some basic internet skills from his brothers; their parents like to curate their gameplay. Recruited via our European Commission-funded (EC) study (Chaudron et al., 2015). *Chapters 2, 3, 4.*

Family 31: Middle income, education/caregiver, White

Ben and Lizzie Coriam have daughter Emily (6) and son Toby (5). Ben is from Germany and is an academic; Lizzie is from South Africa and recently went back to work teaching English. They are anxious about their children keeping up in terms of digital skills but leave it to the children's school to teach them. Recruited via EC study. *Chapter 1.*

Family 32: Middle income, creative/education, White

Elena and Henry Stoddard have Lewis (16), Hugo (13), and Bryony (6). Both parents used to work in the creative industries. Henry is from a working-class background, became a music producer, and now has a small web design business. Elena worked in TV and is now a childminder. Recruited via EC study. *Chapter 7.*

Family 33: Middle income, administration/creative, White

Pawel and Lara Mazur have son Tomas (6). Lara is from Brazil and works as a secretary; Pawel is from Poland and works as a chef. They have some disagreements about how to handle Tomas's media use. Recruited via EC study. *Chapters 1, 2.*

Family 34: Low income, precarious, Black

Cecilia Apau is a single mother from Ghana raising Esi (12), Eugene (8), and Eric (4). The family is Christian. Cecilia works as a grocery store cashier and has no help from the children's father. Eugene takes part in code club at Bluebell Primary School. *Chapters 2, 3, 6.*

Family 35: Low income, health care, Black

Leila Mohammed has daughters Nareen (10) and Safia (8). Leila is Muslim, from Ethiopia; she works part time as a health care assistant. Nareen is good with computers and can fix the family computer when things go wrong. Leila was recruited through friendship with Habiba Bekele (family 25). *Chapters 2, 3, 7.*

Family 36: Low income, precarious/administration, White

Elizabeth Jackson and Andrew Travers have daughters Sara (7) and Amina (6) and son Neo (1), and Elizabeth is pregnant. Sara and Amina attend Bluebell Primary School.

Both parents were raised in a working-class area of South London and have recently converted to Islam. Elizabeth bakes cakes for neighbors and Andrew works at a job center. The family is keen on digital technologies.

Family 37: Middle income, creative, White
Nicole and Jeff Saunders have daughters Eloise (3) and Cora (6 months). Nicole runs a successful parenting blog and works as a social media manager; Jeff works in public relations (PR). Eloise loves *The Gruffalo* and watching *Star Wars* with her dad. *Chapters 2.*

Family 38: Middle income, creative/professional, White
Melissa and Mike Bell have son Milo (4) and daughter Ella (3). Melissa runs a blog and works with brands on their social media presence; Mike works in telecom. Melissa likes to take Milo and Ella on outdoor adventures or trampoline in the garden. *Chapters 4, 7.*

Family 39: High income, professional/caregiver, White
Lily Haas-Strickland and Roger Strickland have daughters Jasmine (13), Terri (11), and Emma (8) and son Aaron (4). Roger is from Austria and is a corporate chairman; Lily has an arts and humanities PhD and is currently a stay-at-home mother. The family attends church and the children are encouraged to learn musical instruments. Recruited through friendship with family 15.

Family 40: Low income, small business, White
Leah Crowe is a single mother to sons Reece (12), Charlie (9), and Will (7). Leah is from Germany and is anxious about money as she establishes her business as a parent coach. She and Reece have conflicts over his use of video games, with each getting frustrated with the other. The younger children attend arts classes at LYA. *Chapter 2.*

Family 41: Middle income, small business, Asian
Anisha Kumar is a single mother of son Rohan (3). She lives with her parents, who share in Rohan's care. Anisha is Asian but born in Liberia, has a blog, and works for her family's import business. She has started a successful parenting group on Facebook. *Chapter 2.*

Family 42: High income, creative/professional, White
Florence and Henry Lewis have son Tony (9) and daughter Caitlin (6). Florence runs a blog and works in PR; Henry works in banking. Tony loves *Minecraft* and has mild to moderate SEN (autism).

Family 43: Middle income, professional/caregiver, Mixed/multiple ethnic groups
Supna and Matt Beale have daughter Willow (7) and son Arthur (3). Supna is from the United States, runs a blog, and is a stay-at-home mother; Matt works as a solicitor.

Family 44: Low income, education/precarious, White
Arnie and Paige Treloar have son Liam (12). Paige is working as a teaching assistant after studying art and illustration; Arnie is on long-term sick leave. Liam is in the animation class at LYA and has mild SEN (dyslexia).

Family 45: High income, professional/health care, White
Peter and Amy Styles have sons Lee (12) and Evan (17). Peter works as an IT manager and Amy as a nutritionist. Evan and Lee both attend LYA, having begun with music

and dance but now studying graphic design and animation; Evan works as a classroom assistant. Their older son, who has mild SEN (attention deficit hyperactivity disorder), also attended LYA and now studies film production. *Chapters 6, 7.*

Family 46: Low income, caregiver, Mixed/multiple ethnic groups
Laura Andrews is a single mother to Zachary (17). Zachary attends programs at LYA and has severe SEN (Down syndrome and physical disabilities). Mother and son are fairly isolated but like to watch TV together and take care of their dogs. *Chapter 5.*

Family 47: Middle income, administration, Mixed/multiple ethnic groups
Rebecca Cox is raising son Owen (14) and daughter Mia (5). Rebecca recently separated from the children's father, although he is also involved in raising them. Owen attends LYA and considers himself a budding entrepreneur. Rebecca works as an administrator in the music industry. *Chapter 6.*

Family 48: Middle income, professional, White
Cameron and Alison Cartwright have two young children, Dylan (2) and Madison (1). Cameron is a digital enthusiast, railroad engineer, and dad blogger. *Chapter 7.*

Family 49: Low income, education, White
Harvey Simon is raising his two sons, Archie (6) and Oscar (4). Harvey is a former teacher but is now home-schooling his boys and running a blog. He and his partner are separated but have shared custody. Harvey is Christian and is moderately physically disabled.

Family 50: Middle income, professional/caregiver, Mixed/multiple ethnic groups
Jack and Fiona Lee have three children, sons Jordan (7) and Ethan (5) and daughter Leah (3). Jack works in marketing, runs a blog, and is a self-described "geek." *Chapter 4.*

Family 51: Middle income, education/caregiver, White
Dennis and Catherine Parrish are raising son Harrison (10 months). Dennis's older children, Max (10) and Phoebe (3), live with his ex-partner. Dennis is a teacher and runs a successful blog with a post that recently went viral.

Family 52: High income, professional/caregiver, White
Kylie and Kit Smithson have son Oliver (12) and twin daughters Anastasia and Jasmine (8). Kylie and Kit met while working in publishing, where Kit still works as Kylie stays home. Oliver likes to play games but has to be dragged to the computer, and wears a Fitbit his mother purchased to encourage him to move more and sleep longer. *Chapters 2, 6, 7.*

Family 53: High income, professional, White
Anne Reynolds and Dave Skelton have daughter Esme (12). Both parents are high-level executives, Anne in market research and Dave in telecom. Esme attends DigiCamp and plays tennis. Both parents enjoy using media with Esme; Dave suggests feminist films and Anne has joined Instagram. Esme has mild SEN (dyslexia). *Chapters 2, 4, 5, 6.*

Family 54: High income, caregiver/professional, Mixed/multiple ethnic groups
Vicki and Jack Marshall have Alice (12) and Jason (10). Vicki is from Poland and is a stay-at-home mother; Jack is a tech entrepreneur. Jason attends DigiCamp and Jack

shares his digital interests, but the parents are also concerned that their children also pursue physical activities like sports.

Family 55: High income, caregiver/professional, White

Julian Street-Woods and Joanna Harrington have Amelia (14), Benjamin (12), and Chloe (9). Julian was a barrister and is now a stay-at-home father; Joanna is a lawyer. Julian, especially, is positive about technology but doesn't always enjoy his children's love of pop culture.

Family 56: Middle income, professional, White

Dani Sykes is raising her boys Josh (12)—who attends DigiCamp—and Michael (9), although the boys live mainly with their other mother, from whom Dani is separated. Dani works in internet security and shares a love of all things "geeky" with Josh. *Chapters, 4, 7.*

Family 57: High income, professional/caregiver, White

Michel and Josephine Thiebault have sons Pierre (18) and Marc (13). Michel is a telecom executive and Josephine is a caregiver. Both sons have attended DigiCamp and similar camps, including at the Massachusetts Institute of Technology (MIT) and Stanford. *Chapters 3, 5, 6.*

Family 58: Middle income, professional/health care, Asian

Sirash and Devika Rajan have daughter Pranita (12). Devika works in pharmaceuticals; Sirash is a dentist. Pranita attends DigiCamp and has a burgeoning career as an actress. She has mild SEN (physical disability). *Chapter 4.*

Family 59: High income, professional, White

Susan Scott and Sven Olsson have sons Niall (16), George (14), and Sean (10). Susan is from the United States and Sven from Sweden. Sven is a corporate executive; Susan runs a literary organization part time. George and Sean attend DigiCamp. All three boys know how to code and have mild SEN (attention deficit disorders). *Chapters 2, 3, 4.*

Family 60: Middle income, creative, White

Peter and Tracy Randall have daughters Liane (13) and Milly (9). Peter is a freelance writer and blogger; Tracy works in fitness and makes art. Peter thinks of his blog as a record of himself to share with his daughters.

Family 61: Middle income, creative, White

Natasha Mason is raising son Jasper (12) alone after the recent death of her husband. She is originally from Bosnia and works as an architect. Jasper attends DigiCamp and is proud of his digital skills, although these cause some conflict with his mother. *Chapters 4, 6.*

Family 62: Low income, creative/health care, Mixed/multiple ethnic groups

Sandra and Jonno Stubbs have son Lucas (9) and live with Sandra's grandparents. Although Sandra and Jonno are separated, they continue to live together for financial reasons. Sandra works as a children's entertainer; Jonno is a mental health nurse but is on sick leave. Lucas attends DigiCamp on a scholarship and has moderate SEN (autism). *Chapters 4, 5, 6.*

Family 63: Middle income, professional/caregiver, White

Minna Nylund and Eric Norris are raising daughter Eja (2). Minna is from Finland and is
    a civil servant and blogger; Eric is a stay-at-home dad. Minna enjoys the creative and
    expressive potential of digital technology.

Family 64: Middle income, creative/professional, White

Andrea and David Foster have children Elsie (6), Layla (3), and Ollie (18 months). Andrea
    is a food and family blogger and writer; David works in marketing. Elsie has been
    recently diagnosed with moderate SEN (autism) and Andrea is considering home-
    schooling her. *Chapters 5, 7.*

Family 65: Middle income, caregiver/professional, White

Nina and Chris Robbins have daughter Iris (7). Nina had a corporate job but is now a
    full-time caregiver to Iris, who is home-schooled; Chris has a corporate job. Nina
    has a blog that recently went viral, and has helped Iris start one as well. Mother and
    daughter play *Minecraft* as part of their home-schooling. Iris has moderate SEN (au-
    tism and sensory integration disorder). *Chapters 2, 5.*

Family 66: Low income, creative/small business, Mixed/multiple ethnic groups

Precious and Jonathan Adams are raising daughter Abby (18); her older sister, Esi (19);
    and two older daughters who no longer live at home. Jonathan works as a market
    trader; Precious is originally from Nigeria and is writing a novel. They define them-
    selves as religious Christians. Recruited via *The Class. Chapter 7.*

Family 67: Middle income, education, White

Eva Gonzalez and Eitan Zaragoza, both from Spain, are raising Adriana (18) and her
    younger brother, while her older sister, Charlotte (20), is away at university. Both
    parents are academics, and this, combined with Charlotte's successes, puts some
    pressure on Adriana, who wants to study midwifery. Adriana has mild SEN (dys-
    lexia/dyspraxia). Recruited via *The Class.*

Family 68: High income, professional, White

Maria and Theo Cantrell have daughter Alice (18), who lives at home, while Ellie (21) is
    away at university. Alice wants to study psychology at university, like her mother,
    and has a developed political critique; she has mild SEN (dyslexia). Recruited via
    The Class. Chapter 7.

Family 69: Low income, administration, Black

Jessica Otunde has four daughters, of whom Dilruba (18), whom we interviewed, is the
    third. Jessica is originally from Mauritius and now works as a community support
    officer. She is raising the girls largely independently of their father and does not in-
    tervene much in the girls' schooling, though she worries about the loss of sociability
    that digital media has brought to their home. Recruited via *The Class.*

Family 70: Middle income, creative, White

Patricia Ellis and Rupert Dixon have separated but have remained living next door to
    one another to raise Giselle (18) and her younger brother, Theo (14). Patricia runs
    a small crafts company and Rupert has a web design business. Giselle is involved
    in many different creative activities and wants to study art. Recruited via *The Class.*

Family 71: High income, professional, White

Isabel Bluestone and Tim Solano have daughters Rosa (23), who has recently returned home after university, and Megan (18). Both parents work in marketing and have raised daughters who are digitally savvy—Rosa works in social media, Megan had a blog, and the girls keep in contact using geolocation on their phones. Recruited via *The Class. Chapter 2.*

Family 72: Middle income, professional/education, Mixed/multiple ethnic groups

Mira Johar and Brian Farnham have daughters Sara (18) and Tabatha (16). Mira's family is originally from India. She is an accountant; Brian is a primary school teacher. Sara is high achieving, off to Oxbridge next year. Mother and daughter are worried about the political climate in Britain. Recruited via *The Class.*

Family 73: High income, small business/professional, White

Debbie and Kevin Cooper have son Sebastian, known as Seb (18). Debbie owns a business that organizes professional events; Kevin is a lawyer. Seb is already working as an assistant in a media studio and wants to go to film school. Recruited via *The Class. Chapter 7.*

References

Adams, V., Murphy, M., & Clarke, A. E. (2009). Anticipation: Technoscience, life, affect, temporality. *Subjectivity, 28*(1), 246–265. doi:10.1057/sub.2009.18

Agar, M. (2008). *The professional stranger: An informal introduction to ethnography* (2nd ed.). Bingley, UK: Emerald Publishing.

Alper, M. (2014). *Digital youth with disabilities.* Cambridge, MA: MIT Press.

Alper, M. (2017). *Giving voice: Mobile communication, disability, and inequality.* Cambridge, MA: MIT Press.

Alper, M. (2018). Inclusive sensory ethnography: Studying new media and neurodiversity in everyday life. *New Media & Society, 20*(10), 3560–3579.

Alper, M. (2019). Future talk: Accounting for the technological and other future discourses in daily life. *International Journal of Communication, 13,* 715–735.

Alper, M., Ellcessor, E., Ellis, K., & Goggin, G. (2015). Reimagining the good life with disability: Communication, new technology, and humane connections. In H. Wang (Ed.), *Communication and the "good life"* (pp. 197–212). New York: Peter Lang.

Alper, M., Katz, V. S., & Clark, L. S. (2016). Researching children, intersectionality, and diversity in the digital age. *Journal of Children and Media, 10*(1), 107–114. doi:10.1080/17482798.2015.1121886

American Academy of Pediatrics. (2011). Policy statement: Media use by children younger than 2 years. Retrieved from http://pediatrics.aappublications.org/content/pediatrics/early/2011/10/12/peds.2011-1753.full.pdf

American Academy of Pediatrics. (2016a). American Academy of Pediatrics announces new recommendations for children's media use. Retrieved from https://www.aap.org/en-us/about-the-aap/aap-press-room/Pages/American-Academy-of-Pediatrics-Announces-New-Recommendations-for-Childrens-Media-Use.aspx

American Academy of Pediatrics. (2016b). Media and young minds: Policy statement. Retrieved from https://pediatrics.aappublications.org/content/138/5/e20162591

Ames, M. (2019). *The charisma machine: The life, death, and legacy of one laptop per child.* Cambridge, MA: MIT Press.

Ames, M. G., Go, J., Kaye, J. J., & Spasojevic, M. (2011). *Understanding technology choices and values through social class.* Paper presented at the Computer Supported Cooperative Work Conference, Hangzou, China.

Ammari, T., Morris, M., & Schoenebeck, S. Y. (2014). *Accessing social support and overcoming judgment on social media among parents of children with special educational needs.* Paper presented at the International Association for the Advancement of Articial Intelligence Conference on Weblogs and Social Media, Ann Arbor, Michigan.

Anderson, C. (2006). *The long tail: How endless choice is creating unlimited demand.* London, UK: Business Books.

Anderson, J. (2015). How to tell if your child's educational app is actually educational. *Quartz.* Retrieved from https://qz.com/544963/how-to-tell-if-you-childs-educational-app-is-actually-educational/

Andrews, M. (2014). *Narrative imagination and everyday life*. New York, NY: Oxford University Press.

Appadurai, A. (2013). *The future as cultural fact: Essays on the global condition*. London, UK: Verso.

Archer, L., Dewitt, J., & Osborne, J. (2015). Is science for us? Black students' and parents' views of science and science careers. *Science Education, 99*(2), 199–237.

Arduino. (2018). Retrieved from https://www.arduino.cc/

Arum, R., & Larson, K. (forthcoming). *Connected learning: Opportunities and challenges*. New York, NY: New York University Press.

Atkinson, P., & Hammersley, M. (1994). Ethnography and participant observation. In N. K. Denzin & Y. S. Lincoln (Eds.), *Handbook of qualitative research* (pp. 248–261). Thousand Oaks, CA: Sage Publications.

Atkinson, W. (2007). Beck, individualization and the death of class: A critique. *British Journal of Sociology, 58*(3), 349–366. doi:10.1111/j.1468-4446.2007.00155.x

Averett, K. (2016). The gender buffet: LGBTQ parents resisting heteronormativity. *Gender & Society, 30*(2), 189–212.

Aynsley-Green, A. (2019). *The British betrayal of childhood: Challenging uncomfortable truths and bringing about change*. Abingdon, UK: Routledge.

Bach, D. (2017). Microsoft broadens the spectrum through hiring program. *The Official Microsoft Blog*, Microsoft.

Baggaly, J. (2017, September). PSHE: For your child's digital future. *Vodafone Digital Parenting*.

Bakardjieva, M. (2005). Conceptualizing user agency. In *Internet society: The internet in everyday life*. (pp. 9–36). London, UK: Sage.

Balakrishnan, J., & Griffiths, M. (2018). Perceived addictiveness of smartphone games: A content analysis of game reviews by players. *International Journal of Mental Health and Addiction, 17*(4), 1–13.

Balestra, C., & Tonkin, R. (2018). *Inequalities in household wealth across OECD countries: Evidence from OECD Wealth Distribution Database*. Paris, France: OECD Publishing.

Banet-Weiser, S. (2018). *Empowered: Popular feminism and popular misogyny*. Durham, NC: Duke University Press.

Baraniuk, C. (2015, August 27). Ashley Madison: Two women explain how hack changed their lives. *BBC News*. Retrieved from https://www.bbc.com/news/technology-34072762

Barassi, V. (2017). BabyVeillance? Expecting parents, online surveillance and the cultural specificity of pregnancy apps. *Social Media + Society, 3*(2), 1–10.

Barron, B. (2006). Interest and self-sustained learning as catalyst of development: A learning ecology perspective. *Human Development, 49*, 193–224.

Barron, B., Martin, C. K., Takeuchi, L., & Fithian, R. (2009). Parents as learning partners in the development of technological fluency. *International Journal of Learning and Media, 1*(2), 55–77. doi:10.1162/ijlm.2009.0021

Barseghian, T. (2013). Money, time, and tactics: Can games be effective in schools? *KQED News*. Retrieved from https://www.kqed.org/mindshift/26776/money-time-and-tactics-can-games-be-effective-in-schools

Bauer, M. W., & Gaskell, G. (Eds.). (2000). *Qualitative researching with text, image and sound: A practical handbook for social research*. London, UK: Sage.

Baumrind, D. (1971). Current patterns of parental authority. *Developmental Psychology*, *4*(1), 1–103.

Bazalgette, C. (2010). *Teaching media in primary schools*. London, UK: Sage.

Beck, U. (1992). *Risk society: Towards a new modernity*. London, UK: Sage.

Beck, U. (1997). Democratization of the family. *Childhood*, *4*(2), 151–168.

Beck, U., & Beck-Gernsheim, E. (2002). *Individualization: Institutionalized individualism and its social and political consequences*. London, UK: Sage.

Beck, U., Giddens, A., & Lash, S. (1994). *Reflexive modernization: Politics, tradition and aesthetics in the modern social order*. Cambridge, UK: Polity in association with Blackwell.

Beck-Gernsheim, E. (1998). On the way to a post-familial family from a community of need to elective affinities. *Theory, Culture & Society*, *15*(3–4), 53–70.

Behar, R. (1996). *The vulnerable observer: Anthropology that breaks your heart*. Boston, MA: Beacon Press.

Bell, D. (2013). Geek myths: Technologies, masculinities globalizations. In J. Hearn, M. Blagojevic, & K. Harrison (Eds.), *Rethinking transnational men: Beyond, between and within nations*. London, UK: Routledge.

Ben-Eliyahu, A., Rhodes, J. E., & Scales, P. (2014). The interest-driven pursuits of 15 year olds: "Sparks" and their association with caring relationships and developmental outcomes. *Applied Developmental Science*, *18*(2), 76–89. doi:10.1080/10888691.2014.894414

Benford, P., & Standen, P. (2009). The internet: A comfortable communication medium for people with Asperger syndrome (AS) and high functioning autism (HFA)? *Journal of Assistive Technologies*, *3*(2), 44–53. http://dx.doi.org/10.1108/17549450200900015

Bennett, S., Maton, K., & Kervin, L. (2008). The "digital natives" debate: A critical review of the evidence. *British Journal of Educational Technology*, *39*(5), 775–786.

Bennett, T., Savage, M., Silva, E., Warde, A., Gayo-Cal, M., & Wright, D. (2010). *Culture, class, distinction*. Abingdon, UK: Routledge.

Berker, T., Hartmann, M., Punie, Y., & Ward, K. J. (Eds.). (2006). *The domestication of media and technology*. Maidenhead, UK: Open University Press.

Bernstein, B. (1990). *Class, codes and control: The structuring of pedagogic discourse* (Vol. 4). London, UK: Routledge.

Besio, S., & Encarnação, P. (2018, March 7). Play for all children: Robots helping children with disabilities play. Retrieved from: https://blogs.lse.ac.uk/parenting4digitalfuture/2018/03/07/play-for-all-children/

Bessant, C. (2018). Sharenting: Balancing the conflicting rights of parents and children. *Communications Law*, *23*(1), 7–24.

Bevan, B., Gutwill, J., Petrich, M., & Wilkinson, K. (2015). Learning through STEM-rich tinkering: Findings from a jointly negotiated research project taken up in practice. *Science Education*, *99*(1), 98–120.

Bilton, N. (2014, September 10). Steve Jobs was a low-tech parent. *New York Times*. Retrieved from http://www.nytimes.com/2014/09/11/fashion/steve-jobs-apple-was-a-low-tech-parent.html?_r=2

Biressi, A., & Nunn, H. (2013). *Class and contemporary British culture*. New York, NY: Palgrave Macmillan.

Blum, L. (2015). *Raising Generation Rx: Mothering kids with invisible disabilities in an age of inequality*. New York, NY: New York University Press.

Blum-Ross, A. (2016). Voice, empowerment and youth-produced films about "gangs." *Learning, Media and Technology* (Special Issue "Voice and Representation in Youth Media Production in Educational Settings: Transnational Dialogues"). doi:10.1080/17439884.2016.1111240

Blum-Ross, A., Donoso, V., Dinh, T., Mascheroni, G., O'Neill, B., Riesmeyer, C., & Stoilova, M. (2018). Looking forward: Technological and social change in the lives of European children and young people. *Report for the ICT Coalition for Children Online*. Retrieved from http://www.ictcoalition.eu/medias/uploads/source/ICT%20REPORT_2018_WEB.pdf

Blum-Ross, A., Kumpulainen, K., & Marsh, J. (Eds.). (2020). *Enhancing digital literacy and creativity: Makerspaces in the early years.* London: Routledge.

Blum-Ross, A., & Livingstone, S. (2016a). *Families and screen time: Current advice and emerging research.* Media Policy Project Policy Brief Series. London, UK: London School of Economics and Political Science.

Blum-Ross, A., & Livingstone, S. (2016b). From youth voice to young entrepreneurs: The individualization of digital media and learning. *Journal of Digital and Media Literacy,* 4(1–2), 1–22.

Blum-Ross, A., & Livingstone, S. (2017). "Sharenting," parent blogging, and the boundaries of the digital self. *Popular Communication, 15*(2), 110–125. doi:10.1080/15405702.2016.1223300

Blum-Ross, A., & Livingstone, S. (2018). The trouble with "screen time" rules. In G. Mascheroni, C. Ponte, & A. Jorge (Eds.), *Digital parenting: The challenges for families in the digital age* (pp. 179–187). Göteborg, Sweden: Nordicom.

Bold Creative. (2017). Digital lives: How do teenagers in the UK navigate their digital world? Retrieved from http://www.boldcreative.co.uk/portfolio-items/digital-lives/

Borchet, M. (1998). The challenge of cyberspace: Internet access and persons with disabilities. In B. Ebo (Ed.), *Cyberghetto or cybertopia?: Race, class, and gender on the internet* (pp. 49–62). Westport, CT: Praeger.

Boston Consulting Group. (2017). The state of social mobility in the UK. Retrieved from https://www.suttontrust.com/wp-content/uploads/2017/07/BCGSocial-Mobility-report-full-version_WEB_FINAL.pdf

Bourdieu, P. (1986). *Distinction: A social critique of the judgement of taste.* London, UK: Routledge.

Bowen, G. (2008). Naturalistic inquiry and the saturation concept: A research note *Qualitative Research, 8*(1), 137–152.

Bowles, N. (2018, February 4). Early Facebook and Google employees form coalition to fight what they built. *New York Times*. Retrieved from https://www.nytimes.com/2018/02/04/technology/early-facebook-google-employees-fight-tech.html

boyd, d. (2011). Social network sites as networked publics: Affordances, dynamics, and implications. In Z. Papacharissi (Ed.), *Networked self: Identity, community, and culture on social network sites* (pp. 39–58). New York, NY: Routledge.

Briant, E., Watson, N., & Philo, G. (2013). Reporting disability in the age of austerity: The changing face of media representation of disability and disabled people in the United Kingdom and the creation of new "folk devils." *Disability & Society, 28*(6), 874–889.

Broadnax, J. (2018). Black girl nerds: For girls like us. Retrieved from https://blackgirlnerds.com/about-bgn/

Brooker, L. (2015). Cultural capital in the preschool years: Can the state "compensate" for the family? In L. Alanen, E. Brooker, & B. Mayall (Eds.), *Childhood with*

Bourdieu: Studies in childhood and youth (pp. 34–56). Basingstoke, UK: Palgrave MacMillan.

Brough, M. (2016). *Game on! Connected learning and parental support in the CyberPatriot program.* Connected Learning Working Papers. Irvine, CA.

Brough, M., Cho, A., & Mustain, P. (forthcoming). Making connections: Encouraging touchpoints, sharing digital authority, and sandboxing among low-income families. In M. Ito et al. (Eds.), *Connected learning: New directions for design, research, and practice.* Cambridge, MA: MIT Press.

Brown, J. D., & Bobkowski, P. S. (2011). Older and newer media: Patterns of use and effects on adolescents' health and well-being. *Journal of Research on Adolescence, 21*(1), 95–113.

Brown, P., Lauder, H., & Ashton, D. (2012). *The global auction: The broken promises of education, jobs, and incomes.* Oxford, UK: Oxford University Press.

Buckingham, D. (2000). *After the death of childhood.* Cambridge, UK: Polity Press.

Buckingham, D. (2007). Digital media literacies: Rethinking media education in the age of the internet. *Research in Comparative and International Education, 2*(1), 43–55.

Burke, A., & Hammett, R. F. (Eds.). (2009). *Assessing new literacies: Perspectives from the classroom.* Oxford, UK: Peter Lang.

Burkitt, I. (2008). *Social selves: Theories of self and society* (2nd ed.). London, UK: Sage.

Carlson, M. J., & England, P. (Eds.). (2011). *Social class and changing families in an unequal America.* Stanford, CA: Stanford University Press.

Carolan, B. V., & Wasserman, S. J. (2014). Does parenting style matter? Concerted cultivation, educational expectations, and the transmission of educational advantage. *Sociological Perspectives, 58*(2), 168–186. doi:10.1177/0731121414562967

Cassell, J., & Cramer, M. (2008). High tech or high risk: Moral panics about girls online. In T. McPherson (Ed.), *Digital youth, innovation, and the unexpected* (pp. 53–76). Cambridge, MA: MIT Press.

Centre for Economic and Business Research. (2017). An updated assessment of the macroeconomic contributions of the arts and culture industry to the national and regional economies of the UK. Retrieved from https://www.artscouncil.org.uk/sites/default/files/download-file/Contribution_arts_culture_industry_UK_economy.pdf

Chambers, D. (2013). Home, families and new media. In *Social media and personal relationships* (pp. 102–120). London, UK: Palgrave Macmillan.

Chambers, D. (2019). Emerging temporalities in the multiscreen home. *Media, Culture & Society.* https://doi.org/10.1177/0163443719867851

Chaudron, S. (2015). Young children (0–8) and digital technology: A qualitative exploratory study across seven countries. Retrieved from http://publications.jrc.ec.europa.eu/repository/handle/JRC93239

Child Poverty Action Group. (2018). The UK poverty line. Retrieved from http://www.cpag.org.uk/content/uk-poverty-line

Children in care, Looked after children. (2007, May 23). Retrieved from https://www.communitycare.co.uk/2007/05/23/children-in-care/

Children of Britain's "digital generation" aiming for careers in technology, study shows. (2018, January 23). *The Independent.* Retrieved from https://www.independent.co.uk/news/education/education-news/british-children-career-ambitions-tech-sector-youtuber-vlogging-software-animation-web-design-study-a8174056.html

The Children's Society. (2019). *The good childhood report 2019.* London, UK: Author.

Ching, D., Santo, R., Hoadley, C., & Peppler, K. (2015). On-ramps, lane changes, detours and destinations: Building connected learning pathways in Hive NYC through brokering future learning opportunities. Retrieved from https://hiveresearchlab.org/2015/04/13/on-ramps-lane-changes-detours-and-destinations-new-community-developed-white-paper-on-supporting-pathways-through-brokering/

Chua, A. (2011). *Battle hymn of the tiger mother*. London, UK: Bloomsbury.

Clark, L. S. (2013). *The parent app: Understanding families in the digital age*. Oxford, UK: Oxford University Press.

Clark, L. S., Demont-Heinrich, C., & Webber, S. (2005). Parents, ICTs, and children's prospects for success: Interviews along the digital "access rainbow." *Critical Studies in Media Communication, 22*(5), 409–426. doi:10.1080/07393180500342985

Clarkson, J., Coleman, R., Keates, S., & Lebbon, C. (2003). *Inclusive design—Design for the whole population*. London, UK: Springer.

Coburn, C., & Penuel, W. (2016). Research–practice partnerships in education: Outcomes, dynamics, and open questions. *Educational Researcher, 45*(1), 48–54.

Coleman, G. (2014). *Hacker, hoaxer, whistleblower, spy: The many faces of Anonymous*. London, UK, and New York, NY: Verso.

Coleman, G. (2017). From internet farming to weapons of the geek. *Current Anthropology, 58*, S91–S102.

Coleman, J. S., Campbell, E., Hobson, C., McPartland, J., Mood, A., Weinfeld, F., & York, R. (1966). *Equality of educational opportunity*. Washington, DC: US Office of Education.

Colombo, F., & Fortunati, L. (Eds.). (2011). *Broadband society and generational changes* (Vol. 5). Frankfurt am Main, Germany: Peter Lang.

Common Sense Media. (2018). Truth about tech: How tech has kids hooked. Retrieved from https://www.commonsensemedia.org/kids-action/truth-about-tech

Cooke, E. (2018, July 9). In the middle class, and barely getting by. *New York Times*. Retrieved from https://www.nytimes.com/2018/07/09/books/review/alissa-quart-squeezed.html?hp&action=click&pgtype=Homepage&clickSource=story-heading&module=second-column-region&region=top-news&WT.nav=top-news

Cooper, M. (2014). *Cut adrift: Families in insecure times*. Berkeley, CA: University of California Press.

Corlett, A. (2017). Unequal results: Improving and reconciling the UK's household income statistics. Retrieved from https://www.resolutionfoundation.org/app/uploads/2017/12/Unequal-results.pdf

Cranmer, S. (2017). Disabled children and young people's uses and experiences of digital technologies for learning. Retrieved from http://www.research.lancs.ac.uk/portal/en/publications/-(08306570-fadd-45b6-8a68-6fa0d6f68e60).html

Crenshaw, K. (1991). Mapping the margins: Intersectionality, identity politics, and violence against women of color. *Stanford Law Review, 43*(6), 1241–1299.

Cribb, J., Hood, A., Joyce, R., & Phillips, D. (2013). Living standards, poverty and inequality in the UK: 2013. Retrieved from http://www.ifs.org.uk/comms/r81.pdf

Critcher, C. (2003). *Moral panics and the media*. Buckingham, UK: Open University Press.

Cross, M. (2013). Demonised, impoverished and now forced into isolation: The fate of disabled people under austerity. *Disability & Society, 28*(5), 719–723.

Csikszentmithalyi, M., Rathunde, K., & Whalen, S. (1993). *Talented teenagers*. Cambridge, UK: Cambridge University Press.

Cunningham, H. (2006). *The invention of childhood*. London, UK: BBC Books.

Curtarelli, M., Gualtieri, V., Shater Jannati, M., & Donlevy, V. (2017). ICT for work: Digital skills in the workplace. Retrieved from https://ec.europa.eu/digital-single-market/en/news/new-report-shows-digital-skills-are-required-all-types-jobs

Cycling '74. (n.d.). Retrieved from https://cycling74.com/products/max/

Daly, A., Ruxton, S., & Schuurman, M. (2016). Challenges to children's rights today: What do children think? A desktop study on children's views and priorities to inform the next Council of Europe Strategy for the Rights of the Child. Retrieved from https://rm.coe.int/CoERMPublicCommonSearchServices/DisplayDCTMContent?documentId=090 0001680643ded

Data & Society Research Institute. (2017). Brief of amici curiae (16–402). Washington DC. Retrieved from https://datasociety.net/pubs/fatml/DataAndSociety_CarpentervUS_Amicus_Brief.pdf

Davies, H., & Eynon, R. (2018). Is digital upskilling the next generation our "pipeline to prosperity"? *New Media & Society, 20*(11), 3961–3979.

Davies, W. (2014). Neoliberalism: A bibliographical review. *Theory, Culture & Society, 31*(7–8), 309–317. doi:10.1177/0263276414546383

de Wolfe, J. (2014). *Parents of children with autism: An ethnography.* New York, NY: Palgrave Macmillan.

Demarrais, K. (2002). What happens when researchers inquire into difficult emotions? Reflections on studying women's anger through qualitative interviews. *Educational Psychologist, 37*(2), 115–123.

Department for Digital, Culture, Media & Sport (DCMS). (2018). Creative industries: Sector deal. London: Crown copyright. Retrieved from https://www.gov.uk/government/publications/creative-industries-sector-deal/creative-industries-sector-deal-html

Department for Education. (2013). Computing programmes of study: Key stages 3 and 4. Crown copyright. Retrieved from https://www.computingatschool.org.uk/data/uploads/secondary_national_curriculum_-_computing.pdf

Department for Education. (2017). Special educational needs in England. Retrieved from https://assets.publishing.service.gov.uk/government/uploads/system/uploads/attachment_data/file/633031/SFR37_2017_Main_Text.pdf

Department for Education. (2018, January 25). Prime minister announces £20 million Institute of Coding. Press release. London, UK: Author.

Dermott, E., & Pomati, M. (2015). "Good" parenting practices: How important are poverty, education and time pressure? *Sociology, 50*(1), 125–142. doi:10.1177/0038038514560260

Deutsch, S. (2017). *The friendship code #1.* New York, NY: Penguin Workshop.

Dickson-Swift, V., James, E., Kippen, S., & Liamputtong, P. (2009). Researching sensitive topics: Qualitative research as emotion work. *Qualitative Research, 9*(1), 61–79.

Dionne, E. (2017). Black nerds reveal what the geek world is mission. *Revelist.*

Domoff, S. E., Miller, A. L., Khalatbari, N., Pesch, M. H., Harrison, K., Rosenblum, K., & Lumeng, J. C. (2017). Maternal beliefs about television and parental mediation in a low-income United States sample. *Journal of Children and Media, 11*(3), 278–294. doi:10.1080/17482798.2017.1339102

Donzelot, J., & Hurley, R. (1997). *The policing of families.* Baltimore, MD, and London, UK: Johns Hopkins University Press.

Doucet, A., & Mauthner, N. (2008). Qualitative interviewing and feminist research. In P. Alasuutari, L. Bickman, & J. Brannen (Eds.), *The SAGE handbook of social research methods* (pp. 328–343). London, UK: Sage.

Douglas, S., & Michaels, M. W. (2005). *The mommy myth: The idealization of motherhood and how it has undermined all women.* New York, NY: Free Press.

Dredge, S. (2014). Coding at school: A parent's guide to England's new computing curriculum. *The Guardian*. Retrieved from https://www.theguardian.com/technology/2014/sep/04/coding-school-computing-children-programming

Drummond, K., & Stipek, D. (2004). Low-income parents' beliefs about their role in children's academic learning. *Elementary School Journal, 104*(3), 197–213.

Duggan, M., Lenhart, A., Lampe, C., & Ellison, N. (2015). Parents and social media. Retrieved from http://www.pewinternet.org/files/2015/07/Parents-and-Social-Media-FIN-DRAFT-071515.pdf

Dunbar-Hester, C. (2014). Low power to the people: Pirates, protest and politics in FM radio activism. Retrieved from http://hdl.handle.net/2027/heb.01134.0001.001

Duncombe, J., & Jessop, J. (2012). "Doing rapport" and the ethics of "faking friendship." In T. Miller, M. Birch, M. Mauthner, & J. Jessop (Eds.), *Ethics in qualitative research* (2nd ed., pp. 107–122). London, UK: Sage.

EA Sports. (2018). FIFA 19. Retrieved from https://www.easports.com/fifa

Education City. (2015). Retrieved from https://www.educationcity.com/us/

Ellcessor, E. (2016). *Restricted access: Media, disability, and the politics of participation* New York, NY: New York University Press.

Ellcessor, E., & Kirkpatrick, B. (2017). *Disability media studies*. New York, NY: New York University Press.

Ellis, K., & Goggin, G. (2015). *Disability and the media*. London, UK: Palgrave Macmillan.

Ely, M., Anzul, M., Friedman, T., Garner, D., & Steinmetz, A. (1991). *Doing qualitative research: Circles within circles*. London, UK: Falmer.

Ensmenger, N. (2010). *The computer boys take over: Computers, programmers and the politics of technical expertise*. London, UK: MIT Press.

Erstad, O., Gilje, Ø., Sefton-Green, J., & Christian Arnseth, H. (2016). *Learning identities, education and community: Young lives in the cosmopolitan city*. Cambridge, UK: Cambridge University Press.

ESOMAR. (2016). ICC/ESOMAR international code on market, opinion and social research and data analytics. Retrieved from https://www.esomar.org/uploads/public/knowledge-and-standards/codes-and-guidelines/ICCESOMAR_Code_English_.pdf

European Commission. (2018). Digital competences and technology in education. Retrieved from http://ec.europa.eu/education/policy/strategic-framework/education-technology_en

Eurostat Press Office. (2016). *Almost 8 out of 10 internet users in the EU surfed via a mobile or smart phone in 2016*. Brussels, Belgium: Eurostat.

Evans, C. A., Jordan, A. B., & Horner, J. (2011). Only two hours?: A qualitative study of the challenges parents perceive in restricting child television time. *Journal of Family Issues, 32*(9), 1223–1244. doi:10.1177/0192513x11400558

Exley, D. (2019). *The end of aspiration? Social mobility and our children's fading prospects*. Bristol, UK: Policy Press.

Faircloth, C. (2013). *Militant lactivism? Attachment parenting and intensive motherhood in the UK and France*. New York, NY: Berghahn Books.

Faircloth, C., Hoffman, D. M., & Layne, L. L. (2013). *Parenting in global perspective: Negotiating ideologies of kinship, self and politics*. Abingdon, UK: Routledge.

Faircloth, C., & Murray, M. (2014). Parenting: Kinship, expertise, and anxiety. *Journal of Family Issues, 36*(9), 1115–1129. doi:10.1177/0192513x14533546

Faucett, H., Ringland, K., Cullen, A., & Hayes, G. (2017). (In)visibility in disability and assistive technology. *ACM Transactions on Accessible Computing (TACCESS), 10*(4), 1–17.

Feiler, B. (2017). App time for nap time: The parennials are here. *New York Times*. Retrieved from https://www.nytimes.com/2017/11/04/style/millennial-parents-parennials.html

Feinstein, L., & Sabates, R. (2006). Predicting adult life outcomes from earlier signals: Identifying those at risk. Retrieved from http://www.pm.gov.uk/files/pdf/PMSU-report.pdf

Fishwick, S. (2017, February 17). London's video game development industry is thriving—from AAA blockbusters to indie mobile games. *London Evening Standard*.

Fisk, N. W. (2016). *Framing internet safety: The governance of youth online*. Cambridge, MA: MIT Press.

Fleischmann, A., & Fleischmann, C. (2012). *Carly's voice: Breaking through autism*. New York, NY: Touchstone.

Flores, M., Musgrove, K., Renner, S., Hinton, V., Strozier, S., Franklin, S., & Hil, D. (2012). A comparison of communication using the Apple iPad and a picture-based system. *Augmentative and Alternative Communication*, 28(2), 74–84. doi:10.3109/07434618.2011.644579

Florida, R. (2014). *The rise of the creative class—Revisited*. New York, NY: Basic Books.

Foer, F. (2017). *World without mind: The existential threat of big tech*. New York, NY: Penguin Press.

Fortunati, L., Taipale, S., & de Luca, F. (2017). Digital generations, but not as we know them. *Convergence: The International Journal of Research into New Media Technologies*, 25(1), 1–18. doi:10.1177/1354856517692309

Friere, P. (1973). *Education for critical consciousness*. London, UK: Continuum.

Fuller, M. (2017). *How to be a geek: Essays on the culture of software*. Cambridge, UK: Polity Press.

Furedi, F. (1997). *Culture of fear: Risk-taking and the morality of low expectation*. London, UK: Cassell.

Furedi, F. (2008). *Paranoid parenting: Why ignoring the experts may be best for your child*. London, UK: Continuum.

Furedi, F. (2014). Forward. In *Parenting culture studies*. New York, NY: Palgrave Macmillan.

Fusch, P., & Lawrence, M. (2015). Are we there yet? Data saturation in qualitative research. *Qualitative Report*, 20(9), 1408–1416.

Gadlin, H. (1978). Child discipline and the pursuit of self: An historical interpretation. *Advances in Child Development and Behavior*, 12, 231–265.

Gee, E., Takeuchi, L., & Wartella, E. (2017). *Children and families in the digital age: Learning together in a media saturated culture*. New York: Routledge.

Gergen, K. J. (2009). *Relational being: Beyond self and community*. Oxford, UK: Oxford University Press.

Gibeault, M. J. (2016). Embracing geek culture in undergraduate library instruction: The TIL Subreddit for resource evaluation and qualitative assessment. *Reference Librarian*, 57(3), 205–212.

Giddens, A. (1991). *Modernity and self-identity: Self and society in the late modern age*. Stanford, CA: Stanford University Press.

Giddens, A. (1992). *The transformation of intimacy: Sexuality, love and eroticism in modern societies*. Stanford, CA: Stanford University Press.

Giddens, A. (1993). *New rules of sociological method: A positive critique of interpretative sociologies* (2nd ed.). Cambridge, UK: Polity.

Giddens, A. (1999). *Runaway world: How globalisation is reshaping our lives*. London, UK: Profile Books.

Gillies, V. (2008). Childrearing, class and the new politics of parenting. *Sociology Compass*, *2*(3), 1079–1095.

Gillies, V. (2011). From function to competence: Engaging with the new politics of family. *Sociological Research Online*, *16*(4), 1–11.

Glover, D., Miller, D., Averis, D., & Door, V. (2005). The interactive whiteboard: A literature survey. *Technology, Pedagogy and Education*, *14*(2), 155–170. doi:10.1080/14759390500200199

Goffman, E. (1963). *Stigma: Notes on the management of spoiled identity*. Englewood Cliffs, NJ: Prentice-Hall.

Goggin, G., & Newell, C. (2003). *Digital disability: The social construction of disability in new media*. Lanham, MD: Rowman & Littlefield Publishers.

Goldberg, A. (2010). Lesbian and gay parents and their children: Research on the family life cycle. In *Contemporary perspectives on lesbian, gay, and bisexual psychology*. Washington, DC: American Psychological Association.

Goldthorpe, J. (2016). Social class mobility in modern Britain: Changing structure, constant process. *Journal of the British Academy*, *4*, 89–111. doi:10.5871/jba/004.089

Gomez, K., & Lee, U.-S. (2015). Situated cognition and learning environments: Implications for teachers on- and offline in the new digital media age. *Interactive Learning Environments*, *23*(5), 634–652. doi:10.1080/10494820.2015.1064447

González, N., Moll, L. C., & Amanti, C. (Eds.). (2005). *Funds of knowledge: Theorizing practices in households, communities, and classrooms*. Mahwah, NJ: Lawrence Erlbaum Associates.

Goodley, D., Lawthom, R., & Runswick-Cole, K. (2014). Dis/ability and austerity: Beyond work and slow death. *Disability & Society*, *29*(6), 980–984.

Google Street View. (2018). Retrieved from https://mapstreetview.com/

Goriunova, O. (2014). *Fun and software: Exploring pleasure, paradox and pain in computing*. London, UK: Bloomsbury Academic.

Gove, M. (2012). "Harmful" ICT curriculum set to be dropped to make way for rigorous computer science. Press Release. Department of Education. Retrieved from https://www.gov.uk/government/news/harmful-ict-curriculum-set-to-be-dropped-to-make-way-for-rigorous-computer-science

Graham, M., Hjorth, I., & Lehdonvirta, V. (2017). Digital labour and development: Impacts of global digital labour platforms and the gig economy on worker livelihoods. *Transfer*, *23*(2), 135–162.

Grant, P., & Basye, D. (2014). *Personalized learning: A guide for engaging students with technology*. Washington, D.C.: International Society for Technology in Education.

Gubrium, J., & Holstein, J. (2009). *Analyzing narrative reality*. Thousand Oaks, CA: Sage Publications.

Guernsey, L. (2012). *Screen time: How electronic media—from baby videos to educational software—affects your young child*. New York, NY: Basic Books.

Guernsey, L., & Levine, M. (2017). How to bring early learning and family engagement into the digital age. Retrieved from http://www.joanganzcooneycenter.org/wp-content/uploads/2017/04/digital_age.pdf

Guernsey, L., & Levine, M. H. (2015). *Tap, click, read: Growing readers in a world of screens*. San Francisco, CA: Jossey-Bass.

Gulliford, R., & Upton, G. (Eds.). (1992). *Special educational needs*. New York, NY: Routledge.

Gutiérrez, K., Zitlali Morales, P., & Martinez, D. C. (2009). Re-mediating literacy: Culture, difference, and learning for students from nondominant communities. *Review of Research in Education, 33*(1), 212–245. doi:10.3102/0091732X08328267

Gutiérrez, K. D., Izquierdo, C., & Kremer-Sadlik, T. (2010). Middle class working families' beliefs and engagement in children's extra-curricular activities: The social organization of children's futures. *International Journal of Learning, 17*(3), 633–656.

Gutiérrez, K. D., & Rogoff, B. (2003). Cultural ways of learning: Individual traits or repertoires of practice. *Educational Researcher, 32*(5), 19–25. doi:10.3102/0013189X032005019

Haddon, L. (2006). The contribution of domestication research to in-home computing and media consumption. *Information Society, 22*(4), 195–203. doi:10.1080/01972240600791325

Hallgarten, J. (2000). *Parents exist, OK!? Issues and visions for parent-school relationships.* London, UK: IPPR.

Hamid, T., Nacu, D., Li, T., Gemmell, J., Stan Raicu, D., Martin, C. K., . . . Pinkard, N. (2016). *Recommender system to support brokering of youth learning opportunities.* Paper presented at the 2016 IEEE/WIC/ACM International Conference on Web Intelligence Workshops (WIW), Omaha, NE.

Hamilton, L. T. (2016). *Parenting to a degree.* Chicago, IL: University of Chicago Press.

Hardyment, C. (2007). *Dream babies: Childcare advice from John Locke and Gina Ford.* London, UK: Francis Lincoln.

Harkness, S., & Super, C. M. (1996). *Parents' cultural belief systems: Their origins, expressions and consequences.* New York, NY: Guilford Press.

Hartas, D., Lee, E., Connect, P., Bristow, J., Faircloth, C., & Macvarish, J. (2014). *Parenting culture studies.* London, UK: Palgrave Macmillan.

Hartmann, M. (2008). Domestication of technology. In W. Donsbach (Ed.), *The international encyclopedia of communication* (Vol. IV, pp. 1413–1415). Oxford, UK: Wiley-Blackwell.

Hays, S. (1998). *The cultural contradictions of motherhood.* New Haven, CT, and London, UK: Yale University Press.

Hays, S. (2004). *Flat broke with children: Women in the age of welfare reform.* Oxford, UK: Oxford University Press.

Heitner, D. (2016). *Screenwise: Helping kids thrive (and survive) in their digital world.* New York, NY: Routledge.

Helsper, E. J. (2017). The social relativity of digital exclusion: Applying relative deprivation theory to digital inequalities. *Communication Theory, 27*(3), 223–242.

Helsper, E. J., & Eynon, R. (2010). Digital natives: Where is the evidence? *British Educational Research Journal, 36*(3), 502–520. doi:10.1080/01411920902989227

Henderson, N. (2011). When Mumsnet speaks, politicians listen. *BBC News.* Retrieved from http://www.bbc.co.uk/news/uk-12238447

Henderson, S., Holland, J., McGrellis, S., Sharpe, S., & Thompson, R. (2012). *Inventing adulthoods: A biographical approach to youth transitions.* London, UK: Sage.

Herek, G. (2010). Sexual orientation differences as deficits: Science and stigma in the history of American psychology. *Perspectives on Psychological Science, 5*(6), 693–699.

Hidi, S., & Renninger, K. A. (2006). The four-phase model of interest development. *Educational Psychologist, 41*(2), 111–127. doi:10.1207/s15326985ep4102_4

Higashida, N. (2013). *The reason I jump.* New York, NY: Penguin Random House.

Hill, M., & Tisdall, E. K. M. (1997). *Children and society.* London, UK: Longman.

Hine, C. (2015). *Ethnography for the Internet: Embedded, embodied and everyday.* London, UK: Bloomsbury.

Hinton, D., Laverty, L., & Robinson, J. (2013). Negotiating (un)healthy lifestyles in an era of "intensive" parenting: Ethnographic case studies from north-west England, UK. In C. Faircloth, D. M. Hoffman, & L. L. Layne (Eds.), *Parenting in global perspective: Negotiating ideologies of kinship, self and politics.* Abingdon, UK, and New York, NY: Routledge.

Hoadley, C. (2012). What is community of practice and how can we support it? In S. Land & D. Jonassen (Eds.), *Theoretical foundations of learning environments* (2nd ed., pp. 287–300). New York, NY: Routledge.

Hochschild, A. R. (1997). *The time bind: When work becomes home and home becomes work.* New York, NY: Metropolitan Books.

Hofer, B., Woody Thebodo, S., Meredith, K., Kaslow, Z., & Saunders, A. (2016). The long arm of the digital tether: Communication with home during study abroad. *Frontiers, XXVIII,* 24–41.

Hoffman, D. M. (2010). Risky investments: Parenting and the production of the "resilient child." *Health, Risk & Society, 12*(4), 385–394.

Hollingworth, S., Mansaray, A., Allen, K., & Rose, A. (2011). Parents' perspectives on technology and children's learning in the home: Social class and the role of the habitus. *Journal of Computer Assisted Learning, 27*(4), 347–360. doi:10.1111/j.1365-2729.2011.00431.x

Holt, J. (2017). *How children learn* (50th Anniversary ed.). Cambridge, MA: Da Capo Press.

Honore, C. (2008). *Under pressure: How the epidemic of hyper-parenting is endangering children.* Toronto: Random House of Canada.

Hoop. (2018). Retrieved from https://hoop.co.uk/

Hoover, S., & Clark, L. S. (2008). Children and media in the context of the home and family. In K. Drotner & S. Livingstone (Eds.), *International handbook of children, media and culture* (pp. 105–120). London, UK: Sage.

Hoover-Dempsey, K., & Sandler, H. (1997). Why do parents become involved in their children's education? *Review of Educational Research, 67*(1), 3–42.

Hulbert, A. (2003). *Raising America: Experts, parents, and a century of advice about children.* New York, NY: Alfred A. Knopf.

Husmann, P., & O'Loughlin, V. (2018). Another nail in the coffin for learning styles? Disparities among undergraduate anatomy students' study strategies, class performance, and reported VARK learning styles. *Anatomical Sciences Education, 12*(1), 6–19.

Inger, M. (2011). Developing the theoretical content in Universal Design. *Scandinavian Journal of Disability Research, 15*(3), 203–215.

Institute for the Future for Dell Technologies. (2017). Emerging technologies' impact on society and work in 2030. Retrieved from https://www.delltechnologies.com/content/dam/delltechnologies/assets/perspectives/2030/pdf/SR1940_IFTFforDellTechnologies_Human-Machine_070517_readerhigh-res.pdf

Ito, M. (2009). *Engineering play: Children's software and the productions of everyday life.* Cambridge, MA: MIT Press.

Ito, M. (2017). What a Minecraft server for kids with autism teaches us about haters and allies. Retrieved from https://medium.com/connected-parenting/what-a-minecraft-server-for-kids-with-autism-teaches-us-about-haters-and-allies-5a151db8dde7

Ito, M., Baumer, S., Bittanti, M., boyd, d., Cody, R., Herr-Stephenson, B., . . . Tripp, L. (2010). *Hanging out, messing around, geeking out: Kids living and learning with new media.* Cambridge, MA: MIT Press.

Ito, M., Gutiérrez, K., Livingstone, S., Penuel, B., Rhodes, J., Salen, K., . . . Watkins, S. C. (2013). Connected learning: An agenda for research and design. Retrieved from http://dmlhub.net/publications/connected-learning-agenda-for-research-and-design/

Ito, M., Horst, H., Bittanti, M., Boyd, D., Herr-Stephenson, B., Lange, P. G., . . . Tripp, L. (2008). *Living and learning with new media: Summary of findings from the Digital Youth Project*. Cambridge, MA: MIT Press.

Ito, M., Martin, C., Cody Pfister, R., Rafalow, M., Salen, K., & Wortman, A. (2018). *Affinity online: How connection and shared interest fuel learning*. New York, NY: New York University Press.

Ito, M., Arum, R., Conley, D., Gutiérrez, K., Kirshner, B., Livingstone, S., Michalchik, V., Penuel, W., Peppler, K., Pinkard, N., Rhodes, J., Salen Tekinbaş, K., Schor, J., Sefton-Green, J., and Watkins, S. C., (2020). The Connected Learning Research Network: Reflections on a Decade of Engaged Scholarship. Irvine, CA: Connected Learning Alliance.

Jack, J. (2014). *Autism and gender: From refrigerator mothers to computer geeks*. Urbana, IL: University of Illinois Press.

Jackson, L. A., Zhao, Y., Witt, E. A., Fitzgerald, H. E., von Eye, A., & Harold, R. (2009). Self-concept, self-esteem, gender, race and information technology use. *CyberPsychology & Behavior, 12*(4), 437–440.

Jackson, S., & Scott, S. (1999). Risk anxiety and the social construction of childhood. In D. Lupton (Ed.), *Risk and sociocultural theory: New directions and perspectives* (pp. 86–107). New York, NY: Cambridge University Press.

James, A. (Ed.). (2013). *Socialising children*. Basingstoke, UK: Palgrave Macmillan.

Jamieson, L. (2007). Intimacy. In G. Ritzer (Ed.), *The Blackwell encyclopedia of sociology*. Malden, MA: Blackwell Publishing.

Jancovich, M. (2002). Cult fictions: Cult movies, subcultural capital and the production of cultural distinctions. *Cultural Studies, 16*(2), 306–322.

Jaysane-Darr, A. (2013). Nurturing Sudanese, producing Americans: Refugee parents and personhood. In C. Faircloth, D. M. Hoffman, & L. L. Layne (Eds.), *Parenting in global perspective: Negotiating ideologies of kinship, self and politics*. Abingdon, UK: Routledge.

Jenkins, H. (1992). *Textual poachers*. London, UK: Routledge.

Jenkins, H. (2006). An occasional paper on digital media and learning. Confronting the challenges of participatory culture: Media education for the 21st century. Retrieved from http://www.digitallearning.macfound.org/

Jenkins, H., Ito, M., & boyd, d. (2016). *Participatory culture in a networked era: A conversation on youth, learning, commerce, and politics*. Cambridge, UK: Polity Press.

Jenkins, H., Shresthova, S., Gamber-Thompson, L., Kligler-Vilenchik, N., & Zimmerman, A. (2016). *By any media necessary: The new youth activism*. New York, NY: New York University Press.

Jensen, T. (2013). "Mumsnetiquette": Online affect within parenting culture. In C. Maxwell & P. Aggleton (Eds.), *Privilege, agency and affect* (pp. 127–145). London, UK: Palgrave Macmillan.

Jensen, T. (2016). Against resilience. In R. Garrett, T. L. Jensen, & A. Voela (Eds.), *We need to talk about family: Essays on neoliberalism, the family and popular culture* (pp. 76–94). Newcastle upon Tyne, UK: Cambridge Scholars Publishing.

Jessop, B. (2002). *The future of the capitalist state*. Cambridge, MA: Polity Press.

Jones, G., O'Sullivan, A., & Rouse, J. (2007). Young adults, partners and parents: Individual agency and the problems of support. *Journal of Youth Studies, 9*(4), 375–392.

Jordan, L. S. (2016, January 6). Writing for the mighty, for my son and with my son. *Washington Post*. Retrieved from https://www.washingtonpost.com/news/parenting/wp/2016/01/06/writing-for-the-mighty-for-my-son-and-with-my-son/

Joshi, K. D., Trauth, E., Kvansy, L., Morgan, A., & Payton, F. (2017). Making Black lives matter in the information technology profession: Issues, perspectives, and a call for action. *ACM SIGMIS Database: The DATABASE for Advances in Information Systems, 48*(2), 2–34.

Kahf, U. (2007). Arabic hip hop: Claims of authenticity and identity of a new genre. *Journal of Popular Music Studies, 19*(4), 359–385.

Kamenetz, A. (2018). *The art of screen time: How your family can balance digital media and real life.* New York, NY: Public Affairs.

Kapp, S., Gillespie-Lynch, K., Sherman, L., & Hutman, T. (2012). Deficit, difference, or both? Autism and neurodiversity. *Developmental Psychology, 49*(1), 59–71.

Katz, J. E., Rice, R. E., & Aspden, P. (2001). Access, civic involvement, and social interaction. *American Behavioral Scientist, 45*(3), 405–419.

Katz, V. S. (2014). *Kids in the middle: How children of immigrants negotiate community interactions for their families.* New Brunswick, NJ: Rutgers University Press.

Katz, V. S., Gonzalez, C., & Clark, K. (2017). Digital inequality and developmental trajectories of low-income, immigrant, and minority children. *Pediatrics, 140*(s2), s132–s136. doi:10.1542/peds.2016-1758R

Katz, V. S., & Levine, M. H. (2015). Connecting to learn: Promoting digital equity for America's Hispanic families. Retrieved from http://digitalequityforlearning.org/wp-content/uploads/2015/12/2015-Katz-Levine_Connecting-to-Learn-brief.pdf

Katz, V. S., Moran, M. B., & Gonzalez, C. (2018). Connecting with technology in lower-income US families. *New Media & Society, 20*(7), 2509–2533.

Kehler, M. (2015). Please don't call me a warrior mom. *The Art of Autism.* Retrieved from https://the-art-of-autism.com/please-dont-call-me-a-warrior-mom/.

Kendall, L., & Taylor, E. (2014). "We can't make him fit into the system": Parental reflections on the reasons why home education is the only option for their child who has special educational needs. *International Journal of Primary, Elementary and Early Years Education, 44*(3), 297–310.

Kerr, A. (2011). The culture of gamework. In M. Deuze (Ed.), *Managing media work* (pp. 225–236). Thousand Oaks, CA: Sage.

Kligler-Vilenchik, N. (2013). "Decreasing world suck": Fan communities, mechanisms of translation, and participatory politics. Retrieved from http://ypp.dmlcentral.net/sites/default/files/publications/Decreasing_World_Suck_6.25.13_0.pdf

Kohn, A. (2016). *The myth of the spoiled child: Coddled kids, helicopter parents, and other phony crises.* Boston, MA: Beacon Press.

Konzack, L. (2006). *Geek culture: The 3rd counter-culture.* Presented at FNG2006, June 26–28, Preston, UK.

Koshy, S., McAlear, F., Martin, A., & Scott, A. (2018). Exploring predictors of computer science outcomes among underrepresented high school students of color. Presentation of the Kapor Center for Social Impact. Retrieved from https://www.kaporcenter.org/wp-content/uploads/2018/08/AERA-2018_-Exploring-Predictors-of-Computer-Science-Outcomes-among-Underrepresented-High-School-Students-of-Color-Alexis-Martin-1.pdf

Krakowiak, P., Goodlin-Jones, B., Hertz-Picciotto, I., Croen, L., & Hansen, R. (2008). Sleep problems in children with autism spectrum disorders, developmental delays, and typical development: A population-based study. *Journal of Sleep Research, 17*(2), 197–206.

Kremer-Sadlik, T., Izquierdo, C., & Fatigante, M. (2010). Making meaning of everyday practices: Parents' attitudes toward children's extra-curricular activities in the United States and in Italy. *Anthropology of Education Quarterly, 4*(1), 35–54.

Kvande, E. (1999). 'In the Belly of the Beast': Constructing femininities in engineering organizations. *European Journal of Women's Studies, 6*(3), 305–328. https://doi.org/10.1177/135050689900600304.

Kvansy, L., Joshi, K., & Trauth, E. (2015). *Understanding Black males' IT career choices.* Paper presented at the iConference, Newport Beach, CA.

Lange, P. G. (2014). *Kids on YouTube: Technical identities and digital literacies.* Walnut-Creek, CA: Routledge.

Lansbury, J. (2014). *Elevating child care: A guide to respectful parenting.* Los Angeles, CA: JLML Press.

Lansdown, G. (2014). 25 years of UNCRC: Lessons learned in children's participation. *Canadian Journal of Children's Rights, 1*(1), 172–190.

Lareau, A. (2011). *Unequal childhoods: Class, race, and family life.* Los Angeles, CA: University of California Press.

Lareau, A., Adia Evans, S., & Yee, A. (2016). The rules of the game and the uncertain transmission of advantage. *Sociology of Education, 89*(4), 279–299. doi:10.1177/0038040716669568

Lee, E., Bristow, J., Faircloth, C., & Macvarish, J. (2014). *Parenting culture studies.* London, UK: Palgrave Macmillan.

Lee, E., Macvarish, J., & Bristow, J. (2010). Risk, health and parenting culture. *Health, Risk & Society, 12*(4), 293–300.

Lee, S. J. (2012). Parental restrictive mediation of children's internet use: Effective for what and for whom? *New Media & Society, 15*(4), 466–481. doi:10.1177/1461444812452412

Lenhart, A., & Fox, S. (2006). Bloggers: A portrait of the internet's new storytellers. Retrieved from http://www.pewinternet.org/files/old-media/Files/Reports/2006/PIP%20Bloggers%20Report%20July%2019%202006.pdf.pdf

Lester, J., & Paulus, T. (2012). Performative acts of autism. *Discourse & Society, 23*(3), 259–273.

Leurs, K., & Georgiou, M. (2016). Digital makings of the cosmopolitan city? Young people's urban imaginaries of London. *International Journal of Communication, 10,* 3689–3709.

LeVine, R., & LeVine, S. S. L. (2016). *Do parents matter?: Why Japanese babies sleep soundly, Mexican siblings don't fight, and parents should just relax.* New York, NY: PublicAffairs.

Levitas, R. (2013). *Utopia as method: The imaginary reconstruction of society.* Basingstoke, UK: Palgrave Macmillan.

Lewiecki-Wilson, C. (2003). Rethinking rhetoric through mental disabilities. *Rhetoric Review, 22*(2), 156–167.

Lieblich, A., Tuval-Mashiach, R., & Zilber, T. B. (1998). *Narrative research: Reading, analysis and interpretation* (Vol. 47). Thousand Oaks, CA: Sage.

Lievrouw, L., & Livingstone, S. (2009). Introduction. In L. Lievrouw & S. Livingstone (Eds.), *New media. Sage benchmarks in communication* (pp. xx–xl). London, UK: Sage.

Lim, S. S. (2018). Transcendent parenting in digitally connected families. When the technological meets the social. In Mascheroni, G., Ponte, C., & Jorge, A. (Ed.), *Digital parenting: The challenges for families in the digital age* (pp. 31–39). Göteborg, Sweden: Nordicom.

Linton, S. (2006). Reassigning meaning. In L. Davis (Ed.), *The disability studies reader* (2nd ed., pp. 161–172). New York, NY: Routledge.

littleBits. (2018). Retrieved from https://littlebits.com/

Littler, J. (2013). The rise of the "Yummy Mummy": Popular conservatism and the neoliberal maternal in contemporary British culture. *Communication, Culture & Critique, 6*(2), 227–243. doi:10.1111/cccr.12010

Livingstone, S. (2002). *Young people and new media: Childhood and changing media environment.* London, UK: Sage.

Livingstone, S. (2009). *Children and the Internet: Great expectations, challenging realities.* Cambridge, UK: Polity.

Livingstone, S. (2012). Critical reflections on the benefits of ICT in education. *Oxford Review of Education, 38*(1), 9–24.

Livingstone, S. (2013). Online risk, harm and vulnerability: Reflections on the evidence base for child internet safety policy. *ZER: Journal of Communication Studies, 18*: 13–28. Retrieved from http://eprints.lse.ac.uk/62278/

Livingstone, S. (2018). iGen: Why today's super-connected kids are growing up less rebellious, more tolerant, less happy—and completely unprepared for adulthood. *Journal of Children and Media, 12*(1), 118–123. doi:10.1080/17482798.2017.1417091

Livingstone, S., & Blum-Ross, A. (2018). *Parenting for a digital future. Appendix A: Methodology.* London, UK: London School of Economics and Political Science. Retrieved from http://www.lse.ac.uk/media-and-communications/assets/documents/research/preparing-for-a-digital-future/Methodology.pdf

Livingstone, S., & Blum-Ross, A. (2019). Imagining the future through the lens of the digital: Parents' narratives of generational change. In Z. Papacharissi (Ed.), *A networked self and birth, life, death* (pp. 50–68). New York, NY: Routledge.

Livingstone, S., Blum-Ross, A., Pavlick, J., & Ólafsson, K. (2018). In the digital home, how do parents support their children and who supports them? Parenting for a digital future: Survey report 1. Retrieved from http://www.lse.ac.uk/media-and-communications/assets/documents/research/preparing-for-a-digital-future/P4DF-Survey-Report-1-In-the-digital-home.pdf

Livingstone, S., Blum-Ross, A., & Zhang, D. (2018). What do parents think, and do, about their children's online privacy? Parenting for a digital future: Survey report 3. Retrieved from http://eprints.lse.ac.uk/87954/1/Livingstone_Parenting%20Digital%20Survey%20Report%203_Published.pdf

Livingstone, S., & Haddon, L. (2017). Risks, opportunities, and risky opportunities: How children make sense of the online environment. In F. Blumberg & P. Brooks (Eds.), *Cognitive development in digital contexts* (pp. 275–302). San Diego, CA: Academic Press.

Livingstone, S., Haddon, L., & Görzig, A. (2012). *Children, risk and safety on the internet: Research and policy challenges in comparative perspective.* Bristol, UK: Policy Press.

Livingstone, S., Hasebrink, U., & Görzig, A. (2012). A general model of determinants of risk and safety. In S. Livingstone, L. Haddon, & A. Görzig (Eds.), *Children, risk and safety on the Internet: Research and policy challenges in comparative perspective* (pp. 323–337). Bristol, UK: Policy Press.

Livingstone, S., & Helsper, E. J. (2008). Parental mediation of children's internet use. *Journal of Broadcasting & Electronic Media, 52*(4), 581–599.

Livingstone, S., & Helsper, E. J. (2012). Gradations in digital inclusion: Children, young people and the digital divide. In J. Hughes (Ed.), *SAGE Internet Research Methods* (pp. 403–412). London, UK: Sage.

Livingstone, S., & Lunt, P. (2013). Mediated frameworks for participation. In N. Pachler & M. Boeck (Eds.), *Transformation of representation: Essays in honour of Gunther Kress* (pp. 75–84). New York, NY: Routledge.

Livingstone, S., Marsh, J., Plowman, L., Ottovordemgentschenfelde, S., & Fletcher-Watson, B. (2014). Young children (0–8) and digital technology: A qualitative exploratory study—national report—UK. Retrieved from http://publications.jrc.ec.europa.eu/repository/handle/111111111/1

Livingstone, S., Mascheroni, G., & Staksrud, E. (2018). European research on children's internet use: Assessing the past and anticipating the future. *New Media & Society, 20*(3), 1103–1122. doi:10.1177/1461444816685930

Livingstone, S., & Ólafsson, K. (2018). When do parents think their child is ready to use the internet independently? Parenting for a digital future: Survey report 2. Retrieved from http://eprints.lse.ac.uk/87953/1/Livingstone_Parenting%20Digital%20Survey%20Report%202_Published.pdf

Livingstone, S., Ólafsson, K., Helsper, E. J., Lupiáñez-Villanueva, F., Veltri, G. A., & Folkvord, F. (2017). Maximizing opportunities and minimizing risks for children online: The role of digital skills in emerging strategies of parental mediation. *Journal of Communication, 67*(1), 82–105. doi:10.1111/jcom.12277

Livingstone, S., & Palmer, T. (2012). Identifying vulnerable children online and what strategies can help them. *Report of the seminar arranged by the UKCCIS Evidence Group.* Retrieved from http://www.saferinternet.org.uk/

Livingstone, S., & Sefton-Green, J. (2016). *The class: Living and learning in the digital age.* New York, NY: New York University Press.

Livingstone, S., & Third, A. (2017). Children and young people's rights in the digital age: An emerging agenda. *New Media & Society, 19*(5), 657–670. doi:10.1177/1461444816686318

Lomas, N. (2018, February 28). AI will create new jobs but skills must shift, say tech giants. Retrieved from https://techcrunch.com/2018/02/28/ai-will-create-new-jobs-but-skills-must-shift-say-tech-giants

Lopez, L. K. (2009). The radical act of "mommy blogging": Redefining motherhood through the blogosphere. *New Media & Society, 11*(5), 729–747. doi:10.1177/1461444809105349

Lopez, M. H., Gonzalez-Barrera, A., & Patten, E. (2013). Closing the digital divide: Latinos and technology adoption. Retrieved from http://www.pewhispanic.org/files/2013/03/Latinos_Social_Media_and_Mobile_Tech_03-2013_final.pdf

Loveless, A., & Williamson, B. (2013). *Learning identities in a digital age—rethinking creativity, education and technology.* Milton Park, UK: Routledge.

Luckin, R. (2018). *Enhancing learning and teaching with technology: What the research says.* London, UK: Institute for Education Press.

Luckman, S., & Thomas, N. (2018). *Craft economies.* London, UK, and New York, NY: Bloomsbury Academic.

Lundby, K. (Ed.). (2009). *Mediatization: Concept, changes, consequences.* New York, NY: Peter Lang.

MacArthur Foundation. (2014). Digital media & learning. Retrieved from http://www. macfound.org/programs/learning/

MacLeod, J. (2005). *Ain't no makin' it: Aspirations and attainment in a low-income neighborhood* (2nd ed.). Boulder, CO: Westview Press.

Macvarish, J. (2016). *Neuroparenting: the expert invasion of family life.* Basingstoke, UK: Palgrave Macmillan.

Makey Makey. (2018). Retrieved from https://makeymakey.com/

Mako Hill, B. (2002). The geek shall inherit the earth: My story of unlearning. *Creative Commons.* Retrieved from https://mako.cc/writing/unlearningstory/ StoryOfUnlearing.html

Mallan, K. M., Singh, P., & Giardina, N. (2010). The challenges of participatory research with "tech-savvy" youth. *Journal of Youth Studies, 13*(2), 255–272.

Mansell, R. (2012). *Imagining the Internet: Communication, innovation, and governance.* Oxford, UK: Oxford University Press.

Mansell, R., & Silverstone, R. (Eds.). (1996). *Communication by design: The politics of information and communication technologies.* Oxford, UK: Oxford University Press.

Mares, M. L., Stephenson, L., Martins, N., & Nathanson, A. I. (2018). A house divided: Parental disparity and conflict over media rules predict children's outcomes. *Computers in Human Behavior, 81,* 177–188.

Marsh, J., Kumpulainen, K., Nisha, B., Velicu, A., Blum-Ross, A., Hyatt, D., . . . Thorsteinsson, G. (2017). Makerspaces in the early years: A literature review. Retrieved from http://makeyproject.eu/wp-content/uploads/2017/02/Makey_ Literature_Review.pdf

Marsh, J., Plowman, L., Yamada-Rice, D., Bishop, J. C., Lahmar, J., Scott, F., . . . Winter, P. (2015). Exploring play and creativity in pre-schoolers' use of apps: Final project report. Retrieved from http://techandplay.org/tap-media-pack.pdf

Martin, A. (2003). The impact of free entry to museums. Retrieved from http://www. culturehive.co.uk/wp-content/uploads/2013/04/Impact-of-free-entry-to-museums-MORI.pdf

Marvin, C. (1988). *When old technologies were new: Thinking about electric communication in the late nineteenth century.* New York, NY, and Oxford, UK: Oxford University Press.

Mascheroni, G., & Ólafsson, K. (2015). The mobile Internet: Access, use, opportunities and divides among European children. *New Media & Society, 18*(8), 1657–1679. doi:10.1177/1461444814567986

Mayall, B. (2015). Understanding inter-generational relations: The case of health maintenance by children. *Sociology of Health & Illness, 37*(2), 312–324.

Mayo, A., & Siraj, I. (2015). Parenting practices and children's academic success in low-SES families. *Oxford Review of Education, 41*(1), 47–63. doi:10.1080/03054985.2014.995160

Mays, N., & Pope, C. (1995). Rigour and qualitative research. *BMJ, 311*(6997), 109–112.

Mazurek, M. O., & Engelhardt, C. R. (2013). Video game use in boys with autism spectrum disorder, ADHD, or typical development. *Pediatrics, 132*(2), 260–266. doi:10.1542/ peds.2012-3956

Mazurek, M. O., Shattuck, P. T., Wagner, M., & Cooper, B. P. (2012). Prevalence and correlates of screen-based media use among youths with autism spectrum disorders. *Journal of Autism and Developmental Disorders, 42*(8), 1757–1767. doi:10.1007/ s10803-011-1413-8

McCarthy, J. (2008). *Mother warriors.* New York, NY: Penguin Group.

McClelland, K., & Karen, D. (2009). Analysis. In J. MacLeod (Ed.), *Ain't no makin' it: Aspirations and attainment in a low-income neighborhood* (pp. 409–463). Boulder, CO: Westview Press.

Mckenzie, L. (2015). *Getting by: Estates, class and culture in austerity Britain*. Bristol, UK: Policy Press.

McRobbie, A. (2015). *Be creative: Making a living in the new culture industries*. Cambridge, UK: Polity Press.

Miller, D. (2009). *Stuff*. Cambridge, UK: Polity Press.

Miller, D. (2011). *Tales from Facebook*. Cambridge, UK: Polity Press.

Miller, D., Costa, E., Haynes, N., McDonald, T., Nicolescu, R., Jolynna, S., . . . Wang, X. (2016). *How the world changed social media*. London, UK: UCL Press.

Miller, T. (2005). *Making sense of motherhood: A narrative approach*. Cambridge, UK: Cambridge University Press.

Millwood Hargrave, A., & Livingstone, S. (2009). *Harm and offence in media content: A review of the empirical literature* (2nd ed.). Bristol, UK: Intellect Press.

Miltner, K. (2018). Girls who coded: Gender in twentieth century U.K. and U.S. computing. *Science, Technology, & Human Values, 44*(1), 161–176.

MIT Scratch Team. (2018). Scratch. Retrieved from https://scratch.mit.edu/

Morgan, D. L. (2008). *Snowball sampling. The SAGE encyclopedia of qualitative research methods* (Vol. 2). Thousand Oaks, CA: Sage Publications.

Morgan, G., Wood, J., & Nelligan, P. (2013). Beyond the vocational fragments: Creative work, precarious labour and the idea of "Flexploitation." *Economic and Labour Relations Review, 24*(3), 397–415. doi:10.1177/1035304613500601

Mumsnet. (2016). Mumsnet blogger network. Retrieved from http://www.mumsnet.com/bloggers/about-us

Nadesan, M. (2005). *Constructing autism—Unravelling the "truth" and understanding the social*. New York, NY: Routledge.

Nathanson, A. I. (1999). Identifying and explaining the relationship between parental mediation and children's aggression. *Communication Research, 26*(2), 124–143. doi:10.1177/009365099026002002

Nathanson, A. I. (2002). The unintended effects of parental mediation of television on adolescents. *Media Psychology, 4*(3), 207–230.

Nathanson, A. I. (2015). Media and the family: Reflections and future directions. *Journal of Children and Media, 9*(1), 133–139. doi:10.1080/17482798.2015.997145

Nathanson, A. I., & Yang, M. S. (2003). The effects of mediation content and form on children's responses to violent television. *Human Communication Research, 29*(1), 111–134.

National Audit Office (NAO). (2018). *Financial sustainability of local authorities 2018*. London, UK: Ministry of Housing, Communities & Local Government.

Nature Canada. (2018). The health impacts of too much screen time. Retrieved from https://naturecanada.ca/wp-content/uploads/2018/12/NOV-23-FINAL-Contact-Info-Nature-Canada-report-Screen-Time-vs-Green-Time.pdf

Nelson, M. K. (2010). *Parenting out of control: Anxious parents in uncertain times*. New York, NY: New York University Press.

Nemorin, S., & Selwyn, N. (2016). Making the best of it? Exploring the realities of 3D printing in school. *Research Papers in Education, 32*(5), 578–595. doi:10.1080/02671522.2016.1225802

Neri, D. (2018). The need for nuance in the tech use debate: A conversation with Amy Orben. *Behavioral Scientist*. Retrieved from http://behavioralscientist.org/need-nuance-conversation-amy-orben/

Nesta. (2017). Guidance for developing a theory of change for your programme. Retrieved from https://www.nesta.org.uk/sites/default/files/theory_of_change_guidance_for_applicants_.pdf

Nesta. (2019). Precarious to prepared A manifesto for supporting the six million most at risk of losing their jobs in the next decade. Retrieved from https://media.nesta.org.uk/documents/Precarious_to_prepared._A_manifesto_for_supporting_the_six_million_most_at_risk_of_losing_their_jobs_in_the_next_decade_v5.pdf

Newell, A. (2003). Inclusive design or assistive technology. In J. Clarkson, S. Coleman, S. Keates, & C. Lebbon (Eds.), *Inclusive design—Design for the whole population* (pp. 172--181). London, UK: Springer.

Newman, J. (2017). *To Siri with love*. New York, NY: Harper.

Nikken, P., & Jansz, J. (2006). Parental mediation of children's videogame playing: A comparison of the reports by parents and children. *Learning, Media and Technology, 31*(2), 181–202. doi:10.1080/17439880600756803

Nikken, P., & Schols, M. (2015). How and why parents guide the media use of young children. *Journal of Child and Family Studies, 24*(11), 3423–3435. doi:10.1007/s10826-015-0144-4

Nutt, D. J., Lingford-Huges, A., Erritzoe, D., & Stokes, P. (2015). The dopamine theory of addiction: 40 years of highs and lows. *Nature Reviews Neuroscience, 16*(5), 305.

Ochs, E., & Kremer-Sadlik, T. (Eds.). (2013). *Fast-forward family: Home, work, and relationships in middle-class America*. Berkeley, CA: University of California Press.

Ochs, E., & Kremer-Sadlik, T. (2015). How postindustrial families talk. *Annual Review of Anthropology, 44*, 87–103.

Ochs, E., & Shohet, M. (2006). The cultural structuring of mealtime socialization. *New Directions for Child and Adolescent Development, 2006*(111), 35–49. doi:10.1002/cd.154

Ofcom. (2017). *Children and parents: Media use and attitudes report*. London: Office of Communications.

Office for National Statistics. (2011). Migration by ethnic group. *2011 UK Census*. Retrieved from https://www.nomisweb.co.uk/query/construct/components/simpleapicomponent.aspx?menuopt=15040&subcomp=

Office for National Statistics. (2016). Population of the UK by country of birth and nationality: 2016. Retrieved from https://www.ons.gov.uk/peoplepopulationandcommunity/populationandmigration/internationalmigration/bulletins/ukpopulationbycountryofbirthandnationality/2016#london-has-the-highest-proportion-of-non-british-nationals

Office for National Statistics. (2017a). Household disposable income and inequality in the UK: Financial year ending 2017. Retrieved from https://www.ons.gov.uk/peoplepopulationandcommunity/personalandhouseholdfinances/incomeandwealth/bulletins/householddisposableincomeandinequality/financialyearending2017

Office for National Statistics. (2017b). Internet users in the UK: 2017. Retrieved from https://www.ons.gov.uk/businessindustryandtrade/itandinternetindustry/bulletins/internetusers/2017

Ofsted. (2018). Retrieved from https://www.gov.uk/government/organisations/ofsted

Ogata, A. (2013). *Designing the creative child: Playthings and places in midcentury America*. Minneapolis, MN: University of Minnesota Press.

Oldenziel, R. (1999). *Making technology masculine: Men, women and modern machines in America, 1870–1945*. Amsterdam, Netherlands: Amsterdam University Press.

Oliver, M., & Barnes, C. (2012). *The new politics of disablement* (2nd ed.). New York, NY: Palgrave Macmillan.

Orgad, S. (2019). *Heading home: Motherhood, work, and the failed promise of equality*. New York, NY: Columbia University Press.

Organisation for Economic Co-operation and Development (OECD). (2018). *The future of education and skills*. Retrieved from https://www.oecd.org/education/2030/E2030%20Position%20Paper%20(05.04.2018).pdf

Ortega, F. (2009). The cerebral subject and the challenge of neurodiversity. *BioSocieties*, 4(4), 425–445.

Osteen, M. (Ed.). (2008). *Autism and representation*. New York, NY: Routledge.

Oster, E. (2019). *Cribsheet: A data-driven guide to better, more relaxed parenting, from birth to preschool*. New York, NY: Penguin Press.

Oxford English Dictionary. (2018). *Negotiate. Oxford English Dictionary*.

Palys, T. (2008). Purposive sampling. In L. M. Given (Ed.), *The Sage encyclopedia of qualitative research methods* (Vol. 2, pp. 697–698). Los Angeles, CA: Sage.

Parker, K., & Livingston, G. (2018). 7 facts about American dads. Retrieved from http://www.pewresearch.org/fact-tank/2018/06/13/fathers-day-facts/

Parks, D., Haron, A., Essien, O., & Vargas, A. (2018). We are geeks of color. Retrieved from https://geeksofcolor.co/about/

Patton, M. Q. (1990). *Qualitative evaluation and research methods* (2nd ed.). Thousand Oaks, CA: Sage Publications.

Pedersen, S. (2016). The good, the bad and the "good enough" mother on the UK parenting forum Mumsnet. *Women's Studies International Forum*, 59, 32–38.

Pedersen, S., & Lupton, D. (2018). "What are you feeling right now?" communities of maternal feeling on Mumsnet. *Emotion, Space and Society*, 26, 57–63.

Pelletier, C., Burn, A., & Buckingham, D. (2010). Game design as textual poaching: Media literacy, creativity and game-making. *E-Learning and Digital Media*, 7(1), 90–107.

Penuel, W., & O'Connor, K. (2018). From designing to organizing new social futures: Multiliteracies pedagogies for today. *Theory into Practice*, 57(1), 64–71.

Peppler, K. (2013). New opportunities for interest-driven arts learning in a digital age. Retrieved from http://www.wallacefoundation.org/knowledge-center/arts-education/key-research/Documents/New-Opportunities-for-Interest-Driven-Arts-Learning-in-a-Digital-Age.pdf

Perrier, M. (2012). Middle-class mothers' moralities and "concerted cultivation": Class others, ambivalence and excess. *Sociology*, 47(4), 655–670. doi:10.1177/0038038512453789

Phillips, N., & Broderick, A. (2014). Has Mumsnet changed me? SNS influence on identity adaptation and consumption. *Journal of Marketing Management*, 30(9–10), 1039–1057.

Pinchevski, A., & Peters, J. D. (2016). Autism and new media: Disability between technology and society. *New Media & Society*, 18(11), 2507–2523. doi:10.1177/1461444815594441

Pink, S., & Leder Mackley, K. (2013). Saturated and situated: Expanding the meaning of media in the routines of everyday life. *Media, Culture & Society, 35*(6), 677–691. doi:10.1177/0163443713491298

Polkinghome, D. (2007). Validity issues in narrative research. *Qualitative Inquiry, 13*(4), 471–486.

Postill, J. (2010). Introduction: Theorising media and practice. In B. Bräuchler & J. Postill (Eds.), *Theorising media and practice.* Oxford and New York: Berghahn.

Prensky, M. (2001). Digital natives, digital immigrants. *On the Horizon, 9*(5), 1–2.

Prensky, M. R. (2010). *Teaching digital natives: Partnering for real learning.* Thousand Oaks, CA: Corwin.

Prince's Trust. (2018). The Prince's Trust Macquarie youth index 2018. Retrieved from London: https://www.princes-trust.org.uk/about-the-trust/news-views/macquarie-youth-index-2018-annual-report

Przybylski, A. K., & Weinstein, N. (2017). A large-scale test of the goldilocks hypothesis: Quantifying the relations between digital-screen use and the mental well-being of adolescents. *Psychological Science, 28*(2), 204–215. doi:10.1177/0956797616678438

Pugh, A. J. (2009). *Longing and belonging: Parents, children, and consumer culture.* Berkeley, CA: University of California Press.

Putnam, L. L., & Fairhurst, G. T. (2015). Revisiting "organizations as discursive constructions": 10 years later. *Communication Theory, 25*(4), 375–392. doi:10.1111/comt.12074

Putnam, R. (2000). *Bowling alone: The collapse and revival of American community.* New York, NY: Simon & Schuster.

Putnam, R. D. (2015). *Our kids: The American dream in crisis.* New York, NY: Simon & Schuster.

Qualtrough, E. (2018). CIOs facing skills and recruitment challenges to drive transformation, 2018 CIO 100 reveals: But CIOs looking to insource and increase headcount to develop in-house capability. Retrieved from https://www.cio.co.uk/cio-career/cios-facing-skills-recruitment-challenges-drive-transformation-3676503/

Radesky, J. S., & Christakis, D. (2016a). Increased screen time: Implications for early childhood development and behavior. *Pediatric Clinics of North America, 63*(5), 827–839. doi:10.1016/j.pcl.2016.06.006

Radesky, J., & Christakis, D. (2016b). Media and young minds. *American Academy of Pediatrics, 138*(5), 1–6. doi:10.1542/peds.2016–2591

Radesky, J. S., Kistin, C., Eisenberg, S., Gross, J., Block, G., Zuckerman, B., & Silverstein, M. (2016). Parent perspectives on their mobile technology use: The excitement and exhaustion of parenting while connected. *Journal of Developmental & Behavioral Pediatrics, 37*(9), 694–701. doi:10.1097/DBP.0000000000000357

Rafalow, M. (forthcoming). *Digital divisions: How schools create inequality in the tech era.* Chicago: University of Chicago Press.

Ramaekers, S., & Suissa, J. (2012). *The claims of parenting—Reasons, responsibility and society.* London, UK: Springer.

Raphael, R. (2017). Netflix CEO Reed Hastings: Sleep is our competition. *Fast Company.* Retrieved from https://www.fastcompany.com/40491939/netflix-ceo-reed-hastings-sleep-is-our-competition

Raspberry Pi. (2018). Retrieved from https://www.raspberrypi.org/

Reay, D. (2004). Gendering Bourdieu's concepts of capitals? Emotional capital, women and social class. *Sociological Review, 52*(s2), 57–74. doi:10.1111/j.1467-954X.2005.00524.x

Reay, D. (2017). *Miseducation: Inequality, education and the working classes.* Bristol, UK: Policy Press.

Reece, H. (2013). The pitfalls of positive parenting. *Ethics and Education, 8*(1), 42–54. doi:10.1080/17449642.2013.793961

Reese, H. W., & Lipsitt, L. P. (1978). Child discipline and the pursuit of self: An historical interpretation. In H. W. Reese & L. P. Lipsitt (Eds.), *Advances in child development and behavior* (Vol. 12, pp. 231–261). New York, NY: Academic Press.

Reeves, A. (2014). Neither class nor status: Arts participation and the social strata. *Sociology, 49*(4), 624–642. doi:10.1177/0038038514547897

Reich, J., & Ito, M. (2017). From good intentions to real outcomes: Equity by design in learning technologies. Retrieved from https://clalliance.org/wp-content/uploads/2017/11/GIROreport_1031.pdf

Reiser, R. A., Williamson, N., & Suzuki, K. (1988). Using Sesame Street to facilitate children's recognition of letters and numbers. *Educational Communication and Technology Journal, 36*(1), 15–21.

Renninger, K. A., & Hidi, S. (2011). Revisiting the conceptualization, measurement, and generation of interest. *Educational Psychologist, 46*(3), 168–184. doi:10.1080/00461520.2011.587723

Resch, A., Mireles, G., Benz, M., Grenwelge, C., Peterson, C., & Zhang, D. (2010). Giving parents a voice: A qualitative study of the challenges experienced by parents of children with disabilities. *Rehabilitation Psychology, 55*(2), 139–150.

Resnick, M., Maloney, J., Monroy-Hernandez, A., Rusk, N., Eastmond, E., Brennan, K., . . . Kafai, Y. (2009). Scratch: Programming for all. *Communications of the ACM, 52*(11), 60–67. doi:10.1145/1592761.1592779

Ribbens McCarthy, J., & Edwards, R. (2011). *Key concepts in family studies.* London, UK, and Los Angeles, CA: Sage.

Ribbens McCarthy, J., Gillies, V., & Hooper, C.-A. (2013). *Family troubles? Exploring changes and challenges in family lives of children and young people.* Bristol, UK: Policy Press.

Richdale, A., & Schreck, K. (2009). Sleep problems in autism spectrum disorders: Prevalence, nature, & possible biopsychosocial aetiologies. *Sleep Medicine Reviews, 13*(6), 403–411.

Rideout, V., & Katz, V. S. (2016). Opportunity for all? Technology and learning in lower-income families. Retrieved from http://www.joanganzcooneycenter.org/wp-content/uploads/2016/01/jgcc_opportunityforall.pdf

Rienzo, C., & Vargas-Silva, C. (2017). Briefing: Migrants in the UK: An overview. Retrieved from https://migrationobservatory.ox.ac.uk/wp-content/uploads/2017/02/Briefing-Migrants_UK_Overview.pdf

Rimini, M., Howard, C., & Ghersengorin, A. (2016). Digital resilience: Empowering youth online. Practices for a safer internet use. A major survey targeting Australia, Japan, Indonesia, Korea and Taiwan. Retrieved from http://www.thinkyoung.eu/research

Ringland, K., Wolf, C., Faucett, H., Dombrowski, L., & Hayes, G. (2016). *"Will I always be not social?": Re-conceptualizing sociality in the context of a Minecraft community for autism.* Paper presented at the ACM CHI Conference on Human Factors in Computing Systems. San Jose: CA.

Robbins, A. (2011). *The geeks shall inherit the earth: Popularity, quirk theory, and why outsiders thrive after high school.* New York, NY: Hyperion.

Roberts, J. (2018). Mumsnet. Retrieved from https://www.mumsnet.com/

Robinson, L., Cotten, S. R., Schulz, J., Hale, T. M., & Williams, A. (2015). *Communication and information technologies annual: Digital distinctions and inequalities*. Bingley, UK: Emerald Publishing.

Robison, J. (2017). Autism parent memoirs: Illuminating or exploitive? Retrieved from https://www.psychologytoday.com/us/blog/my-life-aspergers/201712/autism-parent-memoirs-illuminating-or-exploitive

Roeder, M. (2014). *Unnatural selection: Why the geeks will inherit the earth*. New York, NY: Arcade Publishing.

Roy, K., Zvonkovic, A., Goldberg, A., Sharp, E., & LaRossa, R. (2015). Sampling richness and qualitative integrity: Challenges for research with families. *Journal of Marriage and Family, 77*(1), 243–260.

Royal Society. (2017). After the reboot: Computing education in UK schools. Retrieved from https://royalsociety.org/~/media/policy/projects/computing-education/computing-education-report.pdf

Rutkin, A. (2016, April 30). How Minecraft is helping children with autism make new friends. Retrieved from https://www.newscientist.com/article/mg23030713-100-how-is-helping-children-with-autism-make-new-friends/

Saldaña, J. (2009). *The coding manual for qualitative researchers*. London, UK: Sage.

Sassen, S. (1991). *The global city: New York, London, Tokyo*. Princeton, NJ: Princeton University Press.

Savage, M. (2015a). Introduction to elites from the "problematic of the proletariat" to a class analysis of "wealth elites." *Sociological Review, 63*(2), 223–239.

Savage, M. (2015b). *Social class in the 21st century*. London, UK: Penguin Books.

Scabini, E., Marta, E., & Lanz, M. (2006). *The transition to adulthood and family relations: An intergenerational perspective*. Hove, UK: Psychology Press.

Schleicher, A. (2011). The case for 21st-century learning. *OECD Observer*, 42–43.

Schor, J. (1991). *The overworked American: The unexpected decline of leisure*. New York, NY: Basic Books.

Schor, J. B. (2004). *Born to buy: The commercialized child and the new consumer culture*. New York, NY: Scribner.

Scott, J. (1985). *Weapons of the weak: Everyday forms of peasant resistance*. New Haven, CT: Yale University Press.

Sefton, J. (2008). The roots of open-world games. Retrieved from https://www.gamesradar.com/the-roots-of-open-world-games/

Sefton-Green, J. (2013a). *Learning at not school: A review of study, theory, and advocacy for education in non-formal settings*. Cambridge, MA: MIT Press.

Sefton-Green, J. (2013b). What (and where) is the "learning" when we talk about learning in the home? Retrieved from http://eprints.lse.ac.uk/54793/

Sefton-Green, J., & Erstad, O. (2016). Researching "learning lives"—A new agenda for learning, media and technology. *Learning, Media and Technology, 42*(2), 246–250. doi:10.1080/17439884.2016.1170034

Sefton-Green, J., & Erstad, O. (Eds.). (2019). *Learning beyond the school: International perspectives on the schooled society*. New York, NY: Routledge.

Sefton-Green, J., Watkins, C., & Kirshner, B. (2020). *Young people's journeys into creative work: Challenges and transitions into the workforce*. New York, NY: Routledge.

Seiter, E. (2005). *The Internet playground: Children's access, entertainment, and mis-education*. New York, NY: Peter Lang.

Selby-Boothroyd, A. (2018). The challenges of charting regional inequality. *The Economist*. Retrieved from https://medium.economist.com/the-challenges-of-charting-regional-inequality-a9376718348

Selwyn, N. (2014). *Distrusting educational technology: Critical conversations for changing times*. Abingdon, UK, and New York, NY: Routledge.

Selwyn, N., & Facer, K. (2007). *Beyond the digital divide: Rethinking digital inclusion for the 21st century*. Bristol, UK: Futurelab.

Sennett, R., & Cobb, J. (1993). *The hidden injuries of class*. New York, NY: W. W. Norton & Company.

Shakespeare, T. (2010). The social model of disability. In L. J. Davis (Ed.), *The disability studies reader* (pp. 266–273). New York, NY: Routledge.

Shane, H. C., & Albert, P. D. (2008). Electronic screen media for persons with autism spectrum disorders: Results of a survey. *Journal of Autism and Developmental Disorders*, *38*(8), 1499–1508. doi:10.1007/s10803-007-0527-5

Share, M., Williams, C., & Kerrins, L. (2017). Displaying and performing: Polish transnational families in Ireland Skyping grandparents in Poland. *New Media & Society* 18(10), 1–18. doi:10.1177/1461444817739272

Sheffer, E. (2018). *The problem with Asperger's*. Retrieved from https://blogs.scientificamerican.com/observations/the-problem-with-aspergers/

Siebers, T. (2008). *Disability theory*. Ann Arbor, MI: University of Michigan.

Silander, M., Grindal, T., Hupert, N., Garcia, E., Anderson, K., Vahey, P., & Pasnik, S. (2018). What parents talk about when they talk about learning. Education Development Center & SRI Education. Retrieved from http://www.edc.org/sites/default/files/uploads/EDC_SRI_What_Parents_Talk_About.pdf

Silberman, S. (2001, December 1). The geek syndrome. *Wired*, *9*.

Silicon Valley. (2018). Retrieved from https://www.hbo.com/silicon-valley

Silverstone, R. (2006). Domesticating domestication: Reflections on the life of a concept. In T. Berker, M. Hartmann, Y. Punie, & K. J. Ward (Eds.), *The domestication of media and technology* (pp. 229–248). Maidenhead, UK: Open University Press.

Silverstone, R., & Hirsch, E. (1992). *Consuming technologies: Media and information in domestic spaces*. London, UK: Routledge.

Skeggs, B. (2004). *Class, self, culture*. London, UK: Routledge.

Skeggs, B. (2015). Introduction: Stratification or exploitation, domination, dispossession and devaluation? *Sociological Review*, *63*(2), 205–222.

SketchUp. (2018). Retrieved from https://www.sketchup.com/

Skinner, J. (2012). *The interview: An ethnographic approach*. London, UK: Berg.

Smale, H. (2015). *Geek girl*. New York, NY: HarperTeen.

Smith, J. (2015). Breck Bednar murder: How Lewis Daynes manipulated his victim. Retrieved from https://www.bbc.com/news/uk-england-essex-30730807

Social Mobility Commission. (2017). State of the nation 2017: Social mobility in Great Britain. Retrieved from https://www.gov.uk/government/uploads/system/uploads/attachment_data/file/662744/State_of_the_Nation_2017_-_Social_Mobility_in_Great_Britain.pdf

Social Mobility Commission. (2018). *Social mobility barometer*. London: Crown copyright. Retrieved from https://assets.publishing.service.gov.uk/government/uploads/system/uploads/attachment_data/file/766797/Social_mobility_barometer_2018_report.pdf

Sousa, A. (2011). From refrigerator mothers to warrior-heroes: The cultural identity transformation of mothers raising children with intellectual disabilities. *Symbolic Interaction, 34*(2), 220–243.

Spangler Effect. (2018). Retrieved from https://www.youtube.com/user/TheSpanglerEffect

Sparrow, M. (2017). Why to Siri with love is a wrecking ball of a book. In S. Des Rochas Rosa, J. Byde Myers, L. Ditz, E. Willingham, & C. Greenburg (Eds.), *Thinking person's guide to autism* (Vol. 12). Redwood City, CA: Deadwood City Publishing.

Spector, J. M. (2016). *Foundations of educational technology: Integrative approaches and interdisciplinary perspectives* (2nd ed.). New York, NY, and Abingdon, UK: Routledge.

Spigel, L. (1992). *Make room for TV: Television and the family ideal in postwar America*. Chicago, IL, and London, UK: University of Chicago Press.

Spradley, J. (1979). *The ethnographic interview*. Long Grove, IL: Waveland Press.

Steiner, L., & Bronstein, C. (2017). Leave a comment: Mommyblogs and the everyday struggle to reclaim parenthood. *Feminist Media Studies, 17*(1), 59–76. doi:10.1080/14680777.2017.1261840

Steyer, J. P. (2002). *The other parent: the inside story of the media's effect on our children*. New York, NY: Atria Books.

Stiglic, N., & Viner, R. M. (2019). Effects of screentime on the health and well-being of children and adolescents: A systematic review of reviews. *BMJ Open, 9*(1), 1–15. doi:10.1136/bmjopen-2018-023191

Stuart, K. (2016). *A boy made of blocks*. New York, NY: St. Martin's Press.

Sugg, Z. (2016). *Girl online: On tour: The first novel by Zoella*. New York, NY: Atria/Keywords Press.

Sutton Trust. (2017). The state of social mobility in the UK. Retrieved from https://www.suttontrust.com/wp-content/uploads/2017/07/BCGSocial-Mobility-report-full-version_WEB_FINAL.pdf

Swartz, M., & Crowley, K. (2004). Parent beliefs about teaching and learning in a children's museum. *Visitor Studies, 7*(2), 1–16.

Takeuchi, L., & Stevens, R. (2011). The new coviewing: Designing for learning through joint media engagement. Retrieved from http://www.joanganzcooneycenter.org/publication/the-new-coviewing-designing-for-learning-through-joint-media-engagement/

Tavory, I., & Eliasoph, N. (2009). Coordinating futures: Toward a theory of anticipation. *American Journal of Sociology, 118*(4), 908–942.

Taylor, C. (2003). *Modern social imaginaries*. Durham, NC: Duke University Press.

Taylor, S. (2004). The right not to work: Power and disability. *Monthly Review, 55*.

Te Riele, K. (2006). Youth "at risk": Further marginalizing the marginalized? *Journal of Education Policy, 21*(2), 129–145. doi:10.1080/02680930500499968

Tech Nation. (2018). The state of the UK tech nation. Retrieved from https://35z8e83m1ih83drye280o9d1-wpengine.netdna-ssl.com/wp-content/uploads/2018/05/Tech-Nation-Report-2018-WEB-180514.pdf

TechUK. (2019). Preparing for change: How tech parents view education and the future of work. Retrieved from http://www.techuk.org/images/documents/future_of_work_FINAL.pdf

Therrien, A., & Wakefield, J. (2019). Worry less about children's screen use, parents told. *BBC News*. Retrieved from https://www.bbc.com/news/health-46749232

Thomas, C. (2013). Disability and impairment. In J. Swain, S. French, C. Barnes, & C. Thomas (Eds.), *Disabling barriers—Enabling environments* (3rd ed., pp. 9–16). London, UK: Sage Publications.

Thompson, C. (2017). The next big blue-collar job is coding. *Wired*. Retrieved from https://www.wired.com/2017/02/programming-is-the-new-blue-collar-job/

Thomson, R. (2011). *Unfolding lives: Youth, gender and change*. Bristol, UK: Policy Press.

Thorton, S. (1996). *Club cultures: Music, media and subcultural capital*. Hanover, NH: Wesleyan University Press.

Threadgold, S., & Nilan, P. (2009). Reflexivity of contemporary youth, risk and cultural capital. *Current Sociology, 57*(1), 47–68.

Tilly, C., & Carré, F. J. (2017). *Where bad jobs are better: Retail jobs across countries and companies*. New York, NY: Russell Sage Foundation.

Tirraoro, T. (2015). SEN figures show 2.5% drop in children with special educational needs in England. Retrieved from https://www.specialneedsjungle.com/sen-figures-show-2-5-drop-in-children-with-special-educational-needs-in-england/

Titchkosky, T. (2001). Disability: A rose by any other name? "People-first" language in Canadian society. *Canadian Review of Sociology/Revue canadienne de sociologie, 38*(2), 125–140.

Tkachuk, A. (2018). Engender creativity in young children to maximise their potential. *RSA*. Retrieved from https://www.thersa.org/discover/publications-and-articles/rsa-blogs/2018/02/engender-creativity-in-children-to-function-in-todays-world

Togni, L. (2015). The creative industries in London. *Working Paper 70*. Retrieved from https://www.london.gov.uk/sites/default/files/creative-industries-in-london.pdf

Tolstoy, L. (1886). *Anna Karenina*. Oxford, UK: Oxford University Press.

Trienekens, S. (2002). "Colourful" distinction: The role of ethnicity and ethnic orientation in cultural consumption. *Poetics, 30*(4), 281–298. https://doi.org/10.1016/S0304-422X(02)00025-6

Tripp, L. (2011). "The computer is not for you to be looking around, it is for schoolwork": Challenges for digital inclusion as Latino immigrant families negotiate children's access to the internet. *New Media & Society, 13*(4), 552–567.

Turkle, S. (2011). *Alone together: Why we expect more from technology and less from each other*. New York, NY: Basic Books.

Turkle, S. (2015). *Reclaiming conversation: The power of talk in a digital age*. New York, NY: Penguin Press.

Turner, F. (2006). *From counterculture to cyberculture: Steward Brand, the whole earth network and the rise of digital utopianism*. London, UK: University of Chicago Press.

Twenge, J. M. (2017). *iGen: Why today's super-connected kids are growing up less rebellious, more tolerant, less happy—and completely unprepared for adulthood (and what this means for the rest of us)*. New York, NY: Atria Books.

UK Digital Skills Taskforce. (2014). Digital skills for tomorrow's world. Retrieved from http://www.ukdigitalskills.com/wp-content/uploads/2014/07/Binder-9-reduced.pdf

UK Government. (2017). Looked-after children. Retrieved from https://www.gov.uk/topic/schools-colleges-childrens-services/looked-after-children

UNESCO. (2015). Leveraging information and communication technologies to achieve the post-2015 education goal. *Report of the international conference on ICT and post-2015 education.* Retrieved from http://unesdoc.unesco.org/images/0024/002430/243076e.pdf

Valkenburg, P. M., Piotrowski, J. T., Hermanns, J., & de Leeuw, R. (2013). Development and validation of the perceived parental mediation scale: A self-determination perspective. *Human Communication Research, 39*(4), 445–469.

Van Dijk, J. (2005). *The deepening divide: Inequality in the information society.* London, UK: Sage.

Victor, D. (2015, August 19). The Ashley Madison data dump, explained. *New York Times.* Retrieved from https://www.nytimes.com/2015/08/20/technology/the-ashley-madison-data-dump-explained.html

Villalobos, A. (2010). Mothering in fear: How living in an insecure-feeling world affects parenting. In A. O'Reilly (Ed.), *Twenty-first-century motherhood: Experience, identity, policy, agency* (pp. 57–71). New York, NY: Columbia University Press.

Villalobos, A. (2014). *Motherload: Making it all better in uncertain times.* Los Angeles, CA: University of California Press.

Vittadini, N., Siibak, A., Reifovà, I., & Bilandzic, H. (2013). Generations and media: The social construction of generational identity and differences. In N. Carpentier, K. C. Schrøder, & L. Hallet (Eds.), *Audience transformations: Shifting audience positions in late modernity* (pp. 65–88). New York, NY: Routledge.

Vygotsky, L. (1934/1986). *Thought and language.* Cambridge, MA: MIT Press.

Wajcman, J. (2004). *TechnoFeminism.* Cambridge, UK, and Malden, MA: Polity.

Wajcman, J., Bittman, M., & Brown, J. E. (2008). Families without borders: Mobile phones, connectedness and work-home divisions. *Sociology, 42*(4), 635–652. doi:10.1177/0038038508091620

Wallis, R., & Buckingham, D. (2016). Media literacy: The UK's undead cultural policy. *International Journal of Cultural Policy,* 1–16. doi:10.1080/10286632.2016.1229314

Ward, M. R. M. (2014). "I'm a geek I am": Academic achievement and the performance of a studious working-class masculinity. *Gender and Education, 26*(7), 709–725.

Warner, J. (2006). *Perfect madness: Motherhood in the age of anxiety.* New York, NY: Riverhead Books.

Warschauer, M., & Matuchniak, T. (2010). New technology and digital worlds: Analyzing evidence of equity in access, use, and outcomes. *Review of Research in Education, 34*(1), 179–225.

Wartella, E., Rideout, V., Lauricella, A. R., & Connell, S. L. (2013). Parenting in the age of digital technology: A national survey. Retrieved from http://web5.soc.northwestern.edu/cmhd/wp-content/uploads/2013/05/Parenting-Report_FINAL.pdf

Watkins, S. C. (2009). *The young & the digital: What the migration to social-network sites, games and anytime, anywhere media means for our future.* Boston, MA: Beacon Press.

Watkins, S. C. (2012). Digital divide: Navigating the digital edge. *International Journal of Learning and Media, 3*(2), 1–12.

Watkins, S. C. (2019). *Don't knock the hustle: Young creatives, tech ingenuity, and the making of a new innovation economy.* Boston, MA: Beacon Press

Webb, P. (2011). Family values, social capital and contradictions of American modernity. *Theory, Culture & Society, 28*(4), 96–123.

Weinstein, N., & Przybylski, A. (2019). The impacts of motivational framing of technology restrictions on adolescent concealment: Evidence from a preregistered experimental study. *Computers in Human Behavior, 90,* 170–180.

Wenger, E. (2000). *Communities of practice: Learning, meaning, and identity* (R. Pea, C. Heath, & L. Suchman, Eds.). Cambridge, UK: Cambridge University Press.

Wessendorf, S. (2014). *Commonplace diversity: Social relations in a super-diverse context.* Basingstoke, UK: Palgrave Macmillan.

Westman, K. E. (2007). Beauty and the geek: Changing gender stereotypes on the Gilmore Girls. In S. A. Inness (Ed.), *Geek chic: Women in popular culture.* New York, NY: Palgrave Macmillan.

Williamson, B. (2010). Policy utopias, sci-fi dystopias, and contemporary contests over childhood in education reform in the UK. *Journal of Children and Media, 4*(2), 206–222.

Williamson, B. (2013). *The future of the curriculum: School knowledge in the digital age.* Cambridge, MA and London, UK: MIT Press.

Williamson, B., Rensfeldt, A., Player-Koro, C., & Selwyn, N. (2018). Education recoded: Policy mobilities in the international "learning to code" agenda. *Journal of Education Policy, 34*(5), 705–725.

Williamson, E., Goodenough, T., Kent, J., & Ashcroft, R. (2005). Conducting research with children: The limits of confidentiality and child protection protocols. *Children and Society, 19*(5), 397–409.

Willis, P. (1977). *Learning to labour.* London, UK: Gower.

Wing, J. (2008). Computational thinking and thinking about computing. *Philosophical Transactions of the Royal Society of London A: Mathematical, Physical and Engineering Sciences, 366*(1881), 3717–3725.

Wood, D., Bruner, J., & Ross, G. (1976). The role of tutoring in problem solving. *Journal of Child Psychology and Psychiatry, 17,* 89–100.

Woodman, D. (2009). The mysterious case of the pervasive choice biography: Ulrich Beck, structure/agency, and the middling state of theory in the sociology of youth. *Journal of Youth Studies, 12*(3), 243–256. doi:10.1080/13676260902807227

Wooldridge, A. (2016). The rise of the superstars. *The Economist.* Retrieved from https://www.economist.com/special-report/2016/09/15/the-rise-of-the-superstars

World Health Organization. (2019). Guidelines on physical activity, sedentary behaviour and sleep for children under 5 years of age. Retrieved from https://apps.who.int/iris/handle/10665/311664

Wortham, S. (2006). *Learning identity: The joint emergence of social identification and academic learning.* Cambridge, UK: Cambridge University Press.

Wright, C., Diener, M., Dunn, L., Wright, S., Linnell, L., Newbold, K., . . . Rafferty, D. (2011). SketchUp™: A technology tool to facilitate intergenerational family relationships for children with autism spectrum disorders (ASD). *Family & Consumer Sciences, 40*(2), 135–149.

Yelland, N. J. (2018). A pedagogy of multiliteracies: Young children and multimodal learning with tablets. *British Journal of Educational Technology, 49*(5), 847–858. doi:10.1111/bjet.12635

Yergeau, M. (2018). *Authoring autism: On rhetoric and neurological queerness.* Durham, NC: Duke University Press.

Zelizer, V. A. (1985). *Pricing the priceless child: The changing social value of children.* Princeton, NJ: Princeton University Press.

Zhang, D., & Livingstone, S. (2019). Inequalities in how parents support their children's development with digital technologies. Parenting for a digital future: Survey report 4. Retrieved from http://www.lse.ac.uk/media-and-communications/assets/documents/research/preparing-for-a-digital-future/P4DF-Report-4.pdf

Index

For the benefit of digital users, indexed terms that span two pages (e.g., 52–53) may, on occasion, appear on only one of those pages.

CPSIA information can be obtained
at www.ICGtesting.com
Printed in the USA
BVHW012344200922
646932BV00008B/11